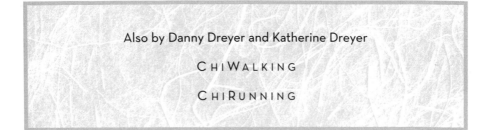

Also by Danny Dreyer and Katherine Dreyer

ChiWalking

ChiRunning

# Chi Marathon

## THE BREAKTHROUGH NATURAL RUNNING PROGRAM FOR A PAIN-FREE HALF MARATHON AND MARATHON

Danny Dreyer

and Katherine Dreyer

A TOUCHSTONE BOOK
PUBLISHED BY SIMON & SCHUSTER
NEW YORK LONDON TORONTO SYDNEY NEW DELHI

Touchstone
A Division of Simon & Schuster, Inc.
1230 Avenue of the Americas
New York, NY 10020

This publication contains the opinions and ideas of its author. It is sold with the understanding that
the author and publisher are not engaged in rendering exercise or health services in the book. The
reader should consult his or her own medical and health providers as appropriate before adopting
any of the exercise programs and suggestions in this book or drawing inferences from them.

The author and publisher specifically disclaim all responsibility for any liability, loss or risk,
personal or otherwise, which is incurred as a consequence, directly or indirectly, of the use and application of any of the contents of this book.

First Touchstone trade paperback edition March 2012

TOUCHSTONE and colophon are
registered trademarks of Simon & Schuster, Inc.

For information about special discounts for bulk purchases,
please contact Simon & Schuster Special Sales at
1-866-506-1949 or business@simonandschuster.com.

The Simon & Schuster Speakers Bureau can bring authors to your live event.
For more information or to book an event contact the Simon & Schuster Speakers
Bureau at 1-866-248-3049 or visit our website at www.simonspeakers.com.

Manufactured in the United States of America

1   3   5   7   9   10   8   6   4   2

Library of Congress Cataloging-in-Publication Data
Dreyer, Danny.
Chi marathon : the breakthrough natural running program for a pain-free
half marathon and marathon / Danny Dreyer and Katherine Dreyer.
        p. cm.
1.  Marathon running—Training.   2.  Tai chi.   I.  Dreyer, Katherine.   II.  Title.
                GV1065.17.T3D74  2012
796.42'52—dc23                                                                    2011038844

ISBN 978-1-4516-1795-5
ISBN 978-1-4516-1799-3 (ebook)

This book is dedicated to the ever-growing Chi Team,
and all of you who support our journey.

# Contents

# Contents

# Foreword

BY CATHERINA McKIERNAN

**Catherina McKiernan winning
London Marathon, 1998.**

I had won three major marathons, Berlin (1997), London, and Amsterdam (both 1998). I had had very fruitful years with four world cross-country silver medals, one European cross-country gold medal, countless national titles, two Olympic games, the Irish records in the 10K, half marathon and marathon, and a smattering of European and world championships achieved.

But I began losing my battle with niggling injury. Irish newspaper headlines regularly led with stories of me pulling out of big events due to injury. *Running is meant to be enjoyed, not endured*, I thought.

I decided to retire in 2004. But as my professional running career was ending, a new and equally satisfying career was about to begin. I got my hands on a copy of Danny and Katherine Dreyer's book *ChiRunning*, and I couldn't put it down. After enduring years of pain and injury and wondering what was the cause of it all, I found that Danny's book was providing me with all the answers. All I could do was laugh as I read what I should have known ten or twelve years previously. I would not swap my successes as a professional athlete for anything, and whatever I was doing during those years, it worked, but I will never stop wondering what might have been had I known about ChiRunning from the start.

After reading Danny's book, I decided that I needed to meet this man. Within months, I was certified as a ChiRunning instructor. And there I was with the perfect transitional job: teaching other people how to run effortlessly and injury-free.

Personally speaking, ChiRunning has given me a lifeline. Despite retiring from competitive athletics, I run every day, naturally, as I did as a child. There is a running boom in Ireland right now, an antidote to our economic crisis, and more and more people want to be able to run and enjoy their running. Luckily, they can come to me to learn about ChiRunning. Of all the thousands of people I have taught, none have come back to say that it has not worked for them. That is job satisfaction.

I was born to run. I loved the outdoors when I was young, and my running successes happened gradually. I had a natural running style and loved the freedom of it. But as training became more intense and training methods kicked in, my free running style changed to suit the demands of professional competition. I lost the natural feel until I came across ChiRunning. It unraveled all of the tenseness and poor style that I had adopted for 24/7 training and competing.

Thanks to ChiRunning, countless numbers of people all over the world have the opportunity to release their fear of injury so that they can enjoy what is so important to them—the ability to get out into the open air and do what is so natural, pacifying, and nourishing to the mind and body. What more could we ask for?

Do I miss competing? It's a question I often get asked, and my answer is most definitely no. There are other athletes who find it hard to step away from the track, but the transformation has been made simple for me because of ChiRunning. My great fear was that I would not be able to run. My life has been running, and more than anything else, the fear of not being able to get out every day for a few miles played heavily on my mind. Fear is the mother of injury in an athlete. But not anymore. There is no fear with ChiRunning.

—Catherina McKiernan, Dublin, Ireland

# Introduction:
# Love Running Forever

## KATHERINE DREYER

ChiRunning is an amazing practice. It takes us back to the roots of running. The desire to run. The pleasure of it. Running becomes a special state: a place of air, gravity, earth, and the runner. —JOE MILLER, A CHIRUNNER

In today's world, good news seems hard to come by. So it is more important than ever to make sure there are positive influences in your life. One suggestion: go to a marathon and cheer on the runners. Better yet, run a marathon yourself and surround yourself with people willing to take on the half or full marathon distance. Drink in the positive inspiration.

Marathons don't look the same today as they did even ten years ago. The hard-bodied runners who previously dominated the sport are now just part of a much broader mix of people with a variety of shapes, sizes, and ages.

This book and program will get you started on your own love affair with running. Making a goal to run a half marathon or marathon is one of the best ways to make running a positive part of your life—if you do it well, and that is a major caveat. The high rate of injury for those who run long distances mars the sport and the joy of running. We want you to experience the kind of running that will make you love running forever; with a profound sense of self-confidence, freedom in your movement, and joy in feeling truly alive. If you follow this program, you too might just love running for the rest of your life.

You might find yourself running longer and longer distances, until you have reached a half marathon, or maybe even a full marathon. Like Forrest Gump, you might not want to stop.

*Chi Marathon* is the result of the need for a new approach to marathon training. The old paradigm is not working for most people. As injury rates rise, what could be a fabulous way to cultivate a lifelong habit of keeping fit becomes a graveyard for once-enthusiastic runners.

Since the ChiRunning book came out in 2004, Danny and I have received the most beautiful letters, thousands upon thousands of them, from readers, runners, and workshop attendees all over the world (the book is currently translated into ten languages, and we have more than 200 Certified Instructors and Instructor Candidates in twenty-one countries), thanking us for ChiRunning with heartfelt gratitude—often with the line "It has changed my life." Okay, so people really appreciate ChiRunning. But why, we ask ourselves, is it changing lives? What is it that impacts people so deeply?

Here is one letter that reflects what so many have written. You'll find similar stories throughout the book, from both clients and Certified Instructors.

Wow, I feel so amazing after my run this morning! I used to *hate* running. I only put up with it because I love biking and swimming, and I tolerated running to do triathlons.

Well, I did two triathlons this summer and finished second in my age group in one and third in my age group in the other! What a thrill to hear my name called out and go up and get my trophy. Thanks to ChiRunning!

After watching the DVD about a hundred times I was finally able to put into practice what I had been watching. This morning my legs felt so light and I ran effortlessly thanks to focusing on my hip rotation and just relaxing enough to let my legs follow along for the ride! I felt like a rock star! My cadence was up where it should be and it was just effortless!

Hills used to kill me, and I mean *kill* me! Now I barely notice the hills. What's even more exciting is that I have no pain, and I get up every day looking forward to learning something new from my ChiRunning. I have had so many breakthroughs with my running this year, it is really life-transforming for me.

I am *forever* indebted to ChiRunning.

—Dean Carpenter, age fifty

# The Ideal Training Triad: Form, Conditioning, and Mastery

In the book *ChiRunning*, we teach the fundamental principles of pain-less, injury-free running. The primary focus in that book is on the Chi-Running technique. We will review that information in Chapter 3. In the rest of this book we talk about how to take those techniques and movement principles and apply them to the half and full marathon distances. The focus is on training your mind and your body to work together as a team (Chapter 4) for long distances. Whether you focus on the half marathon or want to complete the full marathon distance of 26.2 miles, it is an endeavor of endurance and conditioning. But let's be clear: forced physical endurance does not get you to the finish line. Deep, healthy conditioning of the body does. This comes from the endurance built by training mindfully for months in advance. If you'd like to run several marathons in a year, it is the endurance that accompanies training regularly and with great awareness. For everyone, it is the endurance that stems from keeping your mind alert and being in tune with your body. This kind of endurance is born of patience, of faith in your body, which is both vulnerable in its mortality and immeasurably strong and miraculous in its potential.

We have all seen countless people of a wide range of ages, body types, running abilities, and running forms crossing the finish line, some with a happy smile, some with a look of pain and suffering in their eyes, and some with the clear confidence of the naturally gifted runner. The question is, did running that marathon add to their lives in a positive way? Or did it cause them pain or injury, or deplete them to their detriment?

You are invited to run a marathon, or a half marathon, with new purpose and intent: not just to cross the finish line, but to do so with the sense of joy and accomplishment that accompanies our long-term approach. It is about discovering the grace and ease with which you can move mindfully through any significant undertaking or challenge in your life. It is about running marathons in a way that substantially benefits your body, mind, and spirit. This is what we call Mastery.

Chapter 5, "The Mastery Phase," is not just for the elite or fast runner; it is for novice marathoners too. In the Mastery Phase of the *Chi Marathon* training, you will focus on race-specific training by practicing *everything* that will be in your actual event: the start, pacing, fueling—right down to running in the clothes you'll wear on race day so that when you actually run your marathon, it is, as Danny often says, like whistling pop tunes—easy and completely enjoyable. Okay, maybe not that easy—running a marathon is a significant event for most people. It should be approached with respect. However, with this program, you can run any distance with great confidence and come away with a deep sense of well-being.

## T'ai Chi and Running

The Chi in ChiRunning can be as off-putting to some people as it is compelling to others. We understood this from the beginning. In the end, however, we decided that because the philosophies of T'ai Chi and Taoism are so much a part of how we approach running, we need to be true to the source of our inspiration. You'll read more about the Chi in *Chi Marathon* in Chapter 1.

Some clients have confessed that they came to ChiRunning out of desperation—they loved to run but were in so much pain that they were willing to try anything. We firmly believe in the age-old (but not heeded often enough) adage that an ounce of prevention is worth a pound of cure. The fact is, more and more people are using the ChiRunning technique for the joy, the speed, and the efficiency of running well. Training for and running a marathon has a daunting but accurate reputation for causing a lot of injuries. But it is not because of the running itself;

rather, it is because the longer you run with biomechanically imbalanced technique, the more likely you are to get hurt.

These converts are in some ways the most rewarding for us: they start out with great skepticism, then become convinced in the best way possible, through their own personal experience. What is the best way to find out if this Chi stuff really works? Try it!

As soon as *ChiRunning* was released we started getting requests for a book about ChiWalking. People who were benefiting from ChiRunning wanted to share their discovery with the walkers in their lives.

T'ai Chi, a fast and powerful martial art, is the source of the foundational principles and philosophies upon which ChiRunning and Chi Walking are based. However, during practice sessions, T'ai Chi is done at very slow speeds in order to engender greater accuracy, and because of this slowness, every incremental adjustment in balance must be deeply felt and diligently maintained. Similarly, since ChiWalking is practiced at a slower pace than ChiRunning, the Form Focuses (specific directions for your movement) require a deeper precision than while running. When you run, that deep, slow work becomes a strong foundation for sound movement. (We'll talk about the Chi Walk-Run program in Chapter 2.) We suggest that you practice many of the key Form Focuses, especially your posture, throughout the day, and whenever you walk.

We now teach ChiWalking in every ChiRunning workshop, and every Certified ChiRunning Instructor is also certified in ChiWalking.

Throughout this book, when we refer to a marathon we include half marathons, marathons, and even ultra marathons, if that is your goal, although we will not address ultra marathon running to any significant degree. The focus here is the half and full marathon.

## Running: An Innate Part of Who We Are

We believe ChiRunning has the effect it has because it helps people discover something that is both an innate need and an innate ability: to move gracefully and to run freely, without force, without pain, and with a deep realization that this is exactly what they are meant be doing. When we wrote the first ChiRunning we did not realize what a primal, elemental need it would satisfy. ChiRunning has helped people discover that running can act as a gateway to deeper internal sensitivity.

In turn, this new awareness can be transferred and applied to everyday life.

> ### INSTRUCTOR STORY
>
> It was a paradigm shift in mind, body, and spirit for me. BC—before ChiRunning—I was all about ego, focusing exclusively on time, distance, and speed. I saw no reason to run unless I was going to train for a race, and I saw no reason to train unless I was going to set a personal record every time. In hindsight I now call that "the dark side." Now I get a much more profound, deeper sense of joy and fulfillment from my daily runs, as well as training for "focused and relaxed events" (aka races), than I ever did beating my body up in order to get a specific number on a stopwatch. It is the ultimate gift that keeps on giving. And, oh yeah—did I mention I haven't been injured in years?
>
> —Christopher Griffin

Humans are meant to run. In fact, according to a 2004 article in the journal *Nature* coauthored by paleoanthropologist Daniel Lieberman of Harvard University and biologist Dennis Bramble of the University of Utah, we are "born to run." The two studied fossil records and surmised that early *Homo sapiens* was higher up the evolutionary ladder than its ancestors because of the structure of the legs and pelvis. This difference in skeletal structure allowed these early humans more mobility to either forage greater distances and feed off the kills of faster animals or to do "persistence hunting"—basically, running down slower prey. Chris McDougall subsequently used the phrase "born to run" as the title to his successful book about the Tarahumara Indians and barefoot running.

The concept that we are born to run is revolutionary because for decades we have been fed the notion that running causes injury. Doctors, with their patients' best interests in mind, have said, "Running hurts your body!" We've been told: "You're injured—stop running." "You're over forty—find another way to keep fit." "Your knees hurt—give up what you love." "You're out of shape—running is too hard for you." "You're older—there is no way you should run."

The language around running a marathon is even worse. "You want to run a marathon? Expect pain, and a lot of it." The language in some marathon books glorifies pain and prepares you for the worst: "The next day, you'll feel like you've been hit by a truck" . . . "terror" . . . "racked with aches and pains" . . . "26 miles of running hell" . . . "like an auto accident" . . . "your worst nightmare" . . . "the 26-mile monster."

When Lieberman's groundbreaking first study came out in 2006, it was big news: with headlines in major newspapers including the *New York Times* and the *Los Angeles Times*. Humans are meant to, and built to, run. We finally felt supported by science in what we had been doing since 1999: teaching people that running is a natural, safe, and effective way to get fit, take control of your health, clear your mind, and feel great.

In 2002, when we signed our first book contract, the old paradigm was still in full force. This was before Lieberman's study had come out, and the ChiRunning concepts of running with a slight lean, landing with a midfoot strike, and running in minimal shoes were considered "out there," as one running magazine wrote. Minimal shoes (discussed in Chapter 2) are now considered common sense, and shoe companies have all jumped on the bandwagon. The ideas that running could be pain- and injury-free and that relaxation and less effort could give you greater speed flew in the face of the hard-core coaches who promoted grit, muscle, and gutting it out. Back then, there was great doubt that running form could or should be taught; now, however, science is showing up on our side, and the idea that you can improve your running form is becoming common sense. Almost.

The real revolution in running is still in its early stages. Much of the current focus in running is on the shoe, which is important, but it's hardly the whole picture. Part of the reason the focus remains here is that shoes are where the money is. We'll talk about shoes in Chapter 2. Barefoot running, minimal shoes, and the midfoot strike are just the tip of the iceberg when it comes to the impact that running form can have on this wonderful but often maligned sport. The emphasis on how the foot strikes the ground is important, but it's just one aspect of the real evolution that is happening in running. There are now more classes about running technique as well, though many are designed with the purpose of selling shoes. Beware of shortcuts that trick you into running well for a few minutes but don't expand your self-knowledge and understanding.

What is important to remember is that everyone's running form has been greatly influenced by years of movement habits. And, just like any habit, movement habits can and should be changed if they are detrimental to your overall health. Our T'ai Chi master, George Xu, told us that all of us are meant to lose the beautiful running form we had as children, as then we may *consciously* relearn how to move. Only with conscious awareness can we master our bodies—how we move while running, and how we move through life. If you are tricked into running without real knowledge and awareness, you will quickly fall back into bad habits.

The fact is that most adults in modern cultures have lost the connection with the body they once had as kids. Subsequently, they lost their innate ability to run with natural, healthy biomechanics. There are two primary reasons for this. First, for the past century we humans have not needed manual labor to survive. Historically, working to clothe and feed ourselves—to get water, grow crops, and hunt animals—kept our bodies strong and supple. Second, running shoes, initially designed to help prevent running injuries, only exacerbated the problem: adding more cushioning to the sole of a running shoe made the foot *less* sensitive to ground contact and proprioception.

For most of us, the desire, ability, and primal need to run is still there, thanks to the conscious (and even cellular) memory of running as a child. It is one of our earliest and dearest memories of freedom.

Good lifestyle choices such as a healthful diet help, but what is most important is that you follow a pretty basic rule: start with good running form and never run longer or faster than your form and conditioning allow. Just don't do it.

Don't run if running is causing you injury or long-term damage of any kind. It is not necessary or smart. If you are in pain, find out what in your running technique is causing the pain and change your technique. Run lower mileage until your form and conditioning can support greater distances or speeds. You will find more on facing challenges throughout this book and specifically in Chapter 4, in the section "Conserving Your Energy."

Too many people who run marathons not only get injured but stop running because of their injuries. This derails the fundamental reason for running a marathon in the first place: the deep sense of personal accomplishment from stepping beyond your current state of being. If you run a marathon and are in pain, injured, or so wiped out that you can't enjoy life, you won't feel the kind of satisfaction you deserve after taking on such a wonderful challenge.

That is the beauty of the Chi Marathon training program. It allows you to experience an internal process that will leave you with the mental and emotional skills to achieve any long-term endeavor, whether it's running a marathon, writing a book, getting a degree, raising a child, or maintaining your health and vitality for a lifetime.

Here's a letter we appreciated:

I have been ChiRunning since November last year and have found it has had a hugely positive impact on my running form, injuries, and my well-being in general. ChiRunning helped me through a very difficult time in my life when the company I work for announced that it was to close at the end of May. The economic climate is such that jobs are hard to come by, and I was at risk of losing everything that I had built up for my family. ChiRunning and ChiLiving helped me to stay focused and fit through dark days, and gave me clear perspective on my situation. I used ChiRunning skills to plan my job campaign, and even used Chi focuses and relaxation techniques in the job interviews; the result is that I acquired a great new job that I have long aspired for.

—Dave

## Finding Yourself in This Book

In Chapter 2 we'll talk more about what stage you're at in terms of running marathons, but as an overview, this book is for anyone who wants to run a half or full marathon, multiple marathons in a year, and even ultra marathon distances. Running events longer than six hours requires a new set of skills that are not directly addressed in this book, but most of the basic principles of distance training still apply: you still have to know what phase of training you are in, rehearse and prepare for the unknown, and most important, make sure your running form and conditioning can handle the distance.

For novice runners who want to run a half marathon or marathon distance, we highly recommend focusing on form for as long as you need to before committing to a specific half or full marathon event. For an absolute beginning runner to run a half marathon, give yourself at least six months; for a marathon, make it a minimum of one year. Consider yourself ready to move up to the half or full marathon training when you can comfortably run a 10-kilometer race (a 10K) with good form. We have excellent 5-kilometer (5K) and 10K training programs available on our website (www.chirunning.com) that will support you in learning the ChiRunning method, as will the book *ChiRunning: A Revolutionary Approach to Effortless, Injury-Free Running* and the *ChiRunning* DVD.

To get started on this program, take a look at the training programs for the half and full marathons in Appendixes A and B. If you are new to ChiRunning, they will probably bring up more questions than answers. In this book you will learn the why and the how of these techniques, which are so key to creating a positive marathon experience.

Chapter 9 covers advanced ChiRunning techniques. It is for when you feel comfortable with the ChiRunning technique and are ready for new skills to improve your technique, speed, and efficiency. Like T'ai Chi, ChiRunning is a practice that can help you refine your body-mind connection until the two become one; thought and movement always acting in unison. Speed is a result not of more power but of removing the impediments to fluid movement and creating the conditions for speed to happen. Energy-efficient speed happens when you do less, not more.

In reality, there is much more in this book than you can practice or learn in one marathon. So it's important to choose what is most important for you and work on those few things that will have the greatest positive effect. As you learn the ChiRunning Form Focuses, we always suggest you start with one Form Focus at a time, eventually practicing two at a time. The same goes for marathon training—focus on some of the suggestions and save others for future events. We hope you'll discover a lifetime of learning within these pages.

We know that, like life, training for a marathon involves both joy and struggle. From first-timers to old-timers, from champions to back-of-the-packers, running the marathon distance exemplifies the strength and courage of human nature and its desire to reach for and go beyond the boundaries we often abide by.

We hope to offer you the tools to make this journey all that you dreamed, and much, much more.

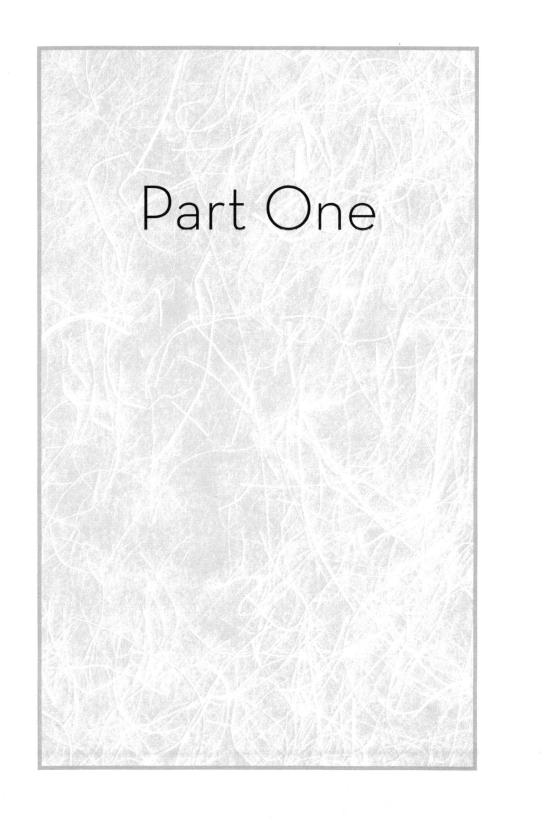

# Part One

# CHAPTER ONE

# The Many Faces of the Marathon

Mildness in action joined to strength of decision brings good fortune.

—I CHING

Like an art museum or a symphony, a marathon is a great place to go when you want to feel good about the potential of the human race. Whether you cheer a friend on from the sidelines, volunteer at an aid station, or run the event yourself, you get to witness and experience a side of humankind that is both elemental and exalted. I love being at marathon events because of the singular connection of spirit that bonds everyone. It's manifested as the innate drive to evolve, to better oneself—to be that bridge between heaven and earth, between the invisible and visible worlds, between mind and body.

You don't need to have expensive or special equipment. Heck, the more low-tech the shoe, the better, these days. The best runners in the world are those who've run barefoot most of their lives. You don't need to be part of an elite club—and yet there are plenty of clubs and groups you can join to enjoy the camaraderie. Going out for a run is one of the quickest and least complicated ways of getting fit.

Along with the elemental beauty of running is the individual story of each runner; every one as inspiring as the next. For some, it is their first marathon. Perhaps they had been significantly overweight or never felt particularly good about their physical abilities; but they decided they too could run and reclaim their health. They have trained for months and are putting themselves at that start line to join in with the thousands of others who also at some point were in their first marathon. Some find that running helps them manage their depression or addictions and celebrate their internal victory by joining the unifying spirit of the marathon. You might find someone running his tenth marathon in as many months and this one being the one hundredth in his life. Story after story is filled with the wonder of the potential of the human spirit to overcome difficulty and sometimes conquer impossible odds. Marathon events are brimming with the excitement of athletes of every level and concern, collectively reaching beyond themselves.

In the lead pack, you'll see human beings who have spent a good deal of their lives dedicated to perfecting their sport, putting everything they have into that event. No matter where you are—cheering from the sidelines, watching from a television screen thousands of miles away, or running in the back of the pack—you can feel the energy of their effort lifting us all up and sparking our imaginations. What can't the human body do? Better yet, what can *this body* do?

In 2009 almost half a million U.S. runners ran a marathon, and more than 600,000 ran a half marathon. The number of female finishers now outpaces the number of men who finish. Not only are the participation numbers in marathons increasing each year, but so is the number of marathons. In 2009 more than twenty-five new marathons were introduced in the United States alone—and this during a downturn in the economy.

There is no comparison to the palpable energy of a marathon event. Where else do thousands of people come together in such a large mass and challenge themselves physically and mentally to such a degree? How often do elite athletes and everyday people get to participate in the same event? Theses events have made long-distance running accessible to anyone willing to stretch herself beyond her perceived limits.

Considering the many health benefits of running, the annual increase in half and full marathon events means that more and more people are getting fit, improving their cardiovascular and aerobic health, releasing excess weight, and feeling mentally more clear and focused. Distance running offers all of those benefits and so many more. Inside every endurance athlete is the desire not only to do something that is beyond the normal but also to step beyond what he has accomplished before, whether it's his first half marathon or his sixtieth marathon by age sixty. Humans live to evolve, and we run with the desire to expand ourselves, to see what's possible and to feel ourselves stretching our limits.

## The Dilemma

There is, however, a downside to our dreams of grandeur. Our minds can be too altruistic and tend to dream without enough consideration of what our bodies are *currently* capable of. Notice the emphasis on *currently*. The human body has a great capacity for learning and for growth. And it is our dreams that motivate and inspire positive change in our lives. Our bodies, however, don't change as fast as our minds (thank heaven). They need time to catch up and collaborate with the ideas in our minds. You wouldn't expect a six-month-old to walk, and it wouldn't be fair to expect your body to run a marathon without being prepared. If you're going to run that far, why not enjoy the entire process from conception to reality? This book is about manifesting your dreams into a healthy, positive physical reality, pain- and injury-free, by following a sensible and sustainable path of learning and growth, one that thrives on the teamwork of the mind and body.

When we push our bodies to longer and longer distances without proper preparation, our chances of getting injured increase astronomically. Running is a high-injury sport when done without proper training. The injury rate among runners generally hovers between 50 and 65 percent, depending on which studies you read. Among marathoners, that number falls between 65 and 90 percent, which is worth taking seriously.

It does not have to be that way, and there is no reason why you should find yourself among these statistics.

As with any sport, your ease, enjoyment, and performance will improve when you train with good technique. At some point in our lives we have all had some kind of instruction in a sport or fitness activity, such as swimming, tennis, golf, or yoga. With almost every sport instruction how best to move is considered the norm. But when it comes to running, we think we can—and most coaches say—"just go out and do it." Unfortunately, for many "it" means getting injured.

Paradoxically, we have an innate ability to run long distances. It is part of our evolutionary makeup, as the studies of Dr. Dan Lieberman and other researchers have shown. It is exemplified in the grace of the East African runners who continue to be so successful in distance running events.

If we are meant to run long distances, then, what is the problem?

Between lack of enough physical movement as we sit in front of computers and TVs to social norms for what looks good, including poor postural habits, our bodies are no longer in good running readiness. Our lifestyle habits have functionally changed how we move. But it is well within us to make the change back to good movement and postural habits. We all just need to choose to do so. It is essential if you want to run a half or full marathon pain-free. You might be able to complete the distance without having good running technique, but don't be surprised if your marathon transforms from an event to an ordeal over the course of those 26.2 miles.

The fact is, there really does not have to be any bad news. Running itself is not the reason for the high rate of injury. It is how you run that is the primary culprit, sometimes fueled by a mind-set that pushes your body beyond sensible limits. Training for a marathon should *build* your body's strength, conditioning, and long-term health and well-being. There is no reason in the world for running, or training for a marathon, to break down your body or cause it long-term damage.

The vast majority of people running a marathon today are following training programs that will train you to increase your weekly long-run distance to build the stamina to make it to the end of a marathon. The problem with this approach is that it doesn't take into consideration the fact that you might be running all those miles in a way that is harmful to your body, given your current biomechanics or weak areas. There is a need to overhaul a faulty, inefficient, and potentially harmful system of training for marathons and replace it with a more holistic approach that considers the needs, abilities, and dreams of *every* athlete.

I can't count the number of people who have told me they ran a marathon and had a very difficult experience. Many wouldn't think of doing it again. Some folks have even given up running altogether. I'm always disappointed to hear this because I know that if they'd been shown how to do it well, they'd still be out there enjoying themselves at what I know to be a safe and very enjoyable sport. Struggle is an option. You can choose to run a marathon on sheer will by gutting it out, or you can learn to take the path of least resistance with a focused body and a relaxed mind. One way feels lousy; the other way is fun. One way feels narrow and limited; the other way can help you grow, move, and understand yourself in ways you never thought possible.

## Pain-Free

In the title of this book is the promise and challenge of running a pain-free marathon. By pain, we mean pain that is in any way detrimental to your long-term health and well-being. If you are a first-time marathoner, you may experience some "productive discomfort" as your body gains the conditioning it needs to run the half or full marathon distance. Many clients will let us know that they feel a slight soreness in their abdominals, and we respond very positively, "Great, that means you're on the right track." Productive discomfort is not the pain we're talking about when we say pain-free. We want every runner to be free of the pain that leads to injury or that hampers your running or your lifestyle in a significant way. Nonproductive discomfort can be the precursor to pain, and you do have to listen to your body and make those judgment calls for yourself. Sharp or throbbing pain or discomfort that lasts more than two to three days is most likely a warning.

In most cases, running with improper technique is what causes pain and injury. What you learn in the *Chi Marathon* program is to minimize the potential for pain and injury by using good technique and a mindful awareness of your body's needs. However, if you are running incorrectly or inefficiently, run farther than your body is conditioned to handle, or continue to run without finding the cause of the issue and correcting it, pain could degrade into injury.

It all boils down to the myth that pain and suffering is a necessary part of the marathon equation. It's that tired old "no pain, no gain" philosophy. As Howard Hanger, a local minister here in Asheville, said, "No pain, no gain? There's enough pain in life—who needs more?"

## The *Chi Marathon* Vision and Challenge

The marathon boom shows one thing: people are willing to work, and work hard, to accomplish their goals. If you're reading this book, at the very least you're in the "I think I can" stage of preparing for a marathon. You also might be in the "I thought I could" stage and hoping for some support to make the training pain-free and enjoyable again. In either case, you're willing to train to run 13.1 or 26.2 miles, and that says a lot about you.

The opportunity and the challenge of *Chi Marathon* is to train in a way that changes your running, for the better, for the rest of your life. As you change your running, you'll change how you relate to your body, and you'll see your movement patterns and your thought patterns change for the better. The beauty of training for a full or half marathon distance is that you have plenty of time to practice. So you might as well make the most of those hours on the road. The ChiRunning Form Focuses and the seven training phases of the *Chi Marathon* program will take you through a process of discovery that makes running long distances easier, more efficient, and more enjoyable. The process is engaging and inspiring as you tap into your innate ability to run.

I have had knee problems ever since a football injury when I was seventeen. While I ran as a young adult and into my fifties, I did okay, but always had knee pain and swelling. I routinely went to orthopedic surgeons and physical therapists to get advice, but I was still limited in how far I could run. Running hills was out of the question. I picked up your book in 2005 and read it but never really applied it like I should. Last year, when I was fifty-seven, I bought the DVD and half marathon training program and really studied them. I'm an engineer, and the descriptions of the physical concept of ChiRunning made a lot of sense to me. The results have been miraculous.

I'm now running faster and longer (even on extreme hills) than I have since I was seventeen. The best news is that I'm having no lingering pain. My forty years of knee pain is gone. I'm swimming, biking, and backpacking without knee pain. My other pains—to shins, Achilles tendon, toes, etc.—are gone.

Thank you so much for your instructions. It really has changed my life.

—Karl Gebhardt

# Natural Running, Barefoot-like Running, Minimalist Running

In 1999, when I first started teaching ChiRunning, Ken Saxton was running marathons barefoot. A quiet man, he did not get quite the press and attention that some barefoot runners get today. Ken ran barefoot because he knew, as I did, that the runners with the best running form, exemplified beautifully in the East African runners who were (and still are) winning most distance events, had run barefoot most of their lives. Their feet and their bodies had been "educated" from childhood by the contact with the ground with each step they ever took.

Dan Lieberman did a follow-up to his "born to run" study and published an article of his findings in the journal *Nature* in January 2010. He wanted to find out if barefoot runners experienced less impact with the ground than runners wearing shoes. So he compared groups of habitually barefoot runners (Kenyans) with groups of runners who habitually wore shoes (Harvard runners) and found that the barefoot runners did indeed experience lower collision forces with the ground. Many people in the running community and the press took this to mean that big, bulky running shoes weren't doing what they were touted to do, which is provide a softer landing and prevent injury. He never said that in his study, but he did suggest that further studies needed to be done in order to find out whether these lower collision forces actually lead to lower injury rates in barefoot runners compared to shod runners.

Between Lieberman's study, Chris McDougall's book, and the growing success of ChiRunning, the running community began to seriously question the need for thick-soled running shoes, and the minimalist shoe industry was born. In 2009, the only minimal shoes available were racing flats. Today all of the shoe companies are building low-profile running shoes—and in my opinion, it's to everyone's advantage. Hence the newly coined term "minimalist running."

Personally, I prefer a more minimal shoe (more on shoes in Chapter 2), but I also feel that switching from wearing overbuilt shoes to running barefoot or running in a minimal shoe is not necessarily the safest or best way to learn to run naturally. It *can* help to strengthen the supportive muscles in the lower leg, which is a good thing. But if you've been running for many years in big, bulky shoes, sitting at a desk, driving a car, not doing regular manual labor, and running with incorrect biomechanics, there's no guarantee that you will automatically run correctly simply because you take off your shoes. It takes time for your body to return to its original state, as when you were a child and ran around barefoot or in low-profile sneakers.

ChiRunning is a whole-body technique that teaches you to run as you would have if you never wore shoes. It is a barefoot-like running style that allows you to run naturally and involves much more than just the contact your foot has with the ground. It is about running from your deep core muscles and letting the rest of your body relax. It is about moving the way you were designed to run, from head to toe. And as we work toward getting back into our natural way to run, it is good to know that modern science agrees with our goal. Our Medical Advisory Board (visit our website) includes MDs, physical therapists, and other health-care practitioners who understand that a more natural running gait is possible, and necessary, if your goal is to run pain-free.

## Intelligent Movement

In the *Chi Marathon* program, rather than training harder, you'll be training smarter. We call it "intelligent movement," and we have seen, in the countless runners we've trained, that the knowledge in your mind can save your body from a lot of unnecessary and unhealthy stress and pain. You'll educate your mind to think in new ways about what training for a marathon really means, and you'll train yourself to work mindfully with your body to be more efficient. You'll learn to manage your energy to the point where you can build energy rather than burn through it like a teenager at the mall with $50.

Intelligent movement can be summed up with these three tenets:

- Energy management and economy of effort
- Having a creative mind and a responsive body
- Seeing challenges in a positive light

Intelligent movement is both a vision and a challenge. The vision is that any average runner can relearn and remember that kidlike, innate running ability that allows them to run joyfully and naturally. The *real* challenge is to approach distance running in a new way and with a new mind-set. Instead of testing how long your body can last, you'll train to improve how your mind and body can work together.

Here are some of the concepts behind *Chi Marathon* training compared to the old paradigm:

| CHI MARATHON | OLD PARADIGM |
|---|---|
| Finesse | Force |
| Intelligent movement | Physical exertion |
| Manage energy | Spend energy |
| Build energy | Burn energy |
| Relax to go faster | Push harder to go faster |
| Core strength | Leg strength |
| Train smart | Train hard |
| Discover, explore | Command, force, dictate, coerce |
| Mind and body | Mind over body |
| Learn from your body | Test your body |
| Listen to your body | Force your body |
| Gradual progress | Right now, at any cost |

## The Key to Effortless Movement

One of the most important keys to effortless movement is good postural alignment. This allows deep relaxation during the support phase of your stride, which is when most injuries occur and where most runners waste the most energy by using too much muscle for support and propulsion.

In T'ai Chi this felt sense of your body being in a perpetual state of "relaxed support" is called *song*. In ChiRunning we call it your Column. In the world of physics it is called tensegrity, a word coined by the famous architect and philosopher Buckminster Fuller, inventor of the geodesic dome. I first came across this term in Rick Barrett's book *Taijiquan: Through the Western Gate*, where he explains, in Western terminology, how relaxed support of the body happens.

Barrett refers to "moving the body in a state of wholeness while relaxing into the intrinsic support of your connective tissue." Running in this way allows your muscles to remain relaxed, especially any muscles that could present any restriction (through held tension) to the natural movement of active muscles. Using muscle power to run is a very inefficient way to move your body compared to that of relying on alignment and relaxation.

Here's how the principle of tensegrity works in your body. Tom Myers, author of *Anatomy Trains*, does a beautiful job of describing how the myofascial system in the body acts much like the stays on the mast of a sailboat. The mast itself can support the weight of the sail, but it would never be able to remain upright if it didn't have guy wires holding it vertically.

In your body your skeletal alignment acts like the mast, while the ligaments and tendons (connective tissue) act like the guy wires that hold your structure upright during the support phase of your stride. Once your bones are lined up (as with the posture focuses in Chapter 3), it's your connective tissue, not your muscle, that allows those bones to remain aligned.

## The Chi in *Chi Marathon*

Tai chi is often described as "meditation in motion," but it might well be called "*medication* in motion." There is growing evidence that this mind-body practice, which originated in China as a martial art, has value in treating or preventing many health problems.

—FROM *HARVARD WOMEN'S HEALTH WATCH*, MAY 2009

ChiRunning and ChiWalking, as well as what we describe here in *Chi Marathon*, are all based on principles of T'ai Chi, the ancient martial art that is showing up in schools, retirement communities, local gyms, and Harvard health publications as a method to improve movement, increase mental cognition, calm the mind, and strengthen the core. In China you can see people of all ages practicing T'ai Chi and Chi Gong in city parks. When we lived in San Francisco we were always inspired by people practicing their movements while waiting for the bus and in groups sprinkled throughout Golden Gate Park.

Chi (pronounced "chee" and also spelled *qi*) is life-force energy—the life-giving, vital energy that unites body, mind, and spirit. The concept has its origins in early Chinese philosophy and has been likened to the yogic concept of *prana*. For thousands of years the Chinese have based their movement principles and medicine on the movement and cultivation of chi.

In 2007, Katherine and I experienced the amazing feats of T'ai Chi grandmasters firsthand. We spent two weeks in China studying T'ai Chi with our teacher, Grandmaster George Xu, and twelve other grandmasters along with a hundred T'ai Chi teachers from all over the world.

Every day in our classes we watched these grandmasters make everyone else look like paper airplanes being tossed about. One day, one of the grandmasters, a small, frail-looking, gray-haired, eighty-six-year-old man, called up from our group a very strong 200-pound man who was a respected T'ai Chi teacher in his own country. Over and over this little old master sent the larger man flying across the room as if he were a toy soldier being flung about. It was clear that the tall, well-built man was doing his best to hold his ground and try to fight back, but to no avail. It was both comedic and truly amazing. During our stay we witnessed many demonstrations of great power and energy that had, from what we could see, very little to do with strength.

T'ai Chi has at its core the concept that your mind directs your chi (energy) and your chi moves your body. The practice cultivates the chi in your body so that it is of the highest quality, like high octane fuel. The better you get at using your chi to move your body, the less you need to use muscles and all the energy they require. In ChiRunning, basic principles of T'ai Chi are employed to optimize the flow of energy in your body to reduce the use of force for moving forward, and thereby reduce the risk of injury. You don't need to know anything about T'ai Chi to benefit from the *Chi Marathon* program. But you can benefit from using the basic principles as we apply them specifically to running long distances.

## The Application of T'ai Chi Principles to Your Running: Creating the Conditions for Energy to Flow

There are many principles found in T'ai Chi that can be transferred into almost any sport or physical activity. Creating the conditions for energy to flow is the overarching theme. In T'ai Chi and in life, you don't want energy to stagnate. In acupuncture, a foundational principle is that where there is pain, the flow of energy has been impeded, and precisely placed needles are used to get it flowing again. In the *Chi Marathon* program you want to keep your energy flowing in order to be able to run 13.1 or 26.2 miles.

Here is a brief overview of three principles of T'ai Chi that are used extensively in this program. (We'll expand on their explanation and application in Chapters 3 and 4.) Holding these principles in the back of your mind during your training will allow you to always have a sense of *why* you're doing any given focus or exercise.

A fundamental principle of T'ai Chi utilized in ChiRunning is Needle in Cotton, which describes the feeling a T'ai Chi student should have when practicing this ancient martial art. The central, vertical axis of your body is the needle. It is your base of support and, when you're running, represents the support provided by your structure during that brief moment between strides when you're on the ground. During the flight phase all of your moving parts—arms, legs, and hips—are relaxed, flexible, and soft as cotton, holding no tension. This allows your energy to flow freely and your body to have maximum freedom of movement.

The ChiRunning terms for needle and cotton are *alignment* and *relaxation*. They demonstrate the balanced and complementary relationship between yin and yang, where yin represents gathering or cohering energy and yang represents expansive energy.

Another principle from T'ai Chi is Gathering and Issuing. Gathering, in terms of ChiRunning, is all about gathering energy to your needle, your centerline, so you have a solid base around which all of the movement in your body takes place. Issuing, on the other hand, is all about energy moving away from your center and out into the world—or, in the case of ChiRunning, being the source of movement for your arms and legs. We'll explore this principle in more depth in Chapter 4, on conditioning, and in Chapter 9, on advanced techniques.

As in T'ai Chi, in the *Chi Marathon* program all your movements and all your workouts are geared to take advantage of principles of physics, the architecture of your body, and the forces of nature to create the conditions for you to move forward with a newfound power and ease that comes from cooperation and awareness rather than hard, mindless work.

## Cooperating with Forces

In T'ai Chi we are taught that when an opponent attacks with a punch or kick we shouldn't meet that force with a punch or kick of our own, but instead move *with* that force in order to neutralize it or redirect it. In running, there are two distinct forces at work on your body: the constant downward pull of gravity and the horizontal force of the oncoming road.

Gravity becomes your ally when you allow your body to gently fall forward into its pull. You then learn to balance yourself in this forward fall, allowing the pull of gravity to do the work of propulsion your legs would normally be doing. If you run with your body in a vertical position (as most adults do), you must rely solely on your legs to push you forward. In the ChiRunning technique the main purpose of your legs is for momentary support between strides, *not* for propulsion. (See figure 1.)

The second force to cooperate with is the approaching ground. Whenever you're running, the ground is moving toward you at exactly the same speed, creating the potential for a lot of force to your body with

**Figure 1—Use legs for support, *not* propulsion**

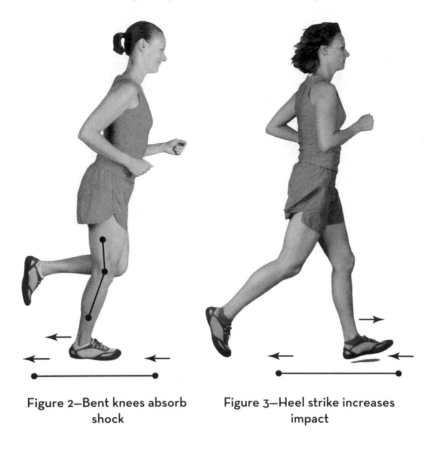

**Figure 2—Bent knees absorb shock**

**Figure 3—Heel strike increases impact**

each foot strike. (See figure 2.) Instead of meeting that force, you'll learn to yield to it by keeping your knees bent and landing in a midfoot strike, directly under your body. This will allow the force of the road to essentially swing your legs for you, in a rearward direction. If you swing your legs forward (toward the oncoming road), you'll land with your feet in front of your body and you'll be opposing the force of the ground, creating greater impact (see figure 3). This increase in the force of impact can lead to the most common running injury of all, the infamous "runner's knee." In Chapter 3 we'll explain in detail how to work with each of these valuable forces and make them your allies.

## The Whole-Body Marathon

As well as cooperating with the force of gravity and the force of the road coming at you, when you're training the *Chi Marathon* way you also utilize all of your body, rather than just your legs, to move yourself down the road. In T'ai Chi, economy of effort is king.

The wise men who developed this martial art wanted to make the most of every move, so they studied efficiency of movement in animals and took the best of what they gleaned into their practice. Some of these key body principles that we bring into ChiRunning are:

- The strongest parts of the body should do the most work.
- The strong core of the body is the most efficient source of power and energy, and should be the place of origination of all movement.
- When the whole body works as one, it is more efficient than separate parts working independently.

You'll get firsthand experience of how these body principles are applied to your running by practicing the Form Focuses in Chapter 3.

## Body Sensing: A Process of Discovery

Having the skills and wherewithal to release tension, move efficiently, pace yourself wisely, and keep your body properly hydrated and fueled are primary goals for anyone thinking about running a marathon. Being mindful means knowing what your body needs in any given moment and how to respond to various internal and external demands as they present themselves. It's being able to make subtle adjustments in your running form from moment to moment while keeping in mind the entirety of the run.

The skill most key to accomplishing this is Body Sensing. Body Sensing is a mindful awareness of your physical, emotional, and energetic state of being in any given moment. When you realize you are carrying tension in your shoulders, you can begin to consciously relax and let the tension go. When you realize you are overstriding, you can learn to shorten your gait, allowing your feet to land softly under you instead of out in front of you with a braking effect.

The beauty of Body Sensing is how much even the most challenged runners improve with just a few hours of paying attention to their body in a new way. While training for a marathon, you'll have ample time to check in with your body, do regular Body Scans, and get to know how your body best functions. You can do a Body Scan anytime, even right now. Close your eyes, drop your focus to your feet, and slowly scan up your whole body as if your mind were an MRI scanner. Notice anything and everything you can: where there is tension, how your body is positioned, how your weight is distributed. Can you feel any places that are tense? Stop and take five deep breaths. We're told to do that all the time, but how often do you actually stop and consciously breathe? Five deep breaths takes only a few seconds and will help focus your mind and feel your body. Pay attention to the thoughts, feelings, and sensations that arise as you "listen" to your body. These messages are worth paying attention to. You don't have to do anything about any of your findings at this stage. Just notice and learn, or make any adjustments that make you more comfortable.

Body Sensing involves taking an active interest in the state of your physical being in the moment, "listening" to your senses to determine if you are functioning optimally and whether you need to make any adjustments. What will help the energy to flow in your body? Some cool water, a deep breath, a stretch? Only you can feel your body and what it needs. No doctor, running coach, or any other human being has the honor of feeling and knowing what your body is telling you. It is a realm that, to me, is totally fascinating because it is what we experience every moment of our lives.

When you get good at Body Sensing you'll discover it is the small adjustments that make a big difference in how you run, how you eat, and how you go through each day. By making those small, incremental choices, you not only affect the course of your workouts but also build the skills and confidence to make the bigger choices when you need to.

Throughout the training programs described in Appendixes A and B, you'll be given Form Focuses for each workout. You'll learn how to do these Form Focuses in Chapter 3. As you practice each Form Focus take the time to sense how it feels in your body.

Body Sensing and the other techniques we talk about in *Chi Marathon* are an invitation to a different kind of adventure. Rather than simply testing your body's strength, we invite you to learn about your body. Listen to it. It is the mind *and* the body working together that makes for the best results. Then, with the proper tools and understanding, use the marathon to expand your awareness of yourself to discover your potential.

## The Seven Phases of Training for a Marathon:
## Technique-Based, Race-Specific Training

Imagine being an actor in a musical. You get your script and practice it day and night before beginning rehearsals. Then you go to rehearsals to learn the songs, the dances, the cues, where to stand, and what is expected of you at any given moment during the production. Weeks go by until finally it's time for the dress rehearsal, where you get to work out any glitches as you see them come up. Then it's opening night. You're excited and totally ready for the lights to go up and the curtain to swing wide. You turn to someone next to you onstage and, with a wide grin on your face, you say, "It's show time!"

Now, imagine going about training for a marathon in a similar way. Just as you'd learn your lines, you spend time perfecting your running form and training your body and mind to respond immediately to almost every conceivable situation that could confront you during your marathon. You practice each of these scenarios by running through repeated mock-ups of challenging situations. By the time race day comes, you know when and where to adjust your technique, when to use your speed and when to rest for an upcoming hill, when to use your upper body, when to fuel, when to drink, how to dress, what pace to go, what to watch out for. The more you can practice ahead of time all that will happen on race day, the more successful your training and race will be.

The psychological advantage to approaching a marathon this way speaks for itself. Imagine standing at the start line feeling thoroughly prepared and ready to have a great day. No worries, no doubts—just pure excitement and the joy that comes from knowing your body can handle anything that comes up. You'll be so ready to put all that practice to work that you'll probably find yourself standing at the start line saying, with a huge grin, "It's show time!"

The process of training for a marathon is like any long-term endeavor. To be successful, you need to break down big goals or complex problems into progressively smaller, more manageable parts. In *Chi Marathon* we've divided the three to six months of training into seven phases. Each phase provides a solid foundation upon which to build the next stage of your training. In each phase the predominant theme and the various focuses help you develop the necessary physical and mental/emotional skills to run your event pain- and injury-free, and to begin to tap into energy and abilities you might not have experienced before.

The seven phases are:

    I. Visioning and Planning
   II. The Technique Phase
 III. The Conditioning Phase
 IV. The Mastery Phase
   V. Taper Time
 VI. The Event
VII. Rest, Renewal, and Next Steps

Here's an overview of each phase.

### PHASE I: VISIONING AND PLANNING

Creating a vision and having a plan is an essential phase of any endeavor and especially when running a marathon where your physical, mental, and emotional skills are all going to be called upon. You'll begin by creating your vision, where you'll see yourself fulfilling your desired outcome. Then you'll assess your strengths and challenges, and finally you'll create a plan that is compatible with your day-to-day life. The mindful approach you cultivate in this phase will also help make the most of each workout. It's important to not gloss over this phase of your training. The most successful athletes, businesspeople, and leaders understand that visioning, assessing, and planning are essential to a positive outcome.

### PHASE II: THE TECHNIQUE PHASE

This is the phase that is missing in virtually every training program, and it is without a doubt the most essential aspect to a pain-free experience. In order to go beyond strength training and enter a truly new paradigm of running, you will first find it necessary to focus on your running form. In the initial weeks of your training you'll be using every workout as a time to learn and practice each of the individual ChiRunning Form Focuses needed to become a highly efficient runner. Think of the Form Focuses as a list of job descriptions for each of the individual body parts involved in your running. Each of the ChiRunning focuses is designed to teach a specific part of your body how to cooperate with all of the other body parts, so that eventually the whole "team" is running in a beautiful

and unified way. When all of your body parts cooperate and work together, each one's job gets easier. True power in running comes not from
stronger muscles but from the freedom of movement that you attain
through good running form. Being a strong athlete will not guarantee
you a successful marathon; being *mindful* will.

### PHASE III: THE CONDITIONING PHASE

After a thorough course in the basics of ChiRunning, we'll introduce
workouts that train you to hold and consistently apply these basic skills
over longer and longer distances. You'll learn all the various types of
workouts and which Form Focuses to emphasize in various workouts.
This does two things: it allows your body to get used to running for extended periods of time by building a strong cardiovascular and aerobic
base, and it trains your mind to focus and be engaged for extended periods of time, a crucial part of preventing the wheels from coming off, so
to speak. The focus will be on learning to relax—yes, relax—and back
off excessive use of force and effort. Workouts will emphasize:

- Sensing and eliminating inefficiencies in your movement
- Using mental focuses to tap into internal energy (chi)
- Applying the principle of stretch and recoil to develop a truly ef-
  fortless leg swing

### PHASE IV: EVENT MASTERY

We call the next few weeks of training the mastery phase because it's
the ideal time to apply your conditioning to the specific requirements
of the marathon or half marathon you've entered. In this race-specific
training, you'll practice each leg of your event: the start, the finish, and
the infamous mile 18, where many "hit the wall." If your course is flat,
you'll learn techniques to freshen your legs; if it's hilly, you'll learn how
to climb without expending extra effort, no matter the height of the
summit. By this time you'll be familiar with most of the ChiRunning
Form Focuses and can customize and adapt them for the specific details
of your event.

Each workout will be a mini dress rehearsal where you practice pacing, fueling, and overcoming challenges. If you are working toward a
personal best, you'll be focusing on managing your energy for optimal
speed without overstressing your body. Event mastery is for everyone,

from beginner to elite runner. If you are seeking greater speed or are well versed in the ChiRunning techniques and want to expand your skills, read Chapter 9, "Advanced ChiRunning Techniques."

## PHASE V: TAPER TIME

The two weeks (one week for the half marathon) immediately prior to your race is spent resting your body while keeping yourself sharp with your focuses. This means a reduction in your mileage but not in your workout speed. You'll be restocking your internal fuel supply in preparation for your race. This is also the time to finalize all the logistics around race day so that everything happens without glitches that might upset the flow of your mental and physical energy.

## PHASE VI: THE EVENT

This phase is the culmination of your training and all you have practiced. The day before, the day of, and the day after the event are all part of the event itself. You'll be so well prepared that the event itself will be a celebration of the training you have done, and after the event, celebrate you should! However, even the most skilled athletes know that the weekend of the event requires a particular set of skills and awareness. In Chapter 7, "Race Weekend," we'll review how to truly enjoy and make the most of the days around the marathon and, of course, how to get the most out of every moment of running those 13.1 or 26.2 miles.

## PHASE VII: REST, RENEWAL, AND NEXT STEPS

The most common testimonials we get are from clients who are surprised at how little recovery time is necessary with ChiRunning. However, no matter how you feel after your marathon, it is important to complete your marathon training cycle by looking at what your body and your being most need. This involves taking deeply into your whole person what you have accomplished, and resting and recuperating. After a few days or a few weeks, you can begin again the process of visioning and assessing your next steps. If you're a multiple marathoner, you'll be planning for your next event. If it's your first event, you'll evaluate what place running has in your life. Renewing your commitment to yourself, your health, and your exercise practice will make the training you did of great value to your whole life.

# It's Your Choice: Choose Quality with Every Step

For every person who runs a marathon, crossing the finish line is a welcome and wonderful moment in time. You've done it. When the medal is put around your neck, it is a powerful symbol of hard work and accomplishment. What you have attained, however, resides in your heart and mind as a positive testament to your ability to focus and to make wise choices, from your strong and upright structure to the deep, powerful core of your being.

The quality with which you move, how you think, and how you relate to the world around you is always a choice in your life. *Chi Marathon* offers you the option to bring the wisdom of the grandmasters into your running and into your everyday life. Every step is about choosing where you place your focus and attention.

When you choose to improve the quality of your running, there is never a bad run, but there is often a good lesson. And there is *always* something you can do to improve the situation. You may need to slow down, or you may just need to make some slight adjustments in your stride, but you'll know that you have options. If you get injured, you'll know that if you change how you run, you can eliminate the cause of that injury. The training you'll get puts the choice in your hands. If you feel pain or fatigue, rather than giving up you can ask, "What can I do, here and now, to change this run into a positive experience?"

*Chi Marathon* is about the process of self-discovery. For anyone who has ever run a marathon, a part of that is finding your limits and learning how to reach beyond those limits without force or aggression, but instead with intelligence, self-awareness, and compassion. As you train for your marathon, the runs get longer, and you have more and more time to practice the Form Focuses, their impact begins to permeate your understanding on other levels, and you'll be met with realizations of how these principles could work in other areas of your life. That process has the potential to take you to new personal frontiers within yourself that are exhilarating and inspiring.

# CHAPTER TWO

# Phase I

## Vision, Goals, and Planning

There are some people who live in a dream world, and there are some who face reality; and then there are those who turn one into the other.

—DOUGLAS EVERETT

I f you run marathons or are even thinking about it, then you're the type of person who dares to dream and dares to turn those dreams into reality. That is why running a marathon is such a highly respected endeavor. Not everyone is willing to take on the challenge. *Chi Marathon* is about tapping into the real reasons you want to run a marathon and then bringing your dreams into a physical reality. Every Form Focus you practice to improve your running technique will translate into the inner resourcefulness to create personal success in your life. This is why we get letters from so many people who tell us that ChiRunning has not just improved their running form but *changed their life*. They are everyday people who have built a bridge between their current state and the vision they have of themselves. They are people who have had a transformative experience by simply paying attention and being willing to try something new.

Let me provide a little backstory. In a matter of twelve months spanning 2004–2005, I started a new career, bought a house, and became a father. Not only did all that new stress add twenty-five pounds to my normally fit physique, but I felt it take a toll on my mental well-being. I had run in the past, though iliotibial band problems in college put an end to that, which I did not really enjoy in the first place. So in 2007 I began running again, pushed hard, and promptly injured myself after about three months. After a six-month layoff, I tried once more, and made it just over four months before the pain of piriformis syndrome sidelined me again. It was Christmas 2008 when a family member introduced me to ChiRunning. I thought it sounded silly. But I was desperate.

I ran 150 and 250 miles, respectively, through my injury-plagued years of 2007 and 2008, completing a fraction of the races I had hoped to run. With the help of ChiRunning and a renewed focus on my breathing, posture, and mechanics, I ran more than 600 miles in 2009 and even won a year-end age group award in my local running club's annual racing series. In 2010, I've set personal records in every distance from the 5K to the half marathon and will cover 850 miles! Most important, every step has been enjoyable and injury-free! I have gone from struggling through a 10K in an hour to racing a 47:07 this fall, something I never thought possible. I've also finally admitted to my wife that I have an addiction: the long run. If I don't knock out 8–12 miles on a Saturday morning, my weekend won't feel complete. A big thank-you to Danny and ChiRunning! Two years later, I'm a true believer.

—Matt Callaway

The unifying of mind and body can be seen on many levels in the ChiRunning, ChiWalking, and Chi Marathon programs.

Alignment, relaxation, leaning, allowing gravity to move you forward: all of the Form Focuses in ChiRunning have a mental and emotional correlation to being successful at any long-term endeavor. The deep core of your body is where your deepest dreams reside, along with the power to make them real. When you strengthen the physical center of your body, you are also strengthening your ability to be centered emotionally. When you learn a new Form Focus, you are also strengthening your mind's ability to stay focused on your goal. When your physical center is strong, it allows the rest of your body to be relaxed, flexible, and responsive to whatever comes your way. When you have a goal to accomplish, you will be most successful when you are strong in your resolve but flexible and responsive to the daily influences that can ultimately create or undermine success.

Alignment in the physical sense means getting your head, shoulders, hips, and ankles in alignment. On another level you are aligning your vision, feelings, and desires with the physical movement of your body to create truly unified movement. Alignment creates ease of movement and ease in fulfilling your goal. Everything you practice on a physical level supports and informs your mental and emotional states, and vice versa.

## The Power of Intention

The literature on the power of intention is vast, from personal growth programs and articles to best-selling business books. Many of the most impressive stories feature top athletes, the best of whom use the power of intention to see, feel, and imagine success in their sport. Studies have even shown that merely imagining yourself doing a workout causes your muscle mass to increase. But don't get too excited—you can't run a pain-free marathon simply by imagining you're training. Your chances of success, however, are greatly increased when you fully utilize the power of intention in each of your workouts.

Muhammad Ali was famous for his use of intention to achieve his goals. "He was not training his body to win. He was training his mind not to lose, at the point when deep fatigue sets in around the twelfth round and most boxers cave in. Ali's most important work was being done, not in the ring, but in his armchair. He was fighting the fight in his head," writes Lynne McTaggart in her book *The Intention Experiment*. Ali is a great role model for all of us. He used all the skills of intention: affirmations, mental imagery, and self-confirmation. Do you remember Ali's repetitive rhymes?

*This brash young boxer is something to see*
*And the heavyweight championship is his destiny.*
*This kid's got a left,*
*This kid's got a right,*
*If he hit you once,*
*You're asleep for the night.*

All of his mantras had meaning and purpose—and they worked. He would publicly say, "I am the greatest," and *Sports Illustrated* agreed by naming him the greatest athlete of the twentieth century.

As you practice the Form Focuses you'll be using the power of your mind and your imagination to educate your body. For example, the hardest part of ChiRunning can be trying to relax. Getting muscles that are used to firing to stop working can be challenging. The rewards in terms of energy efficiency and injury prevention are well worth the effort, though. It is the mind that will direct the tight, active muscles to relax and give them an image of soft cotton to emulate. You use your mind when you are Body Sensing. It's the mind that focuses on the body. It is the mind that eventually connects with the body so well that they can respond and react intuitively as one.

Here is a four-step process that will help you get aligned with your intentions and reasons for running a half or full marathon.

**Step 1: Assess yourself.** Look at yourself in terms of your running, your physical health, and your mental and emotional strengths and challenges.

**Step 2: Write a vision.** Take the big perspective of what you want to achieve through running a half or full marathon.

**Step 3: Create specific goals.** These are measurable goals that are either physical or emotional.

**Step 4: Choose an event.** Train specifically for that event.

## Personal Assessment

Look well into thyself; there is a source of strength which will always
spring up if thou wilt always look there.

—MARCUS AURELIUS

Before you write your vision and set specific, tangible goals, it is important to clearly assess your present state of marathon readiness, not just physically but also mentally and emotionally. These assessments will help you choose the right marathon event, figure out what training program to follow, and create a road map for your training. To fulfill your vision and complete your event, you have to start somewhere. That somewhere is right now.

One of the most important tools in evaluating yourself is developing what we call the Observer. The Observer is the part of yourself that simply takes in information without judging whether it is "good" or "bad." It is the part of your mind that receives input from your five senses—touch, sight, sound, taste, smell—and any factual information that you know to be true. What is really helpful in assessing any given moment is to simply start with information rather than jumping to conclusions too quickly. However, the nature of the mind is to quickly attach judgments to the information it takes in, and it takes some self-awareness to notice when this is happening.

Let's take the example of pain. You're on a run and you feel a twinge of pain in your knee. When you've developed a strong Observer, you notice the pain, and rather than seeing it as bad or scary or upsetting, you remain calm; you notice the twinge as a piece of information. You can then review your toolkit for eliminating knee pain. Maybe you'll try some things you'll learn in this book. Or you might make a note to visit the ChiRunning website and look up how to eliminate knee pain and then practice those Form Focuses on your next run.

From a centered and calm place you'll think, "This is interesting. I have some knee pain. I need to make an adjustment in my running. I've probably slipped back into heel striking, or maybe my foot is rotating laterally." The knee pain actually becomes a good thing, as you recognize that it is a message that you need to hear to improve your running technique.

Without the Observer, knee pain might send you into a downward spiral of fear and identification with the pain. *I can never get past mile 5 without getting this pain!* you might think. *I shouldn't be running. How the heck can I run 13 miles if I can't run 5? I give up.* The negative emo tions take over, and you've lost your rational perspective and your ability to create positive change.

The Observer is the master of the Chi skill of Non-identification, which we've written about in the *ChiRunning* and *ChiWalking* books. Non-identification means putting aside all your personal ideas and pref- erences and responding to what *is* in any situation. You'll be building a strong, centered, and neutral Observer throughout this program.

Whatever you're experiencing is not good or bad; it just is. It's a lot easier to untangle and respond to things appropriately and with clarity when you're dealing with the facts. Approach both the assessments in this chapter and your training with your Observer, not your judge.

We suggest you choose a place to keep all your observations and train- ing data. Our online training program provides a place for you to write, edit, and refer to your vision, goals, personal assessments, and training information. If you prefer to put pen to paper, we also offer a *Daily Fit- ness Journal* that has space for all this information. If you have yet to keep a fitness log, you'll find it invaluable in keeping track of your basic health stats. Measuring your progress week by week will become an incredibly useful resource that will help you become your own best coach.

## RUNNING ASSESSMENT

Here you're going to assess your running skills to determine what train- ing program is best for you and how long you need to train. This will help you determine your running goals.

**ChiRunning Skills:** If you are new to ChiRunning, we highly rec ommend that you spend four to eight weeks on the technique phase of your training. In all honesty, many people have done well with much less time than that; we've had people learn just a few concepts the day before their marathon, such as shortening their stride and leaning slightly, and benefit from those during their race. On the other hand, some people need more time in order to be able to feel and use the Form Focuses well. We highly recommend that you take plenty of time for the technique phase and learn the skills that will be a solid foundation for your event and for the rest of your life. We'll review all the marathon training programs and the time allotted for the technique phase later in this chapter.

If you already use the ChiRunning technique, here are some questions to help you assess your ChiRunning skills:

1. How long have you practiced the ChiRunning Form Focuses?
2. What Form Focuses do you feel most comfortable with?
3. What Form Focuses do you need to practice the most?
4. Have you gotten to the stage where you can feel the relaxation of running with good form?

**Running Statistics:** Note the following to get a picture of yourself in numbers:

1. Distance or time of your longest current long run:

2. Average mileage per week:

3. Average running pace (if you don't know, don't worry):

4. Average race pace (if you run marathons or other events):

5. Number of 5Ks or 10Ks run:

6. Number of half marathons run:          Number completed:

7. Number of full marathons run:          Number completed:

8. Number of marathons (half or full) in the last twelve months:

9. Number of marathons in your life:


**Physical Assessment:** A physical assessment is a fabulous way to track your progress.

Age:


Height:


Weight:


BMI:


Blood pressure:


Resting heart rate (RHR; see box on p. 32 for how to determine this):


General level of fitness and health (where 1 is poor health and 10 is optimal health):


General level of energy in daily life (where 1 is low energy and 10 is optimal energy):


Are you satisfied with your overall health?


Are you satisfied with your weight?

Have you had a health evaluation from a professional in the last eighteen months?

What health conditions or concerns do you need to consider?

Are you addressing these health conditions in your life?

Do you have aches or pains or feel restricted in your movement? If so, what are the specifics?

Do you have any current injuries or specific running injuries?

Are you addressing these injuries?

It is possible you'll resolve the causes of injury or pain as you learn and practice ChiRunning. However, you must determine if you need a professional assessment. Many people who have been told not to run have found that ChiRunning has made it possible for them to run without pain and injury. But if you have a running issue that will affect your long-term health, don't run.

To determine your resting heart rate (RHR), take your pulse by pressing your pointer and middle fingers on your neck beneath your lower jaw, just to either side of your throat. Count the number of beats in fifteen seconds and multiply by 4 to get the number of beats per minute. Check your RHR first thing in the morning, before you get out of bed. As you get into better shape from your training, you may find your RHR gets lower, which is good news.

**Mental/Emotional Assessment:** Spend some time thinking about where you are mentally and emotionally.

What are your mental and emotional strengths (i.e., determination, self-confidence, going with the flow, positive attitude, resourcefulness, creativity)?

What are your mental and emotional challenges (i.e., negative voices or attitudes, being stressed out a lot of the time, reactivity, inability to focus, a tendency to give up easily)?

Generally, do you tend to push yourself too hard or give up too easily?

Are you able to keep focused on whatever activity you are doing, or does your mind tend to wander and skip around from subject to subject?

As you review your strengths and challenges, you'll begin to notice what needs to be strengthened or improved in your physical, mental, and emotional makeup. After doing your assessment, write a vision of how you would like to be, during your training, during the marathon, and in your life, if you'd like to take it that far. Then, you can write down specific goals and intentions to help you achieve your vision.

CREATING A VISION AND SETTING INTENTIONS

A meaningful vision is the center around which all your efforts will orbit; it is your guiding star. Without a strong vision of what you want, long hours of training could become hollow and empty. *What the hell am I doing out here?* you might begin to ask yourself. Your vision is your answer: *I'm reclaiming my health. I'm finishing something for the first time in my life. I'm discovering my real power. I'm running in the name of my sister, who died too young. I'm learning something new so I can run for the rest of my life. I'm supporting an important cause.* An intention is your vision encapsulated into one or more powerful statements.

A vision is about the big picture. Running a marathon is a very practical, physical goal. How you run that marathon and how you want to feel the day of, the day after, and the weeks and months after the event is your vision. A vision is about qualities, not quantities (the latter is what goals are for), and you should infuse it with guiding principles. As you go through the training, you may find that your vision is changing. *I ran my fastest marathon ever* may evolve into *I feel energized and physically strong.* Or *I finished!* may evolve into *I qualified for Boston!* Or *I want to live with less stress and angst* may become *I want to relax and enjoy my life more.* Of course, you have to be careful if your vision devolves; you don't want to let a vision go just because of a few difficult runs. A powerful vision does not die easily; rather, it can be adjusted and recrafted as needed.

What will make a vision most powerful is Body Sensing. Here's why. When most people sit down to write a vision or goals or a plan, they primarily use their mind to think about what it is they want. Yes, the mind rules, but what kind of ruler doesn't listen to the wisdom of advisors? A despot, a tyrant, an oppressor—that's what kind. When your core, your heart and your emotions are integral to creating a vision, you are taking into account much more than your ideas of what you want. Learning to listen to more than just your mind, to the small quiet voice of intuition, is essential for a pain-free marathon and for creating a vision that will inspire and fuel your training.

**Write Your First Draft:** A great way to begin your visioning session is to do a Body Scan. You don't have to think about anything; just take a couple of deep breaths and scan your body from head to toe. Feel your feet on the ground and go up the body. The more time you can take with this, the better. Then let your mind rest on your center, two inches down from the navel and a few inches in toward the spine. Ask, *What do I want from running a marathon?* The word *question* contains the word *quest*, deriving from the Latin *quaestus*, "to ask" or "to seek." When you run a marathon, you can think of yourself as being on a quest, the outcome of which is your vision.

Take up to thirty minutes to write what comes up for you. Write down the main reasons you want to run a marathon and how you want to feel as you run the event, as you cross the finish line, and for the days, weeks and maybe years after.

The best answer will come from a strong internal pull, but it also might reveal itself over time, so remember that this is a first draft. You can also ask yourself while you're out running and write down your answers when you get back. The best way to utilize the power of your mind is to kinesthetically allow yourself to experience the event before it happens. Imagine how you will feel as you cross the finish line of the event. Don't just think about it. Put yourself fully into the experience and allow your body to go through all the positive responses and emotions. With focused concentration, allow the full impact of your accomplishment to wash through you, as if it is actually happening.

Then take your vision and write a few intentions in a positive voice and in the present tense:

"I feel physically stronger and healthier than any other time in my life."

"I feel like I can accomplish anything."

"I am so happy and satisfied with all my efforts."

"I feel relaxed, stress-free, and able to cope with anything that comes my way."

"My body feels well used and tired, but healthier than ever."

"I raised $2,000 for a cause that is meaningful, and I feel truly proud and part of something bigger than me."

"I feel so much energy from the connection and camaraderie of running with my friends."

"I did it, I ran my best time ever, and I have energy to spare!"

"I am capable and strong and feel so alive."

Experience your success now. That's what the best athletes do. They put themselves into the moment fully and feel what it feels like to succeed. Write with as much detail as you'd like. Your vision could be anywhere from fifty to a thousand words or more. A few strong intentional statements will make it easier for you to keep your vision with you while training.

Keep your vision handy. Post it in an obvious place in your home or office. Read it whenever the going gets tough. Edit it as needed. This is the deep, up-front preparation that will pay off when you need inspiration throughout your training.

SETTING GOALS

Setting goals is different than writing a vision, or intentions, in that goals are shorter term, specific, and measurable. Goals are the small but essential stepping-stones to making your vision a reality. The beauty of running a marathon is that it is a very specific, measurable goal around which you can create lots of smaller, but tangible goals.

The seven phases of the *Chi Marathon* training program and the training schedule have built-in goals such as weekly mileage and Form Focuses to practice and learn. These benchmarks let you know where you are in your training cycle. Writing goals that are tied into your vision, and that take into account your assessments, will help personalize your training.

Here are some ideas to get you going:

**Race-Specific Goals**
Finish without injury or pain
Finish in a specific time
Run negative splits (second half faster than the first half)
Feel great at mile 18 (to not "hit the wall")
Have energy for a Surge in the last mile
Hydrate consistently
Qualify for Boston
Place in your age group
Win

**Physical Goals**
Train without injury
Learn to manage my weight
Increase speed with less effort
Lose weight
Improve on any of the Form Focuses (see Chapter 3; these goals are built into the training programs, but you can choose the Form Focuses that you need to work on)

**Mental and Emotional Goals**
Be more positive
Be more centered and focused
Face challenges rather than being intimidated or backing off
Gain clear perspective on how pushing harder is not always the solution

In Chapter 10 we'll discuss the lifestyle issues that come with training for a marathon. A common concern is finding the time to train without feeling guilty about the time not spent with family or at work. When you create goals that also support you being a better person, parent, spouse or employee, then the benefits of training expand beyond the marathon event.

## CHOOSING AN EVENT

Timing is everything when it comes to choosing an event. There are many other factors to consider as well: location, terrain, time of year, support at the event, and with whom you'll run and train. Let's not exclude inspiration and intuition. If you have always wanted to run the Big Sur Marathon for its breathtaking beauty, or one of the Rock 'n' Roll events because of how fun they are, let that inspire you. If running in a marathon in Paris or Honolulu would be a dream come true, make it happen. Just make sure the timing works for thorough training and that you train for the hills of Big Sur or the crowds at the big marathon events. Dream big, and keep your feet planted firmly on the ground when it comes to the details of choosing your event or events.

Be aware of making a spontaneous decision about running a marathon without really considering the training. Too many groups and programs lure you in with a very short training cycle that can be a recipe for injury and put a halt to an activity that you could otherwise enjoy for the rest of your life. Bottom line? Give yourself *plenty* of time for training.

The location of your event is an important choice. Running in a local event is ideal. It makes logistics easy on every level: not having to travel, having friends and family nearby, and being able to train on the actual course (our favorite reason for running locally). Phase IV is all about race-specific training, and when the event is local you have the home team advantage of knowing every hill and turn.

Traveling has its logistical issues, but running a marathon is a great reason to travel, see a new place, and enjoy the benefits of the large marathon events. The excitement of a big event is very energizing and inspiring. You just have to make sure you don't lose your center, your plan, and yourself in the excitement. This topic will be discussed later in the book, but it needs to be part of your decision-making process. Terrain should also be considered. If you're a novice marathoner or returning after injury, don't pick one with a lot of hills. Many marathon events are pretty flat for optimal speed, but not all of them are, so review elevation gains and losses on your list of possible events before making a final decision.

**Choosing Multiple Events:** For those of you who have already run one or more marathons, once you run comfortably using the ChiRunning technique, you can probably rethink how many marathons you might be able to run each year. If you run half marathons, running a number of events is not really an issue. With full marathons, when much of the effort has been taken out of your running technique, the option to run multiple marathons every year becomes a very real possibility. In all the reading I've done, most coaches tell marathoners to do no more than two per year, maybe three if you're a real hot shot. That's to give your body plenty of time to recover from the "harshness" of running 26.2 miles all on the same day. The same coaches say that it takes about a month to recover from a marathon, after which you need to build slowly up to the point where you can begin training again.

I would conservatively say that a well-practiced ChiRunner could comfortably run four marathons per year. Remember, one of the reasons you're working to make distance running easier is so that you will need less recovery time after your workouts and races. We've received countless letters from folks who run a marathon and come away feeling as though they want to run the next day.

### INSTRUCTOR STORY

I ran my first marathon in 2000 at the age of twenty in 4:16. I was in so much knee and shin pain for a few weeks afterward because of heel striking (which I wasn't aware of at the time) and wearing the wrong kind of shoes. I was also disappointed because I walked several miles in the late stages. I thought I didn't have the right body type to run long distance. Fast-forward eight years and my decision to retire from soccer and pick up my love for running again. I found ChiRunning right at this critical time in my running, and when I ran my second marathon ever, a few months after reading the book and training using ChiRunning, I ran 3:43! I have since gone on to run a total of nineteen marathons in the last three years since learning about ChiRunning, and my personal record has dropped to 2:43:02. I have a goal to run sub-2:30, and the best part is that Chi-

Running has allowed to me to run more than I ever thought possible pain-free, efficiently, and sometimes effortlessly. I have won two marathons and also run the Boston and New York City marathons in 2010 in 2:47 each.

—Bryan Huberty

When you are running multiple events in a year, the need for your Observer and Body Sensing to be part of the equation increases exponentially. Running multiple marathons requires skill and self-awareness, and the body does require some amount of rest and rejuvenation. Deciding *not* to do an event can be harder for some people, emotionally, than actually running a marathon. The multiple-marathon lifestyle can be a great way to manage your health and enjoy life, but if your Observer is not engaged, you can lose perspective on why you are running marathons. If your temperament is one that tends to push too hard, did you note that in your self-assessment? Is it something you need to balance in your life with a dose of non-identification? When it's kept in balance, the multiple-marathon lifestyle can increase your energy, improve your overall health, and keep the pressures of life in perspective in balance. Just be sure to plan wisely and be flexible as you stay on course for your bigger vision.

When you live the multiple-marathon lifestyle, it is important to pay close attention to your phases of training so that you don't shortchange focused training. It's very easy to slip into ongoing conditioning. If your half marathons are eight weeks apart, you may instead spend a week in recovery, one week learning new focuses and reviewing the basics, three to four weeks in the conditioning phase, one to two weeks in the mastery phase for your upcoming event, and the final week in taper time.

For full marathons, you'll want ample time to go through all the phases. As your Body Sensing skills improve, you'll know when you need more rest and when to spend time improving performance. Here's what we suggest. It's important to maintain your distance base, so don't totally back off on your LSD (Long Slow Distance) runs. After each marathon take it a little easier for a couple of weeks by doing shorter midweek workouts and running 10–12 miles for your LSD. Then, after two weeks, pick up your training at week twelve in the ChiRunning Intermediate

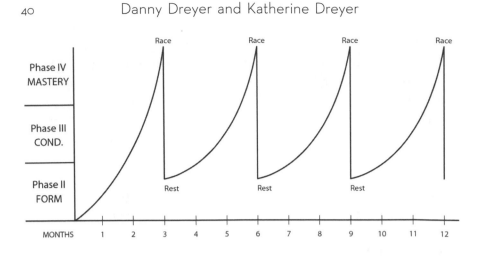

Marathon Training Program (not included in this book; see our website, www.chirunning.com) and run a half marathon for your first long run. Pick races that allow you to create a cycle of training. (See figure above.) Divide your training into the necessary phases for each race and you'll see it's not as big a deal as many people think it is when you do it with good running technique anchored in a deep base of conditioning.

Whether you're going for three marathons a year or more, it's always important to start at week twelve of our Intermediate Program to give yourself two months to train specifically for your race. You can always back up into earlier weeks if time allows.

## Choosing a Training Program

Training with a group is a fabulous way to keep motivated, get and give encouragement, and stay on track and accountable. You'll have people you know, who know how to help you, right by your side. The camaraderie of group training is a fuel unto itself, enriching the whole experience. The only issue is making sure you don't push yourself into running faster or farther than your technique and conditioning can support. Running with other ChiRunners is a great option, as individuals in your group can call out Form Focuses throughout your training. If you are not in a ChiRunning group, make sure you practice Body Sensing, allow yourself to go at your own speed, decrease the distance if it's too much of a push, and learn to practice your Form Focuses while running with other people. You might prefer to work on your own technique while running alone in your shorter, midweek workouts and run with a group for your long runs, where having company during those long miles is a godsend.

You'll also find lots of support on our website, with online groups and Certified Instructors who offer group training programs.

Your personal assessments along with the guidelines below will help you choose the *Chi Marathon* program that is best for you if . . .

## Beginner Half Marathon: 16 Weeks
You can comfortably run or run-walk a 5K
You are willing and able to train at least four days per week
You are a beginning runner wishing to increase distance
You are a beginning runner graduating from a run-walk program
You have run other half marathons but wish to do so with greater ease and enjoyment
You are new to ChiRunning or wish to improve your ChiRunning technique
You want to complete but not race a half marathon

## Intermediate Half Marathon: 12 Weeks
You have run other half marathons
You can comfortably run a 10K
You are new to ChiRunning or wish to improve and expand your knowledge of ChiRunning
You are willing and able to train five days per week
You are interested in increasing speed and performance
You are a triathlete training for a half Ironman

## Beginner Full Marathon: 24 Weeks
You can comfortably run a 10K
You are willing and able to train at least four days per week
You are new to ChiRunning or you want to improve your ChiRunning technique
You are running your first marathon
You have run other marathons but want to do so with greater ease and enjoyment
You have been injured and want to prevent further injury
You want to complete but not race a marathon

**Intermediate Full Marathon: 20 Weeks**

You have run other marathons

You can comfortably run a half marathon

You are new to ChiRunning or wish to improve and expand your knowledge of ChiRunning

You are willing and able to train five days per week

You are interested in increasing speed and performance

You are a triathlete training for an Ironman

### RUN-WALK TRAINING PROGRAM

ChiRunning and ChiWalking are the perfect combination if you use a run-walk program to complete your marathon event. By improving your walking and running techniques you'll be increasing your efficiency and speed while decreasing your risk of pain or injury. What you might find, however, is that when you learn to run with good technique, you don't need to take walking breaks as frequently. In Phase III, which focuses on conditioning, you will learn many techniques to rest and recover while running, so that you become less dependent on walk breaks.

If you intend to use a run-walk program throughout your marathon event, we highly recommend getting our *Run-Walk* DVD to support the process of transitions between walking and running and show you how to maintain your Chi techniques throughout. You may want to deepen and improve your ChiWalking skills and understanding with the *Chi-Walking* book and DVD. We also offer beginner 5K and 10K training programs that include weekly run-walk workouts.

## The Anatomy of the Ideal Workout

A great workout will feel like a ritual that you perform with regularity and consistency. My dog can tell it's time to go for a walk when I go to the front closet to grab a jacket; her whole body wags in anticipation. When you create a ritual around your running, your mind and body will also begin to fall into certain patterns (and maybe even wag with enthusiasm). It's really important to make those patterns positive imprints. That ritual could easily become a sacred part of your life: a time for you, a time to take care of your body and your health, a time when your mind focuses on the moment, on how you feel, and on what you need. When I put on my running clothes, I can feel my mind and body move into a different state of being, one of aliveness and anticipation. I am so used to Body Sensing when I run that I drop into my workout mode as I get ready for the run. I feel my Observer wake up and become more sensitive and alert.

The key to a great workout is understanding the importance of transitions in your life. Practicing the art of transitioning into and out of your workouts will help you learn to make smoother transitions into and out of your daily life. If you have ever felt jolted by the transition from being at work to going home to small children, you know what I mean. At work you might be dealing with adults all day, but then you need to go home and put on the hat of parent and caregiver. If you take a few minutes to consciously make that adjustment, the transition will have less friction and less of a jarring effect, and your whole life will feel like more of a continuum.

You have the option to add quality and mindful awareness to every move you make; making each run a special event, like a Japanese tea ceremony. This doesn't mean you can't enjoy yourself, have fun with your friends, and relax. You can also internally connect with yourself, your vision, and your goals, and savor them during your transitions. Treat them as a special time for *you*.

Here are guidelines for you to create your own ritual around your runs and practice transitioning into and out of your workouts.

- **Have a clear intention.** Know beforehand what type of run you'll be doing: long run, Form Focus intervals, Fun Run, speed intervals (you'll learn the specifics of all the runs in Chapter 4). Know what Form Focuses you'll be practicing.
- **Body Sense how you feel.** Stand for a few moments in your best posture (see Chapter 3). Do a Body Scan and feel for any tension you might be holding. If you sense any tension, take a few deep breaths and direct your attention only to the focus at hand, letting go of the tension. Then open your eyes and begin walking or running while holding your specific focus in your mind and placing your attention on the area of your body where the focus is involved.
- **Do Body Looseners.** Studies show that stretching before a workout can cause muscle pulls and injury. But ChiRunning Body Looseners loosen joints, relax muscles, and begin the warm-up process. Many of our clients would not do a workout without first doing their Body

Looseners. The Body Looseners are covered thoroughly in the Chi-Running book, or you can see them done on the *ChiRunning* DVD.

- **Warm up.** Start *every workout* very slowly in what we call first gear (you'll learn about gears in Chapter 3) for five to ten minutes, depending on the length of your run. At this slow pace, practice aligning your posture with every step you take. This will form the background of any of the focuses you've chosen to work on in this workout.
- **Focus your mind, engage your core, relax your body, and enjoy your run.** Once you're warmed up, gradually shift into a comfortable aerobic pace (second gear) and instate the focuses you have chosen for the day. Specifics of each workout can be found in the training programs. Do regular Body Scans throughout.
- **Experience what relaxation feels like in your body.** How does it affect your movement? How does it feel when you let go of tension held in your muscles? When I'm running, my level of enjoyment is directly proportional to my level of relaxation. Sometimes if I feel a general tension in my body, I'll stop and shake my whole body, like a dog coming out of a lake, and then proceed with my run, dropping all of my tension into the earth with each stride.
- **Cool down.** At the end of your workout, drop back into first gear for five minutes, then walk for three to five minutes. Stretching after you run will help move any lactic acid through your system and will help keep muscles loose and flexible.
- **Do an end-of-run review.** During your post-run walk, take a few minutes to mentally review your run. This will help you incorporate the benefits of the run into the rest of your day. Then do another Body Scan. Note or write down how your body feels, what went well, what was challenging, and what you need to work on in your next workout. Once a week, preferably after your long run, take a little more time and review how your training is going. Writing down your comments will help you incorporate what you've learned and help you see where you could improve.

## Your Training Schedule

In Chapter 10, "Training the Whole Person," we'll discuss training and exercise as part of a healthy lifestyle and getting the support you need from family, friends, and co-workers. To run a pain-free marathon, you need a minimum of four days a week for novices, and five for intermediate runners. You'll have one long run a week, and eventually you'll need two to five hours to complete it. Once you choose a training program or decide to use the beginner plans in Appendixes A or B, map out the days you can run and the day for your long run, and put them on your calendar. Treat each run like an important appointment. There truly is nothing more important than your health. With it, you can do anything. Without it, the quality of your life suffers. By choosing to run a pain-free marathon, you're making a positive choice that can have far-reaching effects.

## Shoes, Accessories, and Clothing

### SHOES

Your chances of finding good shoes and information about what is the best shoe for you have increased dramatically in recent years. In 2002, when we wrote the first edition of ChiRunning, we were considered "out there" because of our suggestion to run in minimal shoes. When a large shoe company invited us to their offices to discuss a midfoot-strike shoe and get our support in promoting them, we learned that the research from the product development team was showing that a midfoot strike reduces impact for runners, but unfortunately, the marketing department was not very enthusiastic about sharing the research with the public and was hesitant to market a shoe that would throw into question the design of their traditional, overbuilt running shoes.

Today, a more minimal, flexible shoe should be considered the norm for every runner. Your foot is a veritable genius when it comes to educating your body how to move well. Running barefoot is a great way to allow your body to feel contact with the ground you're running on, but with all the great minimalist shoe options available today, it's not necessary to forgo shoes altogether. Minimalist shoes are very flexible and have a wide toe box that allows your foot to spread out and make thorough contact with the ground. There are plenty of options out there now that would have seemed outlandish a few years ago—for example, who thought shoes with toes would become the rage?

Running barefoot is definitely an option. We don't, however, suggest barefoot running as the only means to educate your body. People who ran barefoot for most of their childhood have good running technique because of many early years of running well. If you're twenty-five or older and have been shod most of your life, taking off your shoes will inform your body, but not necessarily educate it on good running technique. A combination of learning good running form and running barefoot or in minimal shoes will help your body to remember how it is meant to run.

Gradual Progress is a Chi skill that applies to choosing your shoes. If you are used to running in a stiff, built-up shoe and you'd like to switch to running in less of a shoe, don't start running with a completely minimal shoe for every workout unless you're willing to take a big drop in your weekly mileage and basically start your distance program from scratch. If, on the other hand, you'd like to keep your mileage but switch to less of a shoe, you can move into a shoe that is in between what you're currently wearing and a minimal shoe. Find a shoe that is less structured than your current shoe and over time move into a more flexible minimal shoe. Your shoe should have a wide, flexible toe box with enough room for your toes to completely spread out. (See figure 4.) They should have less heel height than your current shoe (the flatter the better) and be completely comfortable, like slippers. They should also be lighter than your current shoes (10–12 ounces per shoe is a good start)—who needs to lug around extra weight?

Never run more than 5 miles in a new pair of shoes. Break in new shoes with three short runs before wearing them on a long run. This means you cannot run your actual event in a brand-new pair of shoes. If you do, you're asking for blisters, pain, and problems. However, you

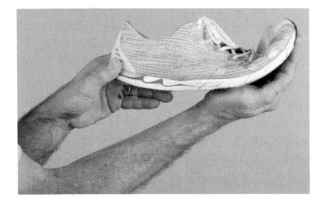

**Figure 4—Flexible forefoot**

don't want to run in old shoes either. When shoes get old, the soles become compacted and deformed, which *really* sends your body the wrong message. You'll need new shoes every 300–500 miles of running. It's a good idea to have two pairs of shoes going all the time and switch them up as you train. Just make sure that for your event you'll have a pair of shoes that are broken in but not too old. Plan ahead. Our training journals have places for you to keep track of the mileage on your shoes.

## ORTHOTICS

If you are reliant on your orthotics, use them, but start running one or two weekly shorter runs without them. We have several podiatrists on our board of medical advisors who support the idea that orthotics are not necessarily the answer. If given the chance, and if you're practicing and improving your running technique, your feet will adjust in a positive way. Your orthotics may be doing the work that your feet can be educated to do on their own. We do not suggest immediately throwing your orthotics away; rather, take the time to gradually allow your feet to become educated and strengthened by your new running technique, and *then* throw the orthotics away when they start to feel like a big lump of plastic in your shoe, which they will. Orthotics can be used to help protect a part of your foot during a healing process, but wearing them forever is like breaking a leg and having your doctor tell you to keep your cast on and use crutches for the rest of your life. When you're working on removing the cause of your foot problems through adjustments in your running technique, you're also working to reduce your need for corrective orthotics.

## ACCESSORIES

You need to be well acquainted with any accessories you plan to use on race day. You will have ample time during your training to learn how to use each tool.

**The Metronome:** The piece of equipment that will best help you learn the ChiRunning technique is a metronome. In the technique phase you'll begin to practice running at a consistent cadence (stride rate) of 170–180 foot strikes per minute. Running at this cadence will be one of the key components to learning good running form. Eventually you can add a cadence, or music that supports that cadence, to your MP3 player.

But in the beginning you'll need to determine your current cadence and adjust it for a few weeks or months until you find the cadence that is right for you. The best metronome we've found clips onto your waistband with several options that optimize your learning process and your workouts. You'll find it on our website along with detailed explanations of how to use it.

**Sports Watch:** A good watch is invaluable when training for a marathon event. You'll need one with a chronometer, a single and double countdown timer, and 30-to-50-lap memory. You'll use the repeat countdown timer as a Form Focus reminder, as a reminder to drink, or as a reminder to do a Body Scan. The dual countdown timer will allow you to get a bit more sophisticated, working a Form Focus for two minutes on, then one minute off. The lap memory function lets you note the time and date of up to fifty runs or up to fifty splits.

**Heart Rate Monitor:** Our favorite use of a heart rate monitor is as a biofeedback tool to help monitor your perceived rate of exertion (PRE). The concept is to see if you can decrease your heart rate while running at a steady pace or to see if you can run slightly faster without increasing your heart rate. In this way you're not just monitoring the efficiency of your running form, but your ability to relax while running faster.

**GPS Tracking System:** You don't have to have a GPS, but one certainly can come in handy to keep track of your favorite runs, know how far and fast you go, and how many calories you burn. The only caution is getting so caught up in technology and in results that you lose track of the real reason you're running. We've found that they are not perfect in terms of pacing unless you're on a totally flat, treeless course. So make sure you use a track or measured course for Time Trials.

A GPS device also comes in handy for keeping track of your miles on your LSD runs because it means you don't have to stick to a specific, premeasured course.

**Water Belts and Bottles:** Hydration is one of the key issues in running long distances. Do not depend solely on water stops at the event if you're running a full marathon. Half marathons do not present as much of a dehydration danger as do longer distances. Hydration will be covered thoroughly in Chapter 4, but for now, know that you will need a water belt of some kind and a small pouch for anything else you will want to carry with you: lip balm, sunscreen, gels, keys, a cap.

**Clothing:** There are two important things to think about regarding your clothing: (1) don't wear anything on race day that you haven't worn in training, and (2) have training-tested clothing available for any kind of weather. Weather can surprise you and, if you're not prepared, make difficult an otherwise perfectly planned event. You think an event is going to be hot, but a freak day could make it unseasonably cold; you expect sunshine, but the desert gets an unexpected cold drenching on race day; you expect cooler temperatures, but the sun is blazing. If you're traveling to an event, bring plenty of tried-and-true options with you. If you're used to a visor, don't buy a hat the day before and wear it. Never wear brand-new shoes, as we've discussed. New shorts may chafe in a way your not-so-pretty but very comfortable shorts never do. Test and choose your clothes for race day during the mastery phase, not the day before the event.

If the weather is cool but expected to warm up, go to a thrift store and buy some throwaway clothing you can leave at the start or along the race course. It's just as bad to wear too much clothing as it is to wear too little. Be conservative in your clothing choices—not too much and not too little.

**Fitness Log or Journal:** When you look at a picture book or notes jotted down from your earlier years, the remembrances can be so vivid and clear, as if it were just the day before. Writing down your experiences, mental notes, or specifics about your training will keep your efforts vital and alive years later. You can also track improvements in your conditioning levels throughout your training.

## Nutrition

In addition to all these aspects of training we've mentioned, good nutrition adds a higher level of quality to your training. You'll learn more about nutrition in Chapter 10.

For Katherine and me, and for many runners, running is a touchstone that helps us live a more centered, balanced life. It doesn't matter if you run to live well or live well to run better; either way you benefit.

As you prepare for training for a marathon, there is a lot to consider and plan for. At the same time, the beauty of the marathon is that it takes time—a commodity that is in short supply for many of us. You want to use it wisely and make the most of the entire process. Enjoy this time to dream your dreams, envision great personal satisfaction, and assess your strengths and challenges. Create specific goals and a plan so that you can train with mindfulness and wisdom. The rewards will far surpass the efforts.

# CHAPTER THREE

# Phase II

## The Technique Phase

**The Runner**
On a flat road runs the well-train'd runner;
He is lean and sinewy, with muscular legs;
He is thinly clothed, he leans forward as he runs,
With lightly closed fists, and arms partially rais'd.

—WALT WHITMAN

Ask me what the single most important aspect of training for a marathon is and I'd answer you in a heartbeat: it's having your technique perfected while being as relaxed as possible. This is arguably more important, in the long term, than conditioning. Here's why: the more relaxed and efficient your running form is, the more easily you'll be able to run any distance and any speed, and enjoy running for as many years as you choose to do so. Whether you're running for an hour, for six hours, or all day, it's never as much fun if your body is hurting or working harder than it needs to.

Most people think that running long miles is the hardest part of marathon training. We'd like you to rethink this outdated approach to marathoning and suspend any disbelief you might have that running a marathon can be easy, fun, and healthy. In my mind the hardest part of a marathon is the effort it takes to train your mind to stay focused and maintain good running technique for the whole distance. The technique phase is about developing an ever-present sense of ease in your running. That ease comes primarily from good running technique, and it allows you to truly embrace that key phrase "Run smarter, not harder."

If you're a novice marathoner, take your time in this phase, and if you feel you need to work more on your technique before moving on to the next phase, by all means take the time before adding more distance. If you're in a training group and you find yourself falling behind or sensing an inordinate amount of fatigue or stress, you might consider doing either a later marathon or a half marathon. Similarly, if you're training for a half marathon and things aren't going as expected, consider doing a 10K or a 10-mile run or opting for a later half marathon.

## The ChiRunning Training Principles

NEEDLE IN COTTON: ALIGNMENT AND RELAXATION
In Chapter 1 we explained the T'ai Chi principle of Needle in Cotton, where the needle represents the alignment of your posture and cotton represents relaxation of all the moving parts of your body. In the technique phase you will be applying this principle functionally to your running. Alignment and relaxation are the guiding principles behind every Form Focus and, more generally, all efficient movement: from carrying a child to kicking a soccer ball to sipping a cup of tea. When you hear these two terms it is important to understand that alignment and relaxation are not two separate entities but actually two sides of the same coin. If efficiency is your goal, you cannot have one without the other. And, as complementary partners of any kind will tell you, each works best when their counterpart is fully included in the activity. There are two types of alignment to be aware of when learning the ChiRunning technique: directional alignment and postural alignment.

**Directional Alignment:** Your efficiency increases when every part of your body is moving in the same direction you are. Examples of breaking this rule include swinging your arms across your centerline, running with your feet splayed out, bobbing up and down, or having your upper body swaying from side to side. Any reduction in up-down or side-to-side motion will ensure that you move more efficiently; and the more efficiently you run, the less energy you'll expend and the less chance you have of ever getting injured.

**Postural Alignment:** Your skeletal structure should support your body weight instead of your muscles having to do the work. Good postural alignment allows chi to flow more easily throughout your body with every stride. Working on your alignment in both ways will significantly reduce your muscle usage and conserve your energy.

**Relaxation:** This is defined as moving with the absence of unnecessary effort. It is a state in which your body does only what is necessary to accomplish the job at hand—nothing more and nothing less. Try to always keep this theme in the back of your mind during your workouts. We'll spend more time focusing specifically on relaxation during the conditioning phase.

## FORM, DISTANCE, AND SPEED

One of our formulas for successful training is FDS, which stands for *form, distance, and speed.* When you are learning how to run, it is always best to work on your form first, as in the technique phase, and then practice holding your form for longer distances, which you'll do in the conditioning phase. Speed is the last to come because it is the by-product of good form and adequate conditioning. For those of you who have done marathons in the past and are looking to improve your times, working on your technique is the most important thing you can do to get the speed and efficiency you want. Even though George Xu is a T'ai Chi grandmaster, he still practices his form regularly to improve it.

As with any skill in life that you'd like to improve, technique is king. Let's say you've always wanted to learn to play the piano. What's the first thing you'd do? Well, since my daughter, Journey, just started taking piano lessons, I can tell you exactly what you'd do: first things first. You'd start by learning how to sit correctly at the piano, then the best way to hold your hands and fingers on the keys, and then how to play scales so that your fingers don't trip over each other. You'd follow this by learning to read music and how each piano key is depicted on the page. You'd spend time getting a feel for how your mind and your body need to work together in order for you to play well. All of the technical aspects are learned early on so that in the future you can enjoy creating beautiful music.

A good training program for a half or full marathon contains all the same elements, and it is how the *Chi Marathon* training system is designed. During the technique phase of your training, you'll be doing just what the name suggests: spending most of your workouts working predominantly on your technique.

We runners can always use some improvement in our technique. It is an ongoing, lifelong process. So for you veterans out there, don't think for a second that you can just get a free pass and skip ahead to the conditioning phase. Sharpening your running skills and biomechanics early on in your training will allow you to get the most out of your training.

## CONVERTING YOUR RUNNING FROM A SPORT TO AN INTERNAL PRACTICE

During these workouts each prescribed Form Focus is designed to improve a specific aspect of your running form, whether efficiency, impact reduction, range of motion, or ground speed. If you consistently study Body Sense, and repeat all of the Form Focuses, your running will become a *practice*. Think of the activities you would call a practice, such as T'ai Chi, meditation, or yoga. The reason why you call some activities a practice is because every time you engage in the activity, you're either trying to perfect your skill or trying to improve yourself by doing the activity. If you approach your running in this way, it will become process-oriented instead of goal-oriented. This transforms your running into an ongoing learning process.

When you are practicing Form Focuses, the best way to get them "hard-wired" into your mind-body system is to repeat them in alternating intervals of engagement and disengagement, which you will do in your Form Focus interval runs, described in detail below. Any action you consistently repeat (for better or worse) will eventually become a habit. It's how our bodies and brains are set up to work. In this case it's a *good* habit of movement you're building into your body.

## GRADUAL PROGRESS: THE SLOW WAY TO LEARN QUICKLY

We've found that the easiest way for runners to learn all the *Chi Marathon* focuses is to divide the learning into small segments. In this chapter we'll go through these segments sequentially, building one upon the other using the Chi principle of Gradual Progress. This is a natural law that says everything should grow incrementally through its own developmental stages, from less to more or from smaller to larger. When a growth process happens gradually, each step forms a stable foundation for the next step. You'll learn the focuses quickly and easily by working on only one area of your technique at a time. In this way you'll gradually develop a clear Body Sense of what each of the focuses does for you and how it feels when it's working.

Another place you'll see gradual progress working is in the way each workout unfolds. At the beginning of every workout, spend the first five minutes warming up at a very easy pace, feeling your body in motion and set up your focuses. Then, as your stride falls into more of a groove, allow yourself to relax even more; you'll find that you shift into a nice second-gear training pace that feels easy and sustainable. By allowing your body to gradually warm up and relax, you'll find your speed is faster yet more relaxed at the end of your run, not because you're trying to run faster, but because you're always focusing on improving your efficiency and level of relaxation.

In keeping with the idea of gradual progress, all running during the technique phase should be done at a comfortable aerobic pace. Learning something new is always easier when speed is left out, so now is not the time to try to run faster. You'll have plenty of time to work on speed later in the conditioning and mastery phases, if that's what you're after. For now, just settle in and take it easy.

---

### INSTRUCTOR STORY

The most important principle of ChiRunning for me is Gradual Progress. For the last four years I've been practicing it in every aspect of my life. When complaining to Danny about the slow speed I was running, he said to me that when doing it correctly, speed will follow. During my training for the marathon, I one day realized that speed came! Just like that!

—Michal Artzi

# The Form Focuses: The Building Blocks of Good Technique

Think of the Form Focuses as a list of job descriptions for each of the individual body parts involved in your running. Each of the ChiRunning focuses is designed to teach a specific part of your body how to cooperate with all of the other parts, so that eventually the whole "team" is running in a beautiful and unified way. When all of your body parts cooperate and work together, each one's job gets easier and you become a highly efficient runner.

We've divided all the focuses into six groups, and each of these groups will be a weekly theme during Phase II of your training. These are the six building blocks of efficient, pain-free running. You will be practicing these focuses for the duration of this training program, and we hope you keep using them for the rest of your running life. As we've noted, weekly training schedules for novice half and full marathon training can be found in Appendixes A and B.

**The Six Form Focus Groups**
1. Posture
2. Lean
3. Lower body
4. Pelvic rotation
5. Upper body
6. Gears, cadence, and stride length

When you first read through all the Form Focuses, the number might seem overwhelming. But don't worry. The sequence of learning the Chi-Running focuses is such that each group of focuses builds a solid base for the next set. You have many months in which to practice them one at a time to build your familiarity and skill with each, so don't pressure yourself to learn all the focuses right away. You'll learn them more quickly and more thoroughly by giving yourself plenty of spaciousness around the learning process. Setting yourself up in this non-pressured way will set a positive tone in training for this and all of your future marathons.

## 1. POSTURE FOCUSES

There are two aspects of your stride that need attention if you'd like to run a marathon with ease. They are the *support phase*, that brief but all-important instant when your body weight is momentarily supported by your structure, and the *flight phase*, when you're not in contact with the ground. In the technique phase you'll focus predominantly on the support phase of your stride. We do this by starting you off with postural alignment. This will build the subtle yet strong internal support system that allows your body to relax and move freely during the flight phase.

In all of our ChiRunning classes we spend the greatest amount of time teaching good posture, which is a significant part of the alignment and relaxation theme central to good technique. The effect that posture has on your running form cannot be overstated for this simple reason: the quality of your posture will affect every step you take for the rest of your life, whether you're walking, running, or skipping. Yes, it's *that* important!

There are two main reasons for refining the support phase of your stride: energy efficiency and injury prevention. The best way to conserve energy while running is to master the support phase of your stride, which spans the period from when your foot first touches the ground until the instant that contact is broken. (See figure 5, page 58.) If your posture is slumped or misaligned during this brief period, your muscles will have to work hard to support your body. By improving the support phase you'll become adept at letting your structure (bones, ligaments, and tendons) support your body weight. Having your entire body supported by structural alignment allows the muscles in your arms, legs, and torso to relax, leading into a natural flow of movement during the flight phase.

In terms of injury prevention, the support phase is when most running injuries happen (overpronation, plantar fasciitis, runner's knee, lower back pain, sore quads, and more), especially if you're a heel striker. Also, most lateral injuries happen during the support phase (hip bursitis, iliotibial [IT] band syndrome), and most of the lower leg and hamstring injuries happen at toe-off (metatarsal stress fractures, plantar fasciitis, calf pulls, shin splints, hamstring pulls). All of these injuries are caused by something that happens between your first impact with the ground and when you leave the ground again. It's an extremely short period of time we're talking about, and anything inefficient or incorrect that goes on during this instant gets repeated many thousands of times during

**Figure 5—Proper alignment**

your workouts. If you learn to treat this instant with the respect it deserves, you will be rewarded exponentially.

In this section you'll practice creating a straight line with your posture, a solid line of support from the crown of your head to the bottoms of your feet. We'll refer to this as your Column, and it will become your biggest ally—closer to you than your shadow, and more helpful.

The ChiRunning technique requires your Column to fall gently forward in a controlled fall, allowing gravity to assist your forward motion. If, for instance, you bend at your waist as you lean forward, your Column is not straight and gravity will pull on the misaligned parts, creating more stress on your bones, muscles, and joints with each stride. It always comes back to your posture and keeping it in alignment with the pull of gravity.

### The Five Steps to Align Your Posture
1. Align your feet and legs
2. Align your upper body by lengthening your spine

3. Engage your core
4. Practice the one-legged posture stance
5. The "C" Shape

**Step 1: Align Your Feet and Legs:** Always run with both feet pointing forward, in the direction in which you're heading. If your feet tend to splay out when you run, it can cause a plethora of running injuries because your lower leg will be rotating laterally with each stride you take. This puts undo stress onto your medial meniscus (front/inside of your knee), your big toe, your groin muscles, your hips, and your IT band (see figure 6) because they are all being asked to move in a way that is not in their job description. Pain in any of these areas should be a red flag telling you to make sure your feet are pointing forward. (See figure 6.)

*How:* While standing, look down at your feet. If either foot is splayed out any amount, lift your upper leg with both hands and rotate that leg medially until your foot is pointing forward. Then set your leg back onto the ground and Body Sense what it feels like to change the direction in which your foot is pointing. Remember that sensation and repeat it as often as necessary whenever you're standing, walking, or running.

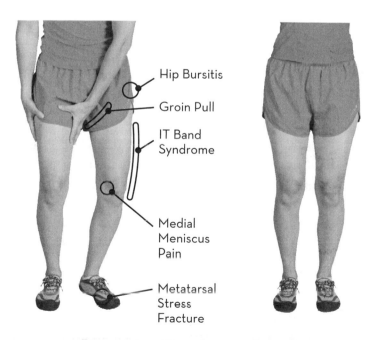

Hip Bursitis

Groin Pull

IT Band Syndrome

Medial Meniscus Pain

Metatarsal Stress Fracture

**Figure 6—Locations of potential injury**

**Tip:** To feel your feet pointing forward, go to a track and run with your feet landing on either side of a lane stripe. Feel what this feels like in your entire leg and replicate that feeling when you're out on the road.

Once your feet and legs are aligned, soften your knees and remember to always keep them slightly bent throughout the support phase. It's a small focus, but it can mean the difference between having healthy knees and having runner's knee.

**Rule of the Road:** If you want to be an efficient runner you need to have as many body parts as possible moving in the same direction you're heading.

**Step 2: Lengthen Your Spine:** This focus lengthens your entire spine and sets your head in a neutral and balanced position at the top of your spine, allowing your back muscles to relax. This frees up tension in your body so it can move quickly and effortlessly. When this is done correctly, you should feel your head floating effortlessly atop your spine and your sacrum dropping toward the earth, creating a balance of lightness above and groundedness below. You'll feel solid support coming from your legs while being light on your feet at the same time—a nice mix.

Lengthening your spine also helps you breathe better by giving your ribs, and subsequently your lungs, more room to expand. You'll need all the oxygen you can get when you're running for hours, and it's difficult to get a deep breath when you're hunched over.

*How:* Stand upright and tall, putting your attention on the crown of your head. Hold your hand about ½ inch above the crown of your head. Now, try to touch your hand by reaching up with the crown of your head. It will feel as though you're lengthening the backside of your neck. Once you have the Body Sense of how this feels, you can try it without using your hand. Then just reach for the sky with the crown of your head wherever you are. (See figure 7.)

**Tip:** This is a focus you can practice all day long, whether you're sitting, standing, walking, or running. Make it a constant habit.

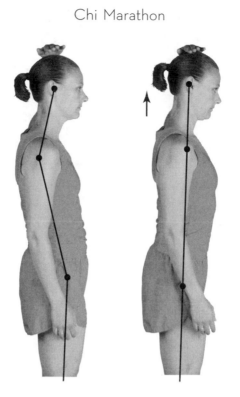

**Figure 7—Lengthen your spine by lifting
the crown of your head**

**Step 3: Engage Your Core by Leveling Your Pelvis:** I'd say conservatively that 75 percent of all Westerners stand with an anterior pelvic tilt (see figures 8 and 9 on page 62), with their core muscles disengaged and their posture in a state of weakness. Engaging your core muscles acts to stabilize your pelvis during the support phase of your stride. Most people's shoulders are behind their hips. This creates a couple of problems. One is that standing in this position compresses the lumbar disks and can lead to back problems, pinched spinal nerves, and sciatica—three things you definitely don't want as a runner. The second is that standing in this position disengages your core muscles, creating instability in your pelvis and torso when you're standing or running. Any lack of stability in your pelvis creates lateral hip motion, which can lead to upper IT band syndrome, hip bursitis, and even lower back pain.

*How:* This exercise is designed to help you feel your core muscles engaging so you can keep your Column straight while in the support phase of your stride. You'll learn this exercise while sitting in a chair. Once you

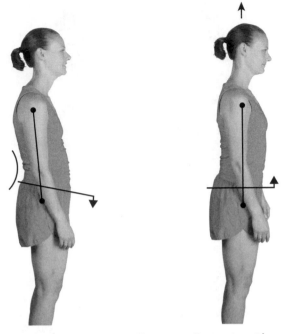

**Figure 8—Incorrect,
shoulders behind hips**

**Figure 9—Correct—with core engaged,
shoulders over hips**

get the feeling of engaging your core, you'll practice it while standing up, and eventually practice the focus while running. As you train yourself to engage your lower abs, make it a point to disengage your glutes. Holding any tension in your glutes can restrict your leg swing and cause other muscles in your legs to work harder. Your glutes should always feel like they're just along for the ride.

Having your core engaged helps you maintain a straight support Column while running (or walking), stabilizes your pelvis during the support phase, and improves the connection between your pelvis and legs, unifying the movement of your whole body.

**Chair Exercise**

Part I

1. Sit upright in a chair with your arms hanging at your sides and with your spine away from the back of the chair.
2. Lengthen your spine as you lift up with the crown of your head. (See figure 10.)
3. Locate your sitz bones directly over your sitz bones.
4. Take a moment to feel what this feels like.

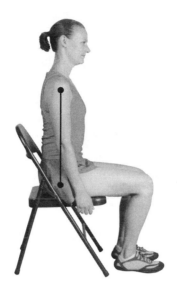

**Figure 10—Sit upright in your chair**

Part II

1. Relax your upper body and slump back into the chair so that your back is resting against the back of the chair. (See figure 11.)
2. While lifting with the crown of your head and contracting your

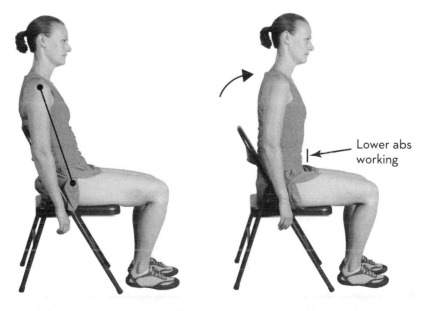

Lower abs
working

**Figure 11—Slump back in your chair**     **Figure 12—Slowly come back to upright**

lower abs (see figure 12), slowly bring your torso back into the original sitting position you had in Part I.

3. Your lower abdominal muscles should be the *only* set of muscles working to do this.

4. Repeat this exercise at least ten times, feeling your lower abs working and your tailbone dropping into the chair seat each time you sit up. Build a clear body memory of the motion of bringing your body into an upright position.

5. Next, stand in front of a full-length mirror, looking at yourself in side view in a slumped posture with your shoulders behind your hips. (See figure 13.)

6. Now, "sit up in your chair" by duplicating the sensation you were just practicing. Feel your lower abs engage and your shoulders move into position directly over your hips. Stop when your shoulders, hips, and ankles are in a straight, vertical line. (See figure 14.)

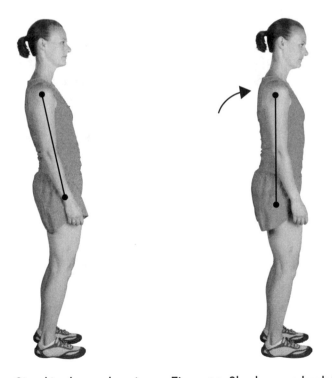

**Figure 13—Stand in slumped posture    Figure 14—Slowly come back to upright**

What you're shooting for is a straight line running through your ears, shoulders, hips, and ankles. This lineup is vertical whenever you're

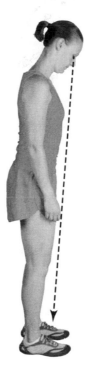

**Figure 15—Look for your shoelaces**

standing still, but it is tilted forward when you run. There are two good ways to check that your alignment is good.

## Look for Your Shoelaces
1. In a standing position, lengthen your spine as described above.
2. While holding yourself in this position, drop your chin and look down to see if you can see you shoelaces. If you can't see them, it means your hips are still too far forward and even though your spine is nice and long, your Column is not in alignment. Your hips need to move into alignment between your shoulders and your ankles. (See figure 15.)
3. Gently move your pelvis to the rear until you can see your shoelaces. This will bring you into alignment, and you'll also feel yourself "sitting up in your chair" even more.

## Side View
1. Look at a side-view reflection of yourself in a full-length mirror or storefront window.
2. Make sure your shoulders, hips, and ankles are aligned (see figure 16).

**Figure 16—Correct postural alignment**

Every time you check in with your postural alignment, make it a point to feel your feet on the ground. This sensation will be there for only a split second during the support phase of your stride, so get really familiar with it. Every time you feel your foot touch the ground you should also feel your entire Column aligned and supported above it.

I have found this to be an incredibly effective way to get runners to feel their core, because in order to bring your shoulders into a position in-line with your hips and ankles, you have to engage your lower abs. In the past, when I'd ask people to level their pelvis, they'd engage their lower abs too much and ended up feeling stiff instead of simply aligned and relaxed in their posture. This way works much better because you can practice it all day: at your desk, in your car, waiting for the bus . . . basically anytime you're not lying down.

**Tip to Remember:** Reach for the sky with the crown of your head and feel the forward movement of your shoulders while moving into the sitting-up position.

**Step 4: The One-Legged Posture Stance: Feel Your Column and Let It Work for You:** The first three steps are used to get your posture aligned properly. Step 4, the one-legged posture stance, is the summation of the three previous steps and is really the most important of all the posture focuses because when you are running you will land in your one-legged posture stance on each leg ninety times every minute. Even though you'll be practicing many other focuses during Phase II, the overarching theme of the first eight weeks is mastering the support phase. Get to the place where you can feel it working with each stride. Feel it supporting you, while all of the other muscles in your body truly relax and move freely and easily.

Remember our metaphor of the sail being supported by both the mast and guy wires? In your body your skeletal alignment acts like the mast while the ligaments and tendons (connective tissue) act like the guy wires that hold your structure upright during the support phase of your stride. Once your bones are lined up (as with the posture focuses) it's your connective tissue, not your muscle, that allows those bones to remain aligned.

**Figure 17—The One-legged Posture Stance**

Your Column is what supports you during your one-legged posture stance. In order for your Column to work most efficiently and truly allow your muscles to rest during the support phase, you must practice setting up the conditions for support and then learn what that support feels like when it's engaged. It's a felt sense of your alignment and connective tissue doing their jobs.

Engage all the posture focuses and then feel your alignment supporting you. Try to sense this on one leg at a time. Feel it working and relax all else. If you sense your muscles working, go back to lifting from the crown of your head. Then, relax, lengthen your spine, drop your sacrum, "sit up in your chair." (See figure 17.)

Once you can get a clear sense of your one-legged posture stance holding you up, practice sensing that support with each and every step you take, whether you're running or walking. Feel the support of your bones and connective tissue, not your muscles. Practice this stance and then try to always feel it happening every time your feet are touching the ground.

**Step 5: The "C" Shape:** In all of our walking and running classes we now have everyone do this easy little exercise. First stand in a slumped position (poor posture), then in one smooth motion reach for the sky with the crown of your head, straightening your spine and lengthening the back of your neck. This upward focus of your attention will quickly straighten your posture and actually lighten your footstep by counteracting the downward motion of your foot coming onto the ground.

Having your neck in the correct position has an effect on the rest of your spine all the way down to your tailbone. (See figure 18.) You'll find it easier to level your pelvis and to relax your shoulders, keeping them low, and it's a crucial part of The "C" Shape. In T'ai Chi it is called *nei-jing*.

Look at the illustration (see figure 19) and you'll see The "C" Shape superimposed on the subject. If you look at the direction the arrows are pointing, you'll see that the arrows begin at T12/L1 (the juncture between your last thoracic vertebra, T12, and your first lumbar vertebra, L1) and move in opposite directions. The arrows on the upper section of The "C" Shape go up (lengthening the back of the neck) and then down the front side of the head, ending at the chin (which is held down). The lower section of The "C" Shape runs down toward the tailbone and then comes back up on the front side of the pelvis, ending at the pubic bone (when leveling the pelvis, you lift up on the pubic bone).

Practice getting yourself into The "C" Shape whenever you're mov-

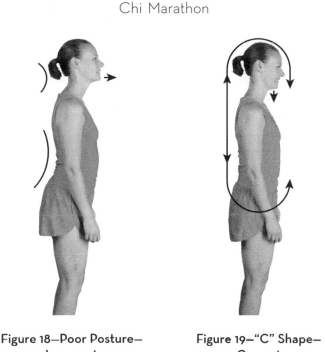

| Figure 18—Poor Posture— | Figure 19—"C" Shape— |
| Incorrect | Correct |

ing into the support phase of your stride. As a backup exercise, you can also remind yourself to do The "C" Shape whenever you feel your posture slipping, whether you're sitting at your desk, standing, walking, or running. It'll have the amazing effect of bringing your mind and your body together, because you'll be engaging your core in the midst of your activity, adding integrity to your spine, and bringing yourself to the physical center of your experience.

### Review
#### The Four Steps to Building Your Column
1. Align your feet.
2. Lengthen your spine
3. Engage your core
4. Practice the one-legged posture stance

#### List of Posture Focuses
- Align your feet and legs (in the direction you're heading)
- Soften your knees (never lock them)
- Reach for the sky with the crown of your head (feel yourself being lifted up)

- Relax your glutes
- Sit up in your chair
- Connect the dots (shoulders, hips, and ankles)
- Level your pelvis (feel your lower abs engaged)
- Practice the one-legged posture stance
- Do The "C" Shape exercise
- Feel your feet at the bottom of your Column

## 2. LEAN FOCUSES

A slight forward lean from your ankles is enough to allow gravity to assist you in falling forward. Here's a nutshell description of the Chi-Running stride: As your Column falls forward, it passes over the foot that's on the ground. The oncoming force of the road sweeps your support leg out behind you, allowing your leading foot to land beneath your center of mass, in a midfoot strike. This leg then momentarily supports your weight as your Column passes over it and the whole cycle happens again. If you're running at a 180 spm cadence, this cycle happens three times every second. (See figure 20.)

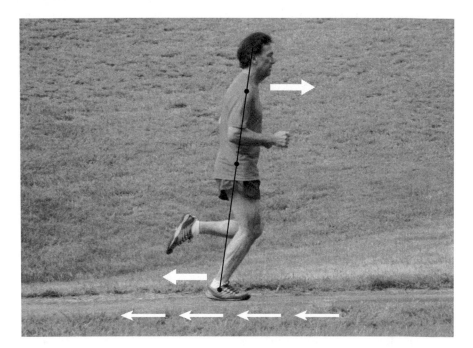

**Figure 20—Running with a lean**

If you don't lean from your ankles, you will run upright (see figure 21), totally changing the physics of your running because you're no longer falling forward assisted by gravity. If you don't lean with your whole Column, your legs have to provide *all* of your propulsion because your center of mass will remain directly over your feet. When you run upright your legs *have* to reach forward and land in a heel strike. Whenever your foot lands in front of your center of mass, you momentarily put the brakes on by creating a force opposite to the direction you're running. It's by far the least efficient way to run, but I'd say conservatively that 75 percent of all runners I see run upright and land with a heel strike, which is synonymous with lower leg injuries. Learn to keep your body falling forward in a balanced lean, slightly ahead of your feet, and you'll never again have to worry about lower leg injuries from either impact or overuse. Running with a slight forward lean allows you to yield to the pull of gravity, thus cooperating with a constant and valuable ally.

Figure 21—Running upright

**Rule of the Road:** Your arms and legs should always swing to the rear as your Column falls forward.

Figure 22

Figure 23

**Relax Your Lower Legs and Ankles:** Leaning should always happen *after* you've first engaged your Column. Once your posture is well aligned, relax your lower legs and ankles and allow your entire Column to fall slightly forward ahead of your feet. You should balance yourself in a slight forward lean instead of engaging any lower leg muscles to hold your lean at the correct angle. Always avoid using any of your lower leg muscles, especially when leaning.

**Lengthen the Back of Your Neck and Lead with Your Forehead:** This will ensure you don't bend at the waist as you lean forward. Bending at the waist can increase stress to your lower legs, knees, quads, and lower back.

Master George Xu suggested I use the image of being pulled by a big kite flying ahead of me, like one of those parasailers or wakeboarders. It's a fun image and you'll get an energizing return for a minimal mental investment.

**Land Midfoot:** Land with your entire foot in contact with the ground in a midfoot (or full-foot) landing. Running on your toes increases the workload to your lower legs, and landing on your heels increases the impact to your knees, quads, and lower back. (See figure 22.)

If you're a barefoot runner, or running in minimalist shoes, you'll land lightly on your forefoot and *immediately* come all the way down onto your midfoot. This will load the elastic tension in the tendons and ligaments in your ankles and feet, allowing a small amount of forward spring into your next stride *without* the use of any muscles.

A simple but effective rule of thumb to help you avoid heel striking is to never step past your knee. If you do, you'll be putting on the brakes every time.

**Upper Body Ahead of Your Feet:** Hold the image of your upper body always being in front of where your feet hit the ground. This will help you maintain a consistent sense of your Column falling slightly forward from your ankles. Use this image: if it's a race between your shoulders and your feet, your shoulders will always cross the finish line first.

**Balance in the "Window of Lean":** Running in the "window of lean" means that when you're running, your Column is not so upright that you lose the sensation of falling, but not so far forward that you have to engage your lower leg muscles for stability or to hold your lean at the correct angle. Balance is the key here. (See figure 23.)

**Your Lean Is Your Gas Pedal:** If you want to run faster, you lean slightly more forward. If you want to run slower, back off your lean a bit. Either way, rebalance yourself in your new angle of lean. You'll feel the change in your core because you'll feel your lower abs and obliques engage more as you lean more. As you lean more, relax your legs more as well.

**The Three Steps to Engage Your Lean:** Every time you change your angle of lean to either run faster or slower, begin by following these three steps to keep yourself from bending at the waist as you change gears.

1. **Feel your Column.** (See figure 24.) Do all of your posture focuses.
2. **Feel your feet.** (See figure 25.) Once you feel your Column, feel your feet at the bottom of your Column.

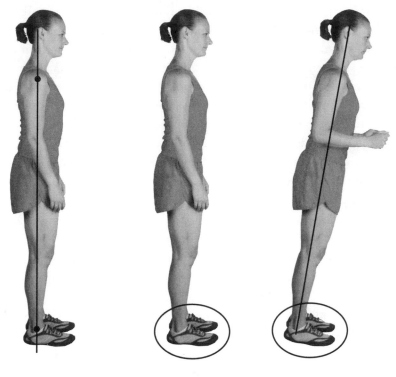

**Figure 24—Step 1:**
**Feel your Column**

**Figure 25—Step 2:**
**Feel your feet**

**Figure 26—Step 3:**
**Fall from there**

**3. Fall from there.** (See figure 26.) Allow your Column to fall slightly forward from your feet.

### List of Lean Focuses
- Relax lower legs and ankles
- Lengthen the back of your neck and lead with your forehead
- Land midfoot
- Your lean is your gas pedal
- Upper body ahead of your feet
- Balance in the "window of lean"
- Three steps to engage your lean
  1. Feel your Column
  2. Feel your feet
  3. Fall from there

### 3. LOWER BODY FOCUSES

The lower body is the moving part of your machine. It's where the rubber meets the road, as it were, and for this reason the focus is on *movement* and how to best allow it to happen in as unhindered a way as possible. The lower body consists of everything below T12/L1, the juncture between your thoracic vertebrae and lumbar vertebrae. (See figure 27.)

If you look at how the lower body is configured, you'll notice that the farther you get from the core area of the body, the smaller the body parts and muscles become. (See figure 28.) It is precisely for this reason that it is important to learn to run with the least amount of leg effort, especially when running a marathon. The smaller, lower leg muscles are not designed for doing sustained work, which is why a high percentage of runners incur lower leg injuries. Your quads, hamstrings, and calves are designed for sprinting relatively short distances (think about the fight-or-flight reaction), where fuel economy is not a factor. That's because

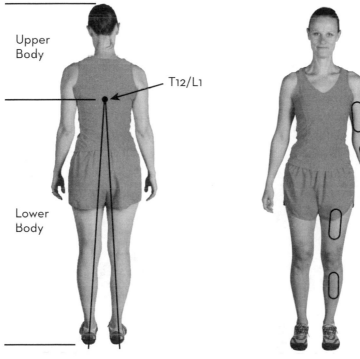
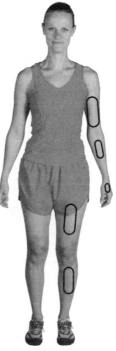

Figure 27—T12/L1
and the Lower Body

Figure 28—Relative
sizes of body parts

you won't be running long enough to burn through all of the glycogen in your body. Using the *Chi Marathon* program, you'll practice running longer and longer distances while using less and less leg muscle. It might sound like an oxymoron, but the farther you run, the less you want to be using your legs for propulsion.

At the end of your stride, allow your foot to simply float up off the ground to keep up with your fall. In this way you won't be relying on your legs for propulsion. You don't have to push yourself forward, because your perpetual forward fall is pulling you forward. We call this the passive leg swing because your legs are used only for support between strides and little else. When you can truly relax your legs (both in and out of the support phase) they are returned forward by the recoil of your hip flexors and your feet land in a midfoot strike beneath your center of mass just in time for another support phase. (See figures 29–32.)

## THE FOUR PHASES OF THE STRIDE CYCLE

Figure 29—The landing phase—
midfoot strike

Figure 30—The support phase—
one-legged posture stance

Figure 31—The lifting phase—peeling
the heel

Figure 32—The flight phase—pelvic
rotation

**Lower Leg Focuses**

### Bend Your Knees but Don't Raise Them

Keep your knees soft and slightly bent during all phases of your stride. This allows your legs to swing more easily because they are, in effect, shorter. Bending your knees lets your feet take more of a circular path (like pedaling a bicycle) instead of swinging like a pendulum. This circular motion allows your foot to come straight down onto the oncoming road instead of swinging into it. This will reduce your impact with the road, significantly reducing any braking motion. (See figures 33 and 34.)

It is important to remember that anytime you raise your knees you're firing your quads and hip flexors, which burns more fuel. Always keep your knees low. The time to lift your knees is while sprinting, not while distance running.

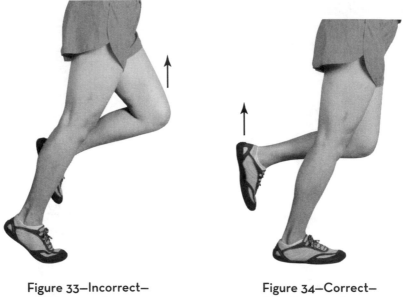

Figure 33—Incorrect—
lifting your knees

Figure 34—Correct—
bending your knees

### Passive Legs: Calves, Shins, Ankles, Feet, and Toes

Always keep your lower legs as relaxed and limp as possible. In fact, shake out your legs whenever you're standing still for any length of time. Use the image of a track star getting ready to run, shaking any tension out of her legs before the gun goes off.

If your lower legs are always limp, you'll never have to worry about any of the common lower leg running injuries: metatarsal stress fractures, Achilles tendonitis, shin splints, plantar fasciitis, or calf pulls. Keep those muscles passively engaged and avoid any intentional flexion or extension of your leg muscles. That's the job for a power runner.

When your legs are truly passive, it allows the recoil motion of your ligaments, tendons, and other connective tissue to swing your legs forward for you. The elastic loading and recoil motion of your legs does not require fuel. The contraction of your leg muscles definitely does.

**Feet and Ankle Focuses:** As we've seen, when it comes to your legs, feet, and ankles, the best idea is to insist they do nothing but support you. Propulsion is not in their job description.

Here are some additional things to focus on.

### Feet Pointed Forward

Before starting your run, make sure your feet are both pointed forward in the direction you're heading.

### Circular Feet with Wheels at the Ends of Your Legs

This was mentioned earlier, but it bears repeating here. You want to create a motion more like circles with your feet, not pendulums. Pretend you have wheels instead of lower legs and you'll be just fine. (See figures 35 and 36.)

**Figure 35—Circular feet—correct**

**Figure 36—Pendulum legs—incorrect**

## Peel Your Foot off the Ground

Instead of feeling your foot coming down onto the ground, a better focus is to feel your heel peeling *off* the ground with each stride, like a sticky note coming off a pad. This will keep you from ever pushing off with your toes and overworking any of those relatively small lower leg muscles.

## Midfoot Strike

As mentioned before, always try to strike the ground under your center of mass to avoid any chance of a heel strike, and never let your foot touch down in front of your knee.

## Review

### Lower Leg Focuses

- Bend your knees
- Limp lower legs: calves, shins, ankles, feet, toes
- Passive legs

### Foot and Ankle Focuses

- Feet point forward
- Circular feet with wheels at the ends of your legs
- Lift your ankles
- Heels up, toes down
- Peel your foot off the ground
- Midfoot strike

## 4. PELVIC ROTATION FOCUSES

Pelvic rotation is when you allow your pelvis to rotate around your central axis with each stride. If your legs swing only at the hip joint, your range of motion is limited by the amount of flexibility at your hip. (See figure 37.) When you allow your entire pelvis to rotate along with the swinging leg, you prevent your legs from ever swinging beyond their own safe range of motion. (See figure 38.) This adds inches to your stride and allows you to run faster without working harder. Additionally, the rotation of your pelvis allows the hip to safely absorb any shock from the road as the foot lands, because it moves rearward with the force of the oncoming road, not against it. If your pelvis does not rotate and "soften the ride," the force of the road will be absorbed by your knees, quads, hips, and lower

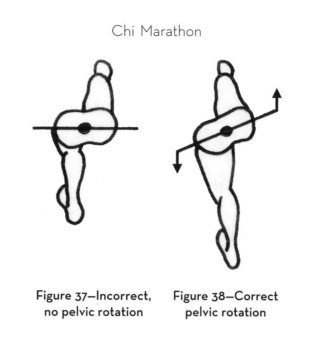

Figure 37—Incorrect,     Figure 38—Correct
no pelvic rotation        pelvic rotation

back. This impact is one of the causes of runner's knee, plantar fasciitis, shin splints, IT band syndrome, and many other lower body injuries. To allow your pelvis to rotate, release your hip when you feel your foot strike the ground and let it be pulled rearward by your leg.

Those who gain this invaluable skill experience a newfound smoothness and ease in their stride that goes beyond anything they've ever experienced in their running, regardless of how long they've been running or what shape they're in. Have you ever driven off without releasing the hand brake in your car? Something doesn't feel right—your car seems a little lifeless. Then, when you finally figure out what's going on and release the brake, it's like you've got a new zippy car under you. When your pelvis swings along with your legs, there's no resistance to your forward movement coming from anywhere in your lower body.

### INSTRUCTOR STORY

I took the ChiRunning certification course in the fall of 2004 and ran the Tucson marathon that December. My mantra during the race was "Three more inches, three more inches," as Danny had taught us how to gain three inches with every step by rotating our pelvis. I felt like I was floating by the other runners three inches at a time. I finished in 3:51—the same time as my first marathon

> twenty-seven years before! ChiRunning seemed to have erased the
> effects of aging.
>
>                                                     —Mary Lindahl

**Feel a Twist at Your Pivot Point:** Feel a gentle twist along your spine and imagine that your legs swing from your Pivot Point at T12/L1 instead of from your hips. This does a number of things: it reduces bouncing in your stride, absorbs the shock of the oncoming road, increases your stride length without hyperextending your hip flexors, and loads your legs for elastic recoil movement.

**Level Your Pelvis:** Keeping your abs engaged whenever you're practicing pelvic rotation will ensure that your pelvis rotates around your central vertical axis. If your pelvis isn't level when it rotates, you'll find yourself wagging your tail like a dog, which is not efficient for forward motion.

**Allow Pelvic Rotation to Happen:** Don't force your pelvis to rotate. Just watch and *allow* it to rotate. Feel your hip go back with your rearward-swinging leg. Every time the road swings your foot and leg to the rear, allow your hip to be pulled rearward with it. This will rotate your pelvis for you, so you don't have to *do* anything.

When you really get this, you'll immediately feel a sense of smoothness taking over your stride and you'll feel your lower back relax.

### Review
#### Pelvic Rotation Focuses
- Feel a twist at your Pivot Point
- Level your pelvis
- Allow rotation to happen

### 5. UPPER BODY FOCUSES

Many runners don't really know how to use their upper body when running, and there are many runners I see whose upper body is actually working *against* them. In order for your legs and lower body to swing as freely as possible, your upper body needs to provide a solid base. I know this might sound a bit backward, but bear with me. Specific topics we address within the upper body are focuses for the head, neck, shoulders, arms, and breathing.

**Rule of the Road:** To help prevent injury, never straighten your legs or lock your knees while running. Keep your knees slightly bent at all times, and *never* let your feet touch down in front of your knees. (See figure 39.)

Figure 39—Never land in front of your knee

**Head, Neck, and Shoulders:** The direction in which your head is pointed determines the direction you're running. So in order to economize your motion, it is important to always have your head and neck relaxed and stabilized in the direction you're headed. The best way to do this is to run with your shoulders square to the front, like the two headlights of your car. I see many runners who swing their shoulders instead of their arms. *Any* amount of upper body rotation will decrease your amount of lower body rotation, create unnecessary tension in your neck, and create an inefficient stride by disconnecting your upper body from your lower body. This is what I meant when I said that some runners' upper bodies are working against them. I highly recommend spending time during every workout disallowing *any* upper body rotation while running.

Many runners don't know if their shoulders are rotating. It's one of those things that can be difficult to sense. The best way to find out is to ask a running partner to watch you, to see whether your shoulders are swinging or if it's just your arms. Set both shoulders facing forward and then experience what it feels like to keep them facing forward as you swing your arms rearward.

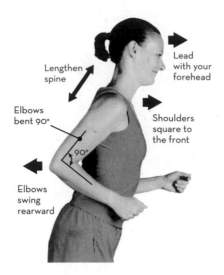

Lengthen spine

Lead with your forehead

Elbows bent 90°

Shoulders square to the front

90°

Elbows swing rearward

**Figure 40—Upper Body Focuses**

### Head, Neck, and Shoulder Focuses
- Keep shoulders low and relaxed
- Shoulders always face forward
- Lengthen back of neck; lengthen spine
- Lead with your forehead

**Arm Swing:** Your arm swing contributes to your ChiRunning technique by creating a counterbalance to your upper body falling forward. Likewise, your upper body falling forward counterbalances your legs and arms swinging to the rear. They're meant to balance each other out. And the more balanced you are in your movement, the easier your running will feel.

### Bend Your Elbows to 90 Degrees
Hold your arms bent at 90 degrees and don't pump your arms. If you always hold your hands above your waistline, you'll never get caught pumping your arms.

### Swing Elbows Rearward
Use the rearward swing of your elbows to counterbalance your forward fall. Also, never let your elbows swing in front of your rib cage or it could throw your leg swing too far forward.

### Shoulders Square to the Front

Pretend your shoulders are like the two headlights of a car, always pointing forward. This allows all of the rotational motion of your pelvis to go into your legs and not into twisting your upper body.

### Curl Fingers, with Thumbs on Top

Avoid holding tension in your hands and forearms by gently curling your fingers inward, like you're holding a butterfly.

### Hands Never Cross Your Centerline

Avoid wasted upper body motion by keeping your hands away from your centerline. Swing your hands in the direction you're heading.

**Breathing:** Last and very crucial is the breath. The quality of your running is directly affected by the quality of your breathing. If with each breath you bring air all the way into the bottom of your lungs, it

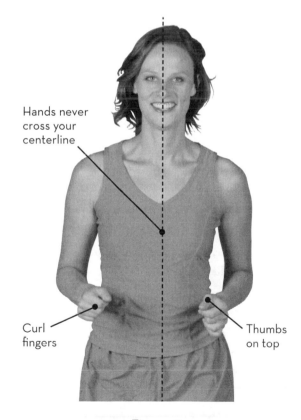

Hands never cross your centerline

Curl fingers

Thumbs on top

**Figure 41**

will significantly increase the amount of oxygen uptake in the capillary beds in the lining of the lower part of the lungs. Shallow, incomplete breaths will not oxygenate your blood as well, and your muscles will burn inefficiently because of the lack of oxygen.

### Belly Breathe

Purse your lips and contract your upper abdominal muscles to expel all the air from the bottom of your lungs. Then, when you inhale, close your mouth and breathe in through your nose, allowing your belly to fill first, followed by your upper lungs (expanding the back of your rib cage).

### Match Breath Rate to Cadence

When I'm running at an easy pace I synch my breath with my stride. I breathe out for three strides and inhale for two. When I'm doing a faster pace I'll breathe out for only two strides and inhale for one. This sets up a nice rhythmical breath rate that's very relaxing at any speed.

### Nose Breathe Whenever Possible

If you want to ensure you're not running beyond your aerobic threshold, the best trick is to always run with your mouth shut, breathing only through your nose. If you run too fast, you won't be able to nose breathe and you'll have to gasp for breath through your mouth. It's a self-limiting method of pacing, and it works like a charm.

## 6. GEARS, CADENCE, AND STRIDE LENGTH FOCUSES

We always talk about gears, cadence, and stride length as a collective unit because they're interrelated. You can work on these areas of focus individually, but eventually you want to be cognizant of all three happening as one big focus.

The goal of ChiRunning is to run with a perceived rate of exertion that stays within a narrow range no matter what speed you're running. When you practice the focuses of relaxation, alignment, and efficient running mechanics, your effort level should not increase substantially while running at faster speeds. So during this marathon training program you'll practice keeping your cadence rock steady and consistent and allowing your stride length to increase and decrease as needed to maintain a sustainable PRE (which we'll discuss more in the conditioning phase).

In bicycles and cars you use a set of gears to help regulate energy expenditure. At slower speeds you use a lower gear, and as your speed increases you use higher gears to keep your workload within a small window of effort and efficiency. Your car's engine gets the best gas mileage when the gears function as they should to regulate the workload on the engine. In ChiRunning, gears come into play in the form of your stride length. Instead of shifting gears the way you would on your bike or in your car, you change your stride length. When you're running slowly (lower gear), your stride length is shorter, and as you speed up (higher gear), your stride length increases.

With all of the changes in your stride length, there's one thing that doesn't change: your cadence, the rate at which your feet hit the ground. This is measured in strides per minute (spm). The best average cadence for most people falls between 170 and 180 spm, with taller runners staying closer to 170 spm and shorter runners at or near 180 spm. If you can keep your cadence at a steady rate, your stride length *has* to lengthen or shorten as you speed up and slow down, and the best way to learn to run with a steady cadence is to use a metronome. Most of the form workouts you'll do in Phase I will be with a metronome because having a steady cadence and an adjustable stride length are must-haves for anyone wanting to become an efficient marathon runner. You can find a clip-on metronome on our website.

Feel what each gear feels like on a scale of 1 to 10, where 1 is easy and 10 is hard:

**First gear:** warm-up pace; very easy, breath rate hardly increases (PRE 1–3)

**Second gear:** aerobic pace; the comfortable speed at which you would run most training workouts, and at which you are able to carry on a conversation and breathe only through your nose (PRE 3–5)

**Third gear:** race pace or aerobic threshold pace; difficult to carry on a conversation (PRE 5–7)

**Fourth gear:** sprint pace or anaerobic pace; short distances, fast running (PRE 8–10)

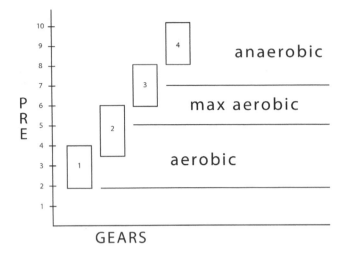

**Figure 42**

### Cadence, Gears, and Stride Length Focuses

#### Feel Your Foot Strike Underneath You, Not in Front of You

Overstriding (landing ahead of your center of mass) is practically ubiquitous among runners and is the main cause of runner's knee, IT band syndrome, and shin splints. So always try to feel your foot striking as close to your body as possible. Your stride length should increase *not* as your legs swing forward but as they swing *rearward.*

#### Run with a Cadence Between 170 and 180 Steps per Minute

As we've noted, tall runners should settle into a cadence closer to 170 spm; shorter folks should be running at a cadence closer to 180 spm. If your cadence is below 170 spm, you're wasting a lot of energy and overstriding. If it's above 180 spm, you're either chasing Kenyans, sprinting, or not rotating your pelvis.

#### Stride Length Changes, Cadence Doesn't

Your stride length will increase as you lean more and pick up speed. Inversely, it will decrease as you back off your lean to run slower. No matter what speed you're running, your cadence never changes. Use a metronome to keep yourself honest and build this crucial tactic for energy-efficient running.

### Feet Are Like Wheels

The "wheels" we spoke of earlier are smaller at slower speeds and larger at higher speeds. A quicker, steadier cadence is much easier to maintain if your feet and legs are rolling like wheels and not swinging like pendulums.

### Relax More as You Increase Your Speed

As you increase your forward lean to run faster, it is crucial that you relax your hips, legs, and feet more so they can swing more freely. Any tension held in your moving parts will show up as an increase in your perceived rate of exertion.

## The Form Focus Workout: Repetition and Accuracy

I had a teacher refer to the concept of "qualitative exactitude." It's a great phrase and perfectly describes the theme of the technique phase.

Your primary workouts during this phase are Form Focus intervals, where you'll spend lots of time practicing, individually and repeatedly, each of the focuses listed in your weekly training schedule. The more accurately you can learn each Form Focus, the more efficiently you'll run. The rest of this chapter is devoted to teaching you the specific Form Focuses. Once you have these basic skills under your belt, you can then work on adaptability, speed, and endurance in the conditioning phase.

Engaging a focus repeatedly throughout a workout allows you to build stronger neural links between your mind and your movement. When each of your new movements is done with a high level of accuracy, the new neural link begins to replace the old one, and inefficient ways of moving simply fall away.

Trust that constant and regular practice will allow the focuses to become so ingrained in your body memory that you can instantly and accurately respond to any situation you might meet on the road. You basically practice until your body can move and respond intuitively in an instant.

When you're given a focus or set of focuses for a workout, spend time studying the description of the focus or watching it on the *ChiRunning* DVD to get a clear image in your mind of how it's done. Then, during your workout, use your *mind* to engage the focus while feeling in your *body* how it works; this constant back-and-forth communication between your mind and your body will accelerate your learning process and work wonders for your Body Sensing skills. Remember, if your mind isn't precise about giving the instruction to your body, it could end up being like a game of telephone, where your body isn't getting the original message that was intended.

## HOW TO DO FORM FOCUS INTERVALS

We'd like you to refer to Appendixes A and B, where you'll find training schedules for the half and full marathon. The technique phase is divided into eight weeks. Each week will have a theme and a list of focuses to be practiced during that week. During these first eight weeks of training, you'll be given specific workouts in which you'll practice the focuses from this chapter.

**Single Form Focus Intervals:** In the first weeks of your training we will have you alternating between two focuses. You'll work on one focus for one minute, then on the other focus for one minute, then take a one-minute mental rest break. Save five minutes at the end of your workout to practice engaging both focuses at the same time.

**Double Form Focus Intervals:** Once you get used to working with single Form Focuses, you'll progress to simultaneously practicing pairs of complementary focuses. In this case, instead of alternating between focuses, you'll simply work for one minute on two focuses followed by a one-minute mental rest break, and so on throughout the workout. The beauty of working focuses in pairs is that your body learns to hold multiple focuses at once. Then, when you can handle working focuses in pairs, you'll progress into working with multiple pairs of focuses. As you can imagine, when you're working at this level, your learning curve can increase exponentially. You can find a helpful list of single focuses and focus pairs in Appendix C, but you're welcome to try pairs that work well for you.

For a more complete and detailed version of these focuses, as well as additional drills and exercises, please refer to the *ChiRunning* book and DVD, available on our website, www.chirunning.com.

## Practice Makes Perfect

This may all seem like a lot to learn, but it's manageable when you take it one focus at a time. Follow the training program, and by the end of the technique phase you'll have a good sense of all of the focuses. Feel each one working in your body. Practice each focus until it's so familiar to you that you can trigger it into action with a thought. Take your time—there's no rush to "get" this. Above all, think of this technique phase as a period of discovery and awakening to what your body can do when you give it good, clear directions and then listen for a response.

Sometimes I feel like I'm still in the technique phase of my running, even though I've been practicing technique for twenty years, because I'm still discovering new and better ways to economize my motion and increase my joy in running

# CHAPTER FOUR

# Phase III

## The Conditioning Phase

Train your mind . . . focus your body.

—ANCIENT CHIRUNNING SAYING

ike T'ai Chi, the focus in *Chi Marathon* is primarily about energy
management: taking energy in, building energy in your body, managing the flow of it through your system, conserving it, containing it, and spending it consciously and for an intended purpose, such as
speed, or making it last for two to six hours while you traverse 13.1 or
26.2 miles. We usually sum all this up by talking about energy efficiency,
but within that phrase are all the nuances of what that entails. In the
technique phase you built the foundation of energy efficiency: good
biomechanics, which reduces your effort, allowing you to expend less
energy for each stride.

In the conditioning phase we refine the uses of the Form Focuses to
manage your energy in more subtle ways as you also build the physical
and mental endurance for the marathon or half marathon distance. As

you might have surmised, we will be working on the distance component of the FDS (form, distance, and speed) formula. With a good base in running technique you will continue to build your cardio-aerobic foundation, as well as tone your muscles to gain the endurance needed for your marathon. All of that is essential. But with *Chi Marathon*, you will also be training in ways that aren't normally covered in most training materials. In every workout you'll increase your mental focus and hone your running and energy management skills.

The complete title of the original ChiRunning book is *ChiRunning: A Revolutionary Approach to Effortless and Injury-free Running*. Effortless does not mean that you put in no effort, because there is some effort needed to get to the point of effortlessness. There is a physical effort to move your body in a new way, but it is not a physically straining effort, or a forcing. It is the effort to make subtle physical changes that make a big difference in how you move. It is also an effort of the mind: to learn, to remember, and to focus. We used the word *approach* because you are working toward that sense of effortlessness in your running. Many of our clients have felt this, and we have countless letters from people who have written us saying, "I felt like I could run forever," but they had to make an effort to get to that place. And holding that level of mastery over your technique for the half or full marathon distance takes both physical and mental conditioning.

For instance, keeping your core engaged to keep aligned with the pull of gravity is a physical and mental effort in the early stages. As your core muscles get stronger and you are better able to hold your alignment, you won't have to exert as much effort to keep aligned, and the energy expenditure required of your legs will diminish exponentially to the point where your legs are truly just used for momentary support between strides, and nothing else! When we get reports of sore abdominals, we always say, "Great news—you're doing it right!" That is what we mean by "productive discomfort." Often we hear that when people use the *Chi Marathon* method, they complete their event and realize they have a lot of energy still in the tank. They realize that they can create new goals for future events, and maybe include speed or go for a personal record.

## Gathering and Issuing

The Chi principle of Gathering and Issuing provides the underpinnings of long-term energy management. There are times to issue and there are times to gather energy, similar to nature's cycles of rest and activity, reflected in the abundant growth cycle of summer and the necessary fallow time of winter. Once you can Body Sense what it feels like to gather and issue, you can then learn when to apply one or the other at the most ideal time in your workout, and you won't end up with an empty well.

Gathering can best be equated to storing or collecting energy. Gathering can also be thought of as preparation for issuing. A good time to focus on gathering energy would be at the beginning of a workout or race, or when you're starting to feel fatigue during an LSD run. The beginning is a time to marshal and conserve your energy, to check in with your posture, to remind yourself to relax and to instate your "C" Shape, which in itself is a gathering posture. In the Chi practice of Needle in Cotton you gather energy to your center by drawing it away from your periphery. That gathered energy adds strength and alignment to your support stance. Your cotton is the soft, supple, and relaxed movement of your arms and legs.

It doesn't matter whether you're a half marathoner, a marathoner, or a working mom with three-year-old twin boys—if you're doing something that takes a lot of energy, your biggest concern should be how to manage your energy so you don't end your day feeling like you just got off a red eye flight. No matter how prepared you are for your marathon, it's still a long way to run, and every ounce of wasted energy could leave your body compromised in some way—it's only a matter of time until the fuel gauge is sitting on E. If this sounds like an economics problem, you're right. Think of the conditioning phase as a course in energy economics. You could even use the word *ergonomics*.

## Functional Relaxation

What we consider the ultimate goal of the conditioning phase is that you get beyond the need to exert effort and learn functional relaxation; where you feel a strong sense of being truly relaxed in your movement and you feel how it benefits your running. You cannot be fully relaxed if you are not first aligned. To refer again to the metaphor of learning to play a piece of music on the piano, the technique phase was where you learned to read the notes and find them on the piano. You can think of that as getting aligned. You are getting the mechanics down. You learned to tap out the melody and add some basic chords. The conditioning phase is where, from weeks of practice, you no longer need the music and your hands know exactly how to move. As you become more comfortable with the piece, your mind and your hands and fingers can relax, and you can add nuance and emotion to your music. It becomes more art than form.

Katherine and I saw the Chinese prodigy Lang Lang perform a Rachmaninoff piano concerto at beautiful Davies Symphony Hall in San Francisco. I have never seen anyone play the piano with such reverence and love. Nor have I ever felt music pierce my heart the way his music did. The packed audience was enthralled. During the intermission you could hear people exclaiming their delight to each other with words such as "direct from heaven," "angelic," "exquisite," "never heard anything like it before." We were all bonded from the shared experience, looking at one another and realizing how lucky we were to have been present for this performance.

I'd like to be at that level with my running. And at times when everything comes together, I feel I touch that place where my running is not about the technique but just about moving through space. It doesn't happen on every run, but I know the potential is there and I am always working toward it, often by just practicing one or two focuses. When I hit that bliss point, when my running feels free, easy, and life-affirming, my spirit soars. It's why I love running so much.

## INSTRUCTOR STORY

I always thought running was the most difficult and boring of all sports. I always wondered why people ran; it never made any sense to me. Then I started running at the age of forty-nine because I wanted to run a half marathon with my daughter. Unfortunately, I was unable to run even a mile. Running was pure torture. I was suffering from severe pain and plantar fasciitis. I was desperate. I read a library's worth of books on running and marathon preparation but was disappointed when none of the books really taught me how to run. I accidentally discovered the *ChiRunning* book. Reading

Danny's book and attending a follow-up workshop changed everything. I became a passionate ChiRunning student and never looked back. I am now fifty and ran four marathons in six months, two of them in seven days. Running has helped me to discover myself. I never knew running could bring so much joy and relaxation. Running has changed my life forever.

—Mariappan Jawaharlal
Mumbai, India

Phyllis Richmond put it beautifully in an article published in the spring 2010 issue of *AmSat News* (the publication of the American Society for the Alexander Technique) in which she talked about the relationship between T'ai Chi and the Alexander Technique. In this article she is referring to practicing T'ai Chi, but she could just as easily be talking about practicing the Form Focuses of ChiRunning.

In practicing the form, once you have learned the rules and can perform the sequence of movements accurately, the next step is to let go of excess tension and get out of the way, so the movements can flow smoothly in accordance with physical principles—gravity, momentum, the rotational movement at the joints, the wind-up tension/release of a spring. First, learn the rules of the form and understand thoroughly what you are doing and why. Then allow yourself to move freely, in accordance with natural principles.

## Body Sensing 2.0

In the technique phase you used your mind to direct your body to do the focuses. Then you "listened" for a response from your body to feel how each focus affected your movement. The flow between your mind and body went something like this: your mind directed your body . . . your body responded to the instruction . . . and then your mind "listened" for the effectiveness of the focus. This mode of mind-body-mind communication is more mind-centric because the learning process is predominantly directed and guided by the mind.

During the conditioning phase you progress to the next level of Body Sensing, where your body initiates the conversation with your mind. It might sound something like, *We're going up a hill and the legs feel like they're working harder. What do we do?* Your mind does a quick search of all the focuses for hills and gives your body one or more focuses specific to the task. The body then takes on the focuses and immediately adjusts to run up the hill in the most efficient way. As your body learns and remembers which focuses to do, you'll begin to run more intuitively and rely less on your mind for direction. As Phyllis Richmond said, "Thinking is a tool: when you don't need it anymore, throw it away."

The mind sets up the conditions for your workout, including which Form Focuses you'll work on, how much fuel you'll need, and how much time you'll be running. The mind can then sit back and relax a bit, being on the alert for messages from the body and aware of energy flow. But it won't have to work as hard as in the technique phase, where you have a steeper learning curve.

## Preparation for the Conditioning Phase

The start of each phase is a transition point, where it's smart to pause, review your last phase, evaluate your current status, and instate a new mind-set for the next phase of training. Think of this as being like the reset button on your computer. First, review the schedule for this phase in your training program and the types of workouts you'll be doing. Explanations of the new types of workouts are in this chapter. If you're behind in your schedule, you'll need to check in with yourself and think about whether it's still realistic to shoot for the race you have scheduled. To be honest with you, good running technique can make up for a lot of lost miles in training. The better your technique, the less crucial high-mileage training becomes. However, don't skimp on practicing good technique. For a pain-free event, I still always recommend doing due diligence by sticking with your program and putting in the miles.

## Review Your Vision and Goals

Now that you've been through weeks of refining your running technique, go back to your original vision and see if anything has changed. Review your physical, mental, and emotional goals. Be thorough, and be honest with yourself because nothing will do more to get you to that finish line than deeply knowing why you're doing what you're doing. It's that connection with your vision that will fuel you when the going gets tough and the training miles seem long; when you're tired and unsure about yourself, and when you have those all-too-human moments of weakness or mental derailment. It happens to all of us. But without exception, the ones who come through to the other side in good shape are those who rely on something stronger than their legs. It usually comes from having three things working together as one unit: your mind (always looking for the best way to respond), your body (well trained and healthy), and your heart, the glue that holds together and guides the other two. Listen very closely to your thoughts, feelings, and sensations, and then move forward with both eyes wide open.

## Assess Your Conditioning and Your Technique

The beginning of this second phase of your training is a good time to assess the strengths and weaknesses of your technique and your level of conditioning so you know what you need to focus on and improve. I strongly suggest getting videotaped so you can see exactly what your form looks like. The camera doesn't lie.

The best way to see what's going on with your running form is to film yourself from a side view, which is most easily done at a track. Run in the outside lane around the curved end of the track and have your cameraperson stand in the center point of the radius (usually under the goal post if there's a football field). Do a warm-up and then have the person film you running the curve beginning at the start of the curve and finishing at the start of the next straightaway. Then turn around and have the person film you running in the opposite direction. You can also have the person film you running toward the camera and away from the camera on a straight section of track.

Our Certified Instructors are experts at video analysis and can provide you with the feedback you need on your form. Check our website for more on how to locate an instructor to get personalized video feedback.

## The Time Trial

Time Trials are a good way for you to periodically monitor your progress in your conditioning throughout the training. Knowing how fast your average running pace is will give you an idea of where you're at relative to your marathon pace goal or how long it will take to run a given distance.

The best way to do a Time Trial is on a track or on a section of road that is flat and measured in 1-mile (or 1-kilometer) increments. To measure your current average pace, warm up for five minutes. When you are ready to run, mark specific start and finish points. Then start your stopwatch and begin running at a sustainable second-gear training pace. At this point your cadence should fall between 170 and 180 strides per minute. Use your metronome to make sure. At the end of your first mile, note your split time and continue running for three more miles, noting your split times for each individual mile (not cumulative times). Afterward, take an average of those four splits.

You can apply this information to find out how long you can expect to be out on your weekly long runs. For example, if your Time Trial pace this week was 9 minutes per mile and you are scheduled to run 13 miles for your LSD, your total run time will be 117 minutes (or 1:57). Running for minutes is easier and less complicated than trying to map out a 13-mile run. You'll note the Time Trial workout in the training programs in Appendixes A and B; however, you can do a Time Trial periodically to confirm your pace until you can tell what pace you are running at any given time. If you are running by time rather than distance, you want to make sure you're running as far as you think you are.

(Note: if you run on a ¼-mile track, run in lane 1 to get an accurate mile. If you're on a 400-meter track, run in lane 2.)

## Pacing and PRE

Your Time Trial is the first lesson in learning pacing and your perceived rate of exertion. During the technique phase you were more focused on the accuracy of your running technique than what speed you were running. In this phase you'll further your skills in energy management by learning good pacing, an invaluable skill every long-distance runner needs to develop. There are two good reasons to practice pacing: (1) to spread out your workload and your fuel supply over a period of hours, which means holding a very steady pace, and (2) to accomplish a specific overall finishing time, which means holding a specific speed for a long period of time.

If you're a novice marathoner and just want to finish your event, you don't have to worry about pacing and PRE as much, but if you want to run a specific time goal, it is essential. In our intermediate and advanced training programs, we ask you to sense your PRE in each workout.

Here's how PRE works. On a scale of 1 to 10 you are asked to Body Sense how hard the workout feels, 1 being at the easy end of the scale, where you sense little or no effort, and 10 being at the top of the scale, where you might feel like you could have a heart attack if you kept it going for more than a couple of seconds.

The easiest way to physically and mentally relate to PRE is to put numbers to each of the four gears we talk about in ChiRunning. Within each gear there is a range of effort level with associated physical symptoms. (See figure 42.) In the description of PRE below I suggest a breath rate for each gear. What I want you to notice is that at a higher gear you breathe more rapidly. Your breath rate does not have to match what I suggest, but breath rate is directly proportional to your effort level. I find it easier to synch my breath rate with my cadence and have listed suggested ratios of breath rate to stride rate below.

## PRE by Gears

**First gear (PRE 1–2):** Warm-up speed. A very easy jog where your heart rate and breath rate barely change.

**Second gear (PRE 3–4):** The aerobic pace at which you will do all of your LSD runs. You could easily carry on a conversation or run breathing only through your nose. Run with a five-stride breath rate, where you exhale for three strides and then inhale for two strides. For novices, be aware that during the later miles of your marathon, you might be in second gear, but your PRE may feel like it's in the 5–7 range. That's okay.

**Third gear (PRE 5–7):** This is the speed at which you'd run a race if you are aiming to improve a previous time. Third gear is the high range of your aerobic capacity, your aerobic threshold pace. Conversation is limited to short sentences. You should not be able to run for very long at this pace with your mouth closed. In third gear I run with a three-stride breath rate, where I exhale for two strides and then inhale for one stride. Your midweek runs will have a mix of second and third gear. Novices or those just wanting to finish may run their entire event in second gear.

**Fourth gear (PRE 8–10):** This is an all-out sprint, or anaerobic pace, where you're giving it all you've got. Breathing is rapid and your heart is starting to leap out of your chest. In fourth gear I run with a single-stride breath rate where I exhale for one stride and inhale for one stride. The *only* time you use this gear or PRE during a marathon is when you can see the finish, and then only if you feel like it.

The best way to get a clear sense of what pace you're running in any given gear is as follows:

- Plan a workout near a local track and do your normal warm-up. Then pretend you're going out for a long run and run at a comfortable, steady pace (PRE 3–4) around the neighborhood near the track (not on the track).
- After ten minutes, make your way to the track with as little disruption in your pace as possible and do a couple of laps on the track, matching as exactly as possible the same physical sense of your pace that you had prior to coming onto the track. Do not look at your watch until after you've completed at least two laps.
- On your third lap start your stopwatch and time yourself for four laps, taking a split after each lap.
- At the end of four laps, stop your stopwatch and check your lap splits. Were they consistent (within one to two seconds of each other)? If all four laps are within two seconds of each other, add up the four splits and that's your speed for a PRE of 3–4.
- If there's a wide range of split times for your laps, throw out the fastest and slowest laps and average the remaining two laps, then multiply by four to find out a closer approximation of your speed.
- Repeat this same sequence for first, second, and third gears to get a clear indication of what speed you're running in each gear and what PRE numbers coincide with the various speeds you're running.

Pacing and PRE both take time to learn, so practice Body Sensing your speed and check in with yourself often by dropping by the track during a run. Within a few weeks you'll begin to feel a familiarity with each pace you're running. Do these random tests of yourself to see what speed you're running relative to any given PRE you're feeling. As your training builds, your PRE will remain within a small range, but you should notice your speed increasing as your heart and lungs get stronger.

Body Sensing, pacing, and PRE are all invaluable skills to have under your belt, whether you're responding to a running situation or dealing with something in your everyday life. If your PRE is too high, you're expending too much energy; learn to manage your energy by slowing down, adjusting your form, shortening your stride, or shifting to a lower gear.

## Functional Workouts

During the conditioning phase you'll be running longer distances, more varied workouts, and more repetitions during interval workouts. These variations all work to increase the cardio-aerobic condition of your body as well as continue to train your mind and body to work as a highly skilled team. You will be working with focus pairs that are specific to certain types of runs. What you're shooting for during these functional workouts is learning to apply the right focus or focuses to respond well to internal and external factors such as hills, fatigue, physical discomfort, pacing, and many other situations. You could call it applied ChiRunning. The key here is responsiveness. As you become more fluent in using the Form Focuses as a natural way to run and as a way to respond to various challenges, you'll begin to discover the real promise of the *Chi Marathon* program.

Next we'll go in depth into making the most of the LSD run, which becomes more and more a simulation of running your event. In the mid-week runs, you'll be improving your cardio and aerobic conditioning as well as your running skills and range of motion by doing intervals, hills, Surges, and tempo runs.

## The LSD Run

The LSD run is the key component of your marathon training. During these runs, you will:

- Increase your aerobic capacity
- Convert your body to a fat-burning machine
- Learn to hydrate and fuel for distance running
- Learn to manage your energy
- Develop the skills to manage adversity

The idea behind all of your long runs is to approach them in such a way that you don't really think of them as being long. It's all in your mind. I've used all kinds of mental images to describe my long runs to myself, so my mind can always see them in a positive light. Think of your long runs as an opportunity to have all the time you need to sharpen any weak areas of your form. I like to make my long runs a nice mix of work and relaxation. By work, I mean focus work. By relaxation, I'm using the image of being out on a nice Sunday drive in the country, looking at the scenery, and taking in lots of fresh air. There's no pace pressure because for most of the run you'll be in a nice, easy second gear. I never think about how far I have to go on my long runs. Instead, I set myself up by thinking about where I'd like to explore.

Figure out your route, then pick two pairs of focuses and alternately work on each set for ten to twenty minutes. Make sure they contain a good mix of work and play. If it gets to be more work than play, your long runs will begin to feel l-o-n-g. Running with other ChiRunners is a great way to get a good mix of conversation *and* help each other with remembering the focuses.

During the last weeks of the conditioning phase you will have the option of doing either shorter hilly runs or longer, flatter LSD runs. Varying the terrain on your long runs is a great way to get conditioned and keep the run interesting, as long as your body can handle it. You do not want to push hard on the hills on your LSD. Either way, whether longer and flat or slightly shorter and hilly, you'll end up in great shape.

## How to Become
## the Ultimate Fat-Burning Machine

In the conditioning phase of the *Chi Marathon* training programs, whether you want to just finish your event or run a personal record, you train for the event at an aerobic pace, not an anaerobic pace. I've come across many runners who think they need to train at their projected marathon pace on every long run in order to meet their pace goal for the actual race. You might ask, "How in the world am I going to run my projected marathon pace for the whole distance if I don't practice running at that pace for the whole distance?" That's a fair question, and a big one to answer. So I enlisted the help of my good friend and fellow ChiRunner Dr. Mark Cucuzzella for an explanation of the science behind aerobic training.

First of all, in order to run farther or faster, your body needs to run more efficiently. One of the important functions of the LSD run is teaching your body to burn fat as a fuel so you can run the marathon distance without bonking. In order to do that, you need to train your body to metabolize fat by running at a pace that is below your maximum aerobic capacity. By training at an aerobic pace, your body learns to burn less glycogen and more fat. Here's an interesting fact: it takes a small amount of glycogen to metabolize fat for fuel. So if you burn through all of your glycogen stores up front (by starting too fast), you won't have any glycogen left for when you need to access fat for fuel later on—and when you run out of glycogen, that's when you hit the wall. Taking in glucose on the run helps, but we are most efficient in economy mode, with the majority of our fuel source coming from metabolized fat.

Aerobic training does two things: (1) it improves your oxygen exchange rate by building more extensive capillary beds in the lining of your lungs and muscle tissue, and (2) it builds more mitochondria, which are sometimes called "cellular power plants" because they produce most of the cells' supply of a substance called ATP (adenosine triphosphate), which is a source of energy.

If you train too fast, you produce less ATP and you don't build capillary beds that are as extensive as they can be. In scientific terms, if you run at an anaerobic pace you create only 2 molecules of ATP per molecule of glycogen, whereas when you run at an aerobic pace you can produce up to 470 molecules of ATP per fat molecule. That's a lot of energy you'll be missing out on if you train too fast.

I'm going to use the modern fuel-burning automobile as an analogy. There are a number of different types of engines used in cars today, and they generally fall into the categories of either speed or efficiency. Speed and economy are inversely proportional—one can't go up without the other going down. The same rule holds true for the human body. When it comes to burning fuel we have two "engines": one for quick accelerations and fast speeds, and a different one that kicks in when you need to run very far but not necessarily very fast.

For running shorter distances at a faster pace, your body utilizes the anaerobic system, which consumes muscle glycogen at a high glycogen-to-oxygen ratio. It's called anaerobic because your body's demand for oxygen outpaces its ability to fill the need, and you go into oxygen debt. To use the car analogy: car engines built for speed and high performance can do what they do because they burn a massive amount of high-octane fuel mixed with a relatively tiny amount of oxygen, creating a hotter explosion in the engine and subsequently providing more power to the wheels. It can be a fun adrenaline rush to drive fast in one of these high-performance vehicles, but basically the faster you drive, the worse your gas mileage gets. It's fun, but it doesn't last long. Sound familiar?

On the other hand, if you need to go on a long car trip and want to save some money, you'd be smart to drive an economy car so you can get more miles for your buck. For long-distance running you'll need to develop the fuel-efficient aerobic system. Your aerobic engine runs on oxygen, blood glucose, and metabolized fat. It's highly efficient and can run all day on minimal added fuel. The system is called aerobic because it burns with a higher oxygen-to-fuel ratio. The physiology is complex, but the practical implications are nothing short of amazing.

A pioneer in this field was New Zealand's Arthur Lydiard, who trained the best middle distance and distance runners in the 1960s. His runners did months of aerobic training followed by measured increases in intensity as their events approached. He invented the LSD run. And he had 800-meter specialists doing long runs of 22 miles and 100-mile weeks in their conditioning phase. Why? To build a massive and resilient aerobic system, upon which everything later would be built.

I drive a Prius, and on the cool dashboard viewscreen I can watch the subtle mixing of gas and electric as I drive. When I drive aggressively I can actually watch my fuel economy drop. On the other hand, if I press lightly and gradually on the accelerator, I can watch my fuel economy go up. I love it. My car is teaching me to drive more economically by Body Sensing how hard or soft I push on the accelerator.

Your body is doing this all the time as you run. If you go faster than your body is conditioned to run, your efficiency drops. When you run at a steady, relaxing, aerobic pace, your efficiency goes way up as your effort level drops. We all need to go easier on the gas pedal and run more aerobically.

## Use of the Heart Rate Monitor

One of the best ways to learn an economical training pace is with a heart rate (HR) monitor. Two modern masters of this technique are seven-time Tour de France champion Lance Armstrong and six-time world

Ironman champion Mark Allen. Armstrong's coach Chris Carmichael describes Lance's training in *The Ultimate Ride*. After his Tour de France recovery, Lance would go into winter/spring aerobic system building, setting his aerobic threshold heart rate at 145 beats per minute, no higher.

Lance rode thousands of miles, became leaner, and generated more and more power and efficiency at the low HR. He ate amazingly little before or during his rides, teaching his body to burn fat. When he was no longer improving at the low heart rate, he knew he could build no more ATP factories and that his economy engine was as large as it could be. It was time now to train the glucose-burning (gas) aerobic system and the glycolytic anaerobic system required for sprints, Time Trials, and breakaways on mountain climbs. Lance had access to a combination of both his engines for these measured efforts, using his economy engine by itself at all other times.

Another master of this is Mark Allen. Earlier in his career he tried to finish each and every run all out. After seasons of inconsistencies and fatigue, he discovered that running harder was not the answer. He heard about Phil Maffetone's lower-effort training (which we discuss on the following pages), and while he was skeptical, he put a heart rate monitor on and set it to beep when he hit 155 beats per minute. He found that at that heart rate he was running an 8:15-per-mile pace, which was much slower than his normal training pace. Convinced to take the slow-burn approach, he spent months running at an HR of 155. During this time he became more efficient and faster at the low heart rate and eventually trained his body to run "easy" 5:30 miles at this heart rate.

These experienced athletes also understood that mixing in hard anaerobic work during the aerobic building phase actually *inhibited* aerobic development. Many athletes are constantly doing cycles of hard intervals week in and week out, year-round, and find themselves fatigued, injured, or lacking joy in their running. Aerobic running is the feel-good zone, where you feel a runner's high. Very short (six- to ten-second) bursts of speed can be done in this phase to develop biomechanical efficiency and neuromuscular movement. But these short bouts of speed do not produce damaging acidosis.

## USING YOUR HEART RATE TO DETERMINE
## THE RIGHT TRAINING ZONE

In order to maximize fat-utilizing aerobic development, plus all the positive cellular and vascular changes that occur along with it, how do you determine what your own maximum training heart rate should be? Most of us do not sense this until it is too late in our efforts. The simplest and most practical way is to apply the "180 formula."

This formula for determining one's maximum aerobic zone was developed by Phil Maffetone, who has been coach and advisor to many world-class marathoners and Ironman triathletes, as well as thousands of recreational athletes. So grab a pencil and paper and let's do the math.

**The 180 Formula:** To find your maximum aerobic heart rate, subtract your age from 180 and then modify the resulting number by selecting one or more of the following categories:

1. If you have, or are recovering from, a major illness (heart disease, any operation, any hospital stay) or are on any regular medication, subtract 10.
2. If you have not exercised before, you have exercised but have been injured, or you are regressing in your running, subtract 5.
3. If you have been exercising for up to two years with no real problems and have not had colds or flu more than once or twice a year, subtract 0.
4. If you have been exercising for more than two years without any problems, making progress in competition without injury, add 5.
5. If you are about 60 years old or older *or* if you are about 20 years old or younger, add 5.

The final result will be your maximum aerobic heart rate for base training. For efficient base building, you should train at or below this level throughout the Form Focus phase and the conditioning phase of your marathon training. As I mentioned before, this doesn't necessarily mean you'll always run the same speed or always run slowly. It just means that when you run, you don't allow your heart rate to go above your maximum aerobic HR.

If you're a seasoned marathoner and are trying to run a faster marathon this time around, do most of your long runs at your max aerobic

HR for the duration of this conditioning phase. If you can hold a consistent max aerobic HR, what you'll notice is that your heart rate will stay the same while your speed gradually increases over the weeks. The emphasis of your work will be to run a sustainable pace without going into your anaerobic zone.

As an example of how this formula works, I've done it for myself. By the time this book is published I'll be sixty-two. So . . .

$$180 - 62 = 118$$

Option 4 applies to me, so I add 5 to my previous number . . .

$$118 + 5 = 123$$

Option 5 also applies to me, so I add 5 more to that number . . .

$$123 + 5 = 128$$

This means that to build my economy engine I need to keep my heart rate below 128 beats per minute throughout the conditioning phase of my training (with the exception of very short bursts of speed or during hill intervals). As a side note, when I'm running in second gear my HR hovers around 120.

Some runners have a good Body Sense of what their aerobic pace is and can run in this easy and efficient zone without the feedback of a monitor. Others might need a monitor to help train their body to recognize what it feels like. Some runners are hard chargers and need a feedback tool to help them slow down to an efficient, fat-burning aerobic pace. It takes months to fully build the aerobic engine, so it is unwise to begin adding speed until the last four to six weeks before your race, depending on whether you're running a half or full marathon. This is done during the mastery phase of the *Chi Marathon* program. Doing speed too early in your training can inhibit aerobic development. There are no short cuts or quick-and-easy ways to build your aerobic engine.

It's a simple rule to follow: you should be running at or below your aerobic threshold on your long runs. Exceptions to this rule during your LSD runs would be when you're running uphill or when you pick up the speed during the last couple of miles (which I highly recommend).

Many runners are training too fast on their LSD runs, not trusting that they'll be able to hold a faster pace during their marathon. If you can discipline yourself to stay in this mode during the conditioning phase, the payback in your performance during the mastery phase, and especially on race day, will blow you away.

## Fueling, Hydration, and Electrolyte Replacement

Glycogen, water, and electrolytes are the three things on which your body relies to keep moving. If you run low on fuel, your body will stop running. If you run low on electrolytes, your muscles will stop firing and you'll get muscle cramps. If you run low on hydration, your blood will thicken and your heart will have to work harder than it already is. You must replace these three things during your long runs and most definitely on race day. Maintaining each of them in your body in the right amounts is a skill you have to learn and practice.

### FUELING

Exercise physiologists generally agree that if your body's stores of blood glucose and glycogen (in the muscles) are topped off, you have about ninety minutes of running in your body before your tank is empty. This, of course, is a very generalized statement because everyone's body is different. Every runner has a different rate of metabolism and runs with a different level of efficiency. However, as your mastery of the ChiRunning technique improves, your glycogen burning will be spread out over a longer period of time because you'll be burning more fat and less glycogen.

Use your LSD runs to practice getting your fueling down to a science, so you can determine approximately at which mile point your body will begin running low on fuel. Practice fueling on the run by experimenting with what works best for you. You're looking for a fuel that provides a sustained energy level, not an energy swing of the sort where you're feeling good one minute and crashing the next. The most important rule is this: don't ingest anything during your event that you have not used and tested in training.

Gels, bananas, dried fruits, energy bars, and even jelly beans can be used to replace glycogen stores. Most marathons offer gels after mile 10. If you plan to use gels, it's important that you train with the gels you will have on race day—whether it's your own supply or what's available from the aid stations.

1. Take them with plenty of water. Gels increase your need for water.
2. Once you begin taking gels, you should continue to take one at least every 4 miles for the rest of the race and no more than every half hour.
3. Find out ahead of time which gel packs will be given at your race and train with those to see how your body responds. During your race, don't eat gels that your body hasn't already tried and approved.

Most races offer bananas. They are loaded with potassium, a cellular electrolyte, and calories. Dried fruits work well and are a good source of glycogen. You can chew them or just hold them in your mouth and let them slowly dissolve. Energy bars can be the least efficient form of energy foods because of the time it takes to digest them, unless they are pure carbohydrate bars. I do not recommend any form of solid protein on the run.

Energy drinks are another source of glycogen, but they can be high in calories, and sometimes the ingredient list can look more like a science experiment than a drink. Do not use gels and an energy drink at the same time or you could be ingesting too much glucose and setting yourself up for a crash.

For more on diet and nutrition, see Chapter 10.

## HYDRATION

There has been lots of controversy over how much water to drink during a marathon, with doctors, exercise physiologists, and race directors urging all runners to "drink a lot, but not too much." Well, that's good advice, but you'd have to agree that it leaves the exact amount for *you* a bit nebulous.

Dehydration happens when you don't drink enough water. It can show up as dizziness or a light headache, a lack of mental focus, fatigue, and, in more extreme cases, a rapid pulse. An important fact to note is that dehydration reduces your body's ability to take up oxygen. So don't let all of that great aerobic training go to waste by not drinking enough water.

Hyponatremia, on the other hand, is a very dangerous state where there is too much water in your body. If you drink too much water it will dilute the salt content in your blood, reducing your body's ability to conduct the subtle electric current needed to fire your muscles and, more important, the neurotransmitters in your brain. If your brain doesn't fire, your life-support systems become compromised, and that's *really* not where you want to go. Some marathoners have died needlessly, and others have had to drop out of their race, all because of drinking too much water. I heard someone once say, "Drink intelligently, not maximally."

Here's a foolproof way to never again have to worry about drinking too much or too little during your race. I set my countdown timer to beep every ten minutes and drink a mouthful of water every time it goes off. This way I never drink too much or too little. When you drink just the right amount you'll never get dehydrated and you'll also never have to stop to pee (which can put a huge hole in your finish time).

## ELECTROLYTE REPLACEMENT

If you're a novice marathoner, you might not be used to taking electrolytes while running, since most of your prior races have been a half marathon or less. But when you begin running beyond 15 miles it no longer becomes an option. Your body sweats out salts as a part of the cooling process, and as long as you sweat, you'll continue to deplete the stores of sodium and potassium in your system.

I train with S! Caps (Succeed! Caps) or Endurolytes (also in capsule form) on LSD runs. They are designed to replace sodium and potassium as well as other minerals. Take one every forty-five minutes in hot weather and every sixty minutes in temperate weather. There's really no reason to take electrolytes sooner than 10 miles into any long run, but once you start taking them, continue on a regular hourly schedule. I tape the capsules to the outside of my race bib with masking tape. This makes it extremely convenient to reach for one when I need it. And they're protected from getting wet from sweat.

I prefer caps over sports drinks for electrolyte replacement because most sports drinks just don't replace enough electrolytes for a marathoner and many contain high-fructose corn syrup, which is not good for your body. If you use the sports drink offered in your race, you might consider backing it up with an electrolyte cap every hour to be safe.

Never drink a sports drink offered to you by an aid station volunteer unless you've already tried that particular drink out on your body. I've heard of lots of runners having to pull out of a race from drinking a sports drink that either upset their stomach or tasted bad. Be wise and find out which sports drink will be offered at your race. Then do your "field testing" on your LSD training runs.

## Managing Your Energy for the Long Run

In this section we'll get into the nitty-gritty of managing your energy:

- Gathering energy
- Focusing energy
- Conserving energy
- Managing adversity

### GATHERING ENERGY

In addition to building your cardio-aerobic base and fueling well, the mind is a crucial tool in building and focusing your energy. We've talked about the importance of vision and goals, but equally important is a positive mental attitude. Your mind is fickle. It can serve your best interests or it can derail your best intentions. And it has a huge impact on how much energy you have in any given moment. Begin to notice how your energy level changes with either a positive or negative thought or feeling. If it's a beautiful day and you're going for a hike with friend, you probably have lots of energy. If, on the other hand, you have to do your taxes and they're late and you owe money, you might feel the energy draining right out of you.

Distance running is easiest when fueled by positive mental thoughts. I look forward to long runs. They are special for me and I feel blessed to have the time. Running with friends, learning something new, and making running fun by exploring new places are all ways to build energy with a positive mental approach. What's important to remember is that every moment you have a choice in how you use your mind. Positive mental thoughts are an unlimited source of energy that you can tap into whenever you need it.

Another source of energy is your environment. Most people think only of food, air, and water as sources of energy, but in reality, your environment and the people in your life are a huge and rich source of energy. Think of a beautiful sunset, a gorgeous vista, a mountain stream, or your running group. They all give you energy and recharge your batteries. Here's an exercise we use all the time to consciously take in the energy of the environment.

**The Window Exercise:** This was taught to me by a teacher many years ago and has always worked to gather and replenish my energy whenever I've needed it. Just think of an open window, like the old houses have, and imagine that your chest, from your collarbone to your navel, is one big picture window that is opened for a fresh breeze to blow into your body. Feel the chi of your environment flowing in through your window as you run along. Imagine you have eyes in your chest and you're "seeing" your environment through those eyes. Bring that energy in through your chest and then feel it flowing down into your pelvis and on down into your legs. Keep this image going for as long as you need it. I have also used the image of my chest being a big dish antenna, receiving energy as I run. Both images work great for gathering energy.

## FOCUSING YOUR ENERGY

All of the Form Focuses are designed to focus your mind and your energy. A lot of people like to let their mind wander when they run, and that is okay to an extent, but a lack of focus can become an energy leak, which we'll talk about. Anytime you feel fatigue or a lack of energy, it is time to refocus your mind. A great exercise to refocus and direct your energy is to engage the power of your y'chi, which we talked about in Chapter 2 in terms of creating a vision, and which we'll now show you how to apply while running.

**Y'Chi: Strengthen Your Mind, Focus Your Body, Run Like the Wind:** Y'chi (pronounced "ee-chee") is the practice of using your eyes to direct your chi to move your body. It's a full mind-body focus and a great skill to have if you want to increase your efficiency and speed. The best example of y'chi is a cat that has just spotted a bird. The cat fixes its gaze on the prey. Without breaking its gaze, the cat begins to slowly and quietly creep toward the bird in a motion that can only be described as "a cat doing T'ai Chi." The cat's limbs move, but its gaze never leaves the bird. The cat's y'chi is pulling it forward.

Using your y'chi is a fascinating and extremely effective way to use your mind to direct your running. It is the skill of directing your chi through your eyes so that your mind can "back off," allowing the energy in your body to naturally flow and respond to external demands. Y'chi works most effectively when your body can hold decent running form without mental prompting. You can use your y'chi anytime you need a boost of energy. One of my favorite times to use it is while running intervals at the track. When I'm running the curves I mentally engage all the Form Focuses I'm working on that day. Then, as I approach the straightaway, I switch my mind from thinking about the Form Focuses to locking my eyes onto a spot at the far end of the track directly ahead of me, and I let that unbroken visual connection energetically pull me to the start of the next curve.

Here's how to practice using your y'chi during your LSD runs. If you're feeling fatigued, just lock your visual focus to a point in the distance greater than 100 meters ahead. It can be a tree, a cloud—anything that you can focus on that will remain straight ahead for a decent amount of time. Let your visual connection with that object pull you forward as if you were hooked up to a bungee cord, while you relax and rest your body. It works only as long as you sustain an *unbroken* focus; if the road curves, change your focal point to another target. You can even use runners who are ahead of you and reel them in like a fish. As your LSD runs increase in distance, it is especially useful to engage your y'chi in the later miles when you need a mental and/or physical break. Whenever you engage your y'chi, be sure to send the message to your body to relax and flow. My experience with using my y'chi is that I arrive at my focus point before I know it. Your y'chi is an endless source of energy, and all it takes is being able to focus your mind and allow your body to relax and be pulled forward.

By gathering and focusing your energy, you can come back from a run with more energy than when you left—more energy, in fact, than you might get from resting on the couch.

## Conserving Energy

Once you've gathered and focused your energy, you'll need to do what you can to hold on to it. Here are some important ways to maintain your energy level.

- **Start off at a comfortable pace.** Don't start any of your runs faster than you hope to finish. On longer runs start slower than your projected average pace and finish only slightly faster. Here's why: if you apply this principle of negative splits to every training run you do, guess what—the same thing will happen when you run your marathon.

- **Increase your pace during a race only when you feel totally comfortable in doing so and when you can do it without increasing your PRE.** During your long runs you can practice increasing your speed *without* increasing your muscle usage. Now there's a form challenge for you.

- **Talk less, and at the right time.** Practice talking less during your runs and especially when racing. My HR monitor shows me that my heart rate jumps at least ten beats per minute as soon as I start talking. Whenever my heart rate increases I know I'm working harder, so I try to keep my talking to a minimum. Talk on the downhill sections if you need to.

- **Practice your Form Focuses regularly.** Know which focuses you'll be working on in every workout and set a repeating ten-minute countdown timer to remind yourself to reinstate any number of the focuses. When you get to the point where you can hold multiple focuses simultaneously, you'll feel a drastic increase in your efficiency. Many hands make easy work.

- **Maintain a steady cadence.** Run at a cadence between 170 and 180 strides per minute and keep that stride rate steady throughout every run. Having a stride rate that fluctuates will cost you valuable energy. What *does* change is your stride length, relative to terrain, effort level, and speed. If you can keep your PRE within a small range, your energy expenditure will be very even-keeled and you'll begin to feel more relaxed at any speed, which burns less fuel.

- **Watch your foot strike.** Whenever your foot strikes in front of your knee you're overstriding, which consumes more of your available energy because you're essentially braking at the same time. It's never efficient to drive with the brakes on. Try to sense where your foot is striking relative to your knee and always have the intention to feel your foot touch down more underneath your body, not in front of it.

- **Release any tension.** Do a Body Scan (head to toe) every ten minutes and feel for muscle tension held anywhere in your body—especially in your shoulders, arms, hips, and legs. If you feel tension in isolated areas, work on relaxing those particular areas with visualization, breathing, and conscious release of the muscle. Sometimes it is easier to relax and let go of a tight muscle if you tense it first, then let it relax into a nice fluid motion.

There are many more ways to conserve your energy, but these are the most effective. If you work only on these and nothing else, you'll be a rock star in terms of energy efficiency, and your friends will wonder what you're on . . . or onto.

## Additional Form Adjustments to Conserve Energy

- Engage your "C" Shape.
- Relax the tension in your shoulders, neck, face, and arms.
- Soften your visual focus.
- Check your cadence. It should be between 170 and 180 spm.
- Synchronize your stride rate with your breath rate. If you're just running to complete your distance, settle into a comfortable, sustainable pace and instate a five-count stride rate: three steps on the out-breath, two steps on the in-breath. (Set your metronome at 36 bpm and it will beep every fifth step.) Or, if your pace is faster, in the third-gear range, instate a three-count stride rate: two steps on the out-breath, one step on the in-breath. (Set your metronome at 60 bpm and it will beep every third stride.)
- Relax your lower back and allow your pelvis to freely rotate.

**Resting on the Run and Overcoming Fatigue:** During this phase your weekly LSD runs will get progressively longer (up to 19 miles for marathoners and up to 13 miles for you half marathoners). What this means is that you have more opportunities to create effortless running. I find that when I get it right, it happens, and there's no mistaking that sense of running and not feeling anything. When I'm not occupying that state of running bliss, I'm left with feeling some sense of effort, usually accompanied by some level of fatigue. I float in and out of these two states often during every run. The important thing to remember when you're feeling tired is that it doesn't necessarily mean that you have expended all your energy and that your tank is empty. Yes, it could mean that, but it could also mean that your mind or your body is doing something that is either blocking or misusing your available energy.

Practice each of these suggestions during your long runs to see which ones work best for you and use them at your event.

- **Walk when you need to.** For you novice marathoners, there's nothing illegal about walking for brief spells if you need to. But walk only until your breath rate and/or heart rate recovers (your heart rate should not drop below 110). Here's the basic rule to remember: run until you feel tired, then walk until you feel guilty.
- **Walk through the aid stations.** Use them as a brief but nourishing interlude in the constant movement of the marathon. One way to gain energy while passing through an aid station is to thank every volunteer you pass. It's even more energizing when you make eye contact.
- **Drop your arms.** Let them dangle at your sides for thirty seconds at a time. This will rest both your arms and your shoulders. A good time to do this is after passing through an aid station, when you're getting back into your run. When your arms feel rested, relax your shoulders, slowly bring your arms back into a 90-degree bend at the elbow, and continue on.
- **Drop into a lower gear.** Take a break from the pace and relax your whole body for thirty seconds. Let your body go floppy, like a rag doll. Shake out any tension and then very slowly bring your body back into a Column again with your posture focuses. If your quads feel pounded, shorten your stride and relax your legs for a brief period (or do some ChiWalking) until they recover.
- **Slow your pace to a more relaxing rate.** This is the ideal alternative to walking because you don't lose any momentum and your cadence doesn't change from faster (running) to slower (walking) and back again.
- **Share the workload.** If one part of your body gets tired, allow it to rest by engaging another part of your body. If your legs are feeling tired, use more lean and arm swing instead. If your calves are feeling tired, or if they're cramping, let them dangle from your knees and direct the emphasis to your hips. If your body is generally fatigued, let your mind take over—engage your y'chi and allow your body to be pulled along.

Working with fatigue is always a creative act and requires you to have your wits about you. First build energy, then conserve it, and do this as much as possible before you get too tired.

**Energy Leaks and Positive Thinking:** There are countless ways we waste our energy when running. For lack of a better term, I call them energy leaks, because it's like punching a hole in your gas tank. Your body wants to move forward, but your brain has some other direction in mind. For some folks leaking energy can become so habitual that it can even turn into a form of self-sabotage. Energy is energy, whether it's mental or physical, and your mind and body both have their own ways of leaking it.

You leak physical energy when you expend more energy than you need to. This can occur for various reasons, but the main culprits here are inefficient running, improper fueling, and carrying tension, all of which we've covered. Some of the ways we consume additional physical energy are subtle: talking too much, running faster than our body is trained to, running with a heel strike, not swinging our arms effectively, and not leaning enough.

You leak mental energy by misusing your mind in the form of negative or doubtful internal conversations. These can include obsessing about how far you need to run, how fast you're running, how much discomfort you're in, or how crowded the race is. Your negative thoughts might sound like this:

"I don't know how I got myself into this mess."

"Everyone is having a great time except me."

"I can't believe I'm only at mile 10. How am I going to ever finish?"

None of the statements listed above will do anything to change or correct your situation. A friend once told me, "There are two times when you should not worry. One is if you can't do anything about the situation. The other is if you *can* do something about it." You get the point. It's all needless and ineffectual mental grumbling. Not only will it *not* help you, it could easily sink your ship.

If you can catch yourself in the midst of negative thinking, you're already heading in the right direction. Just pretend you're surfing through the channels on your TV and happen to land on one that you don't like. What do you do? You change the channel to something else, preferably something that makes you feel better. The best "channel" to switch to while running is your "focus channel." It's always there to help you out of any mental conversation that's heading south. It also helps to look up and around at what's going on outside your head. Smile, or laugh at yourself. Take a deep breath and focus on feeling your feet touch the ground with each step. This will direct your focus away from your head and into your body, which is always a safer place to be.

Lastly, missing a training run is an energy leak that affects almost every marathoner I've ever met. Don't sweat missing a midweek run. It is not that big a deal as long as it's not happening regularly. Missing a single LSD run is not a big deal either. But missing more than one can start to detract from your training plan and leave you obsessing about being in shape for the big day. If you find yourself slipping, go back and reread your vision. It'll recharge you with positive energy. If that doesn't work, you should think seriously about running in a later or shorter event.

As you can see, none of us has any problem finding ways to waste energy. But now you have some tools to help stop the energy leaks before they hijack your plans.

## MANAGING PHYSICAL ADVERSITY: REMEMBER THE OBSERVER

The highest form of spiritual practice is self-observation without judgment.

—SWAMI KRIPALU

Adversity is anything that challenges your copacetic state: mild discomfort, pain, emotional angst, physical ailments or injuries, the weather, or even just having a plain old bad day. That being said, adversity is never really a problem. I like to think of it as a lesson masquerading as a challenge. It's your *response* to adversity that could either wreck your day or be a learning opportunity that could change your life. This is where your Observer comes in handy.

For years I've repeated the following phrase to myself whenever I find adversity in my lap: "My present situation, *subject to change*, is _____." This statement has the immediate effect of pulling me out of identification with my dilemma. It gives me the space to think of a clear-headed response, instead of being caught up in an emotional reaction, which gets me nowhere. This simple approach can help you immeasurably in training for long-distance running.

It might go something like this: "My present situation, subject to change, is that my right knee is killing me." At which point the words "subject to change" would kick in, and I would then search my memory to see what I could do to alleviate knee pain. Then I would hear, "Shorten your stride . . . rotate your leg medially . . . keep your upper body ahead of your feet . . . *relax.*" Inevitably one of the suggestions would work and I'd be on my merry way, problem solved, within minutes. I'm not saying it will always be that easy, but it *can* be. In your journal or end-of-week review, write down some of your own responses that consistently turn adversity around for you.

If you're experiencing discomfort, pain, or injury, it's your body trying to tell you something, in no uncertain terms. Listen to what it's saying and do your best to address the issue and make any corrections as soon as possible. The best way to avoid physical problems is to cover the basics as well as you can. This means always paying close attention to your running form, fueling, hydration, and electrolyte levels.

Here's a list of ways to address physical problems:

- **Ask yourself if the pain is productive.** Or is it nonproductive discomfort?
- **If you have an injury, look for what *you* did to cause it.** If it's a technique problem, focus on the specific aspect of your technique that, if changed, could help alleviate the problem.
- **If you're feeling pain, it usually means chi is blocked from flowing through the area of pain.** The solution lies in going back to the dual theme of alignment and relaxation. Look for the areas in your body where you're either not aligned or not relaxed and do your best to make the necessary adjustment(s).
- **Know your limits and adjust accordingly.** This usually means either slowing down or shortening your stride. If you slow down, run just below the pain threshold.
- **Know your weak points, what they feel like, and how to work with each one.** Improve your weak areas through technique first (Form Focuses), then through strengthening.
- **If you're in pain, take NSAIDs (non-steroidal anti-inflammatory drugs) only if the pain is significant and acute.** Don't take them for lesser pain, and never take them for long periods. Taking painkillers during training or racing is risky at best and should be done cautiously. They can prevent you from feeling your discomfort accurately and may inhibit your ability to respond accordingly. A 2006 study of fifty long-distance runners done by lead researcher David Nieman,

director of the Human Performance Lab at Appalachian State University in North Carolina, and reported in the journal *Brain, Behavior, and Immunity* compared runners who took ibuprofen regularly during training and in their event to a group of runners who abstained from taking any painkillers. After their race Nieman found that the runners on ibuprofen actually had 50 percent *more* inflammation in their bodies along with mild kidney impairment and mild endotoxemia, which can be potentially dangerous.

- **Get physical therapy or treatment if you need it.** Yoga, Pilates, acupuncture, ART, and deep tissue massage all work wonders to help reset your body.
- **Keep moving if you can.** And always move as symmetrically as possible (no one watching you should be able to tell you're injured).
- **Go to our website, chirunning.com.** There you'll find lots of specific information and support about managing pain and specific injuries.

**Dealing with Weather Challenges:** Appropriate clothing is always necessary. Here are some specifics.

### Heat
- Wear sunscreen.
- Wear a light-colored hat, and wet it if the weather is really hot. The evaporation will cool your head.
- Douse your head, neck, and wrists with water every chance you get. These are the points on the body that are most efficient at regulating your body temperature.
- Slow down if needed, or take more walk breaks. Use ChiWalking during the breaks to reinstate your pelvic rotation and help smooth out your stride.

### Cold
- Wear light wool or wicking clothing.
- Layer with clothes you can drop on the way, either handing them to a friend along the course or hiding them along the course knowing that they might not be there after the race.
- Nylon vests are a great temperature regulator in cold conditions.
- Regulate your body temperature by covering or uncovering your neck and/or head.

**Rain**

- If it's warm, pretend you're a duck.
- If it is cold, wool keeps you warm even if it's wet.
- Wear tech clothing. It doesn't get heavy when it's wet.
- Be careful of slipping on oily spots on the course. A strong core helps create good balance, so level your pelvis and shorten your stride.

**Wind**

- If it's at your back, thank your lucky stars.
- In a strong headwind, treat it like a hill: take shorter strides and lean into it.
- With a strong side wind, add mental focus and integrity to the side of your body bearing the brunt.
- Work with a running partner or group to take turns blocking the wind and drafting each other.

## Midweek Training Runs: Expanding Your Running Horizons

Most runners training for a half or full marathon do their long runs on weekends because it's when they have the largest chunk of time. Since most of us work during the week, we tend to do shorter, more intensive training runs then. There are four completely different midweek workouts in the ChiRunning training program, and each one has its own flavor and purpose in rounding out your training.

The following are descriptions of each type of run you'll do in the conditioning phase. We'll also tell you how each run contributes to your conditioning.

### INTERVALS

Intervals are designed to help you learn new patterns of movement in the quickest and most efficient way—through repetition. They also are a great way to build your ability to focus. In these workouts you'll be practicing your Form Focuses for short periods of time (usually one to three minutes).

In the ChiRunning training program there are four types of intervals.

- **On/off Form Focus Intervals.** During this workout you'll be asked to concentrate as precisely as possible on the focus at hand for the time period allotted, followed by a rest period where you're not focusing per se but taking a mental break. You'll be alternating this sequence throughout your workout. Each time period of focusing is called an interval.

- **Alternating Form Focus Intervals.** In this workout you'll be asked to pick two Form Focuses to concentrate on (sometimes we'll suggest them). You will then focus on one of them for one, two, or three minutes. When the specified time period is up, switch to the second focus for the prescribed time period. Go back and forth, alternating the two focuses in this way, for the first two-thirds of your workout. During the last third of your run, try to do both focuses at the same time. In this type of Form Focus interval workout there is no "off" interval. You're always focusing on one or the other. Later in your training you'll be asked to pick two pairs of focuses and alternate them the same as you would single focuses.

- **Speed Intervals.** This is the workout where you practice the Form Focuses that allow you to run faster (if you feel the need). But be very clear: a speed interval is not about trying to run faster. It's about creating the conditions for speed to happen. Speed intervals are simply Form Focus intervals done with more lean and more relaxation. This workout is best done on a track, a measured flat loop, or a measured straight stretch of road. Resist the temptation to do your speed interval workouts with your local track club. The atmosphere at track workouts is usually very competitive and will draw your attention away from running the workout that is best for you.

    *How to:* Begin each interval at a slow pace and slowly increase your lean as you progress to the finish (that is, go from second gear to third gear). It is important to do speed workouts with a metronome because it trains you to relax your hips and pelvis and lengthen your stride as you increase your lean. You should never feel wiped out at the end of a speed interval. If you do, you're pushing yourself too hard. Lighten up! Remember, you're working on technique first and foremost, and speed is just a by-product of good technique.

    Always follow the Chi principle of Gradual Progress. Your first interval should be the slowest and your last one the fastest. If you do the intervals correctly, your exertion level (PRE) should feel the same from the first interval to the last.

- **Hill Intervals.** This is a great cardiovascular workout that also adds upper-body strength and lower-body stretch into your running. Find a low paved hill that goes up and over symmetrically (that is, it has roughly the same incline and distance on each side of the hill). Ideally the hill from the low point on one side to the low point on the other side is around 200 meters, with about a 25-foot elevation gain from bottom to top. To start with, it should not be a particularly steep hill, though you can switch to a steeper one once your conditioning is ready for it. Each hill interval will consist of beginning at the bottom of the hill, running up and over the top and down the other side to a point equal distant from the top as the beginning. The best way to mark off a hill interval is to go to the top of the hill and slowly run down about thirty seconds in each direction; at the bottom of the hill on each side, mark your turnarounds with something clearly visible.

*How to:* Run uphill with all of your concentration on your upper body, really working the uphill focuses (see "Hill Runs," page 126). When you go down the other side, you're concentrating on the lower-body focuses, especially pelvic rotation, stride lengthening out the back, and getting as loose as you possibly can while keeping your cadence consistent. When you reach the bottom of the other side of the hill, downshift to first gear and jog for one minute. Then repeat this cycle up and over the hill again. Do the number of repetitions that is prescribed in the schedule. The Chi principle of Gradual Progress also applies to this workout: if you do it right, your first interval should be the slowest and your last should be the fastest, with your PRE staying about the same.

## SURGES

This is a high-end aerobic workout that will add greater performance capacity to your lungs and heart while teaching you to add some stretch to your stride. The beauty of this workout is that it doesn't need to be done on a track. It can be done on flat or hilly terrain.

*How to:* Warm up for at least ten minutes. At the end of your warm-up, settle into a comfortable second-gear aerobic pace. This will be your base pace, which you will return to after each Surge. A Surge is a light pickup in your speed brought on by adding a little lean while increasing your pelvic rotation and relaxing your legs. More lean, more relaxation . . . that's the formula for doing a Surge. Increase your lean very gradually over a two-minute period. At the end of your Surge you should be running a speed that feels fast, but you shouldn't feel as if you're killing yourself. Don't force your speed by pushing harder. Do it by using your technique—by leaning and relaxing. At the end of your two-minute Surge, return to your base pace. After one minute of running at your base pace, do another Surge. Repeat this cycle throughout your run. When you're nearing the end, try to hold your Surge pace for three to five minutes and then do a cool-down jog for three minutes. During your two-minute Surges practice one or two Form Focuses. During your one-minute breaks just focus on relaxing your entire body. Every two to three weeks you can increase your Surge time by one minute until you get up to four minutes of Surge time with a one-minute break.

## TEMPO RUNS

Tempo runs offer the opportunity to practice running at your projected race pace (whatever that might be for you), if it applies. These runs are generally 4–8 miles in length, depending on your conditioning level. We recommend this for runners with a good command of the ChiRunning technique and Form Focuses. The goal of this workout is to familiarize your body with what your eventual race pace feels like.

*How to:* Start off in second gear and slowly increase your lean over the length of the run until you finish in third gear. During this run, practice all of your Lean Focuses and always remember to relax more as you increase your lean. Your goal with this run is to move with a steady cadence and to slowly increase your speed throughout the run without increasing your effort level. This means you're not working on getting stronger and faster, you're working on getting better at creating the conditions for speed to happen by making the necessary adjustments to your technique. Use your metronome to keep your cadence steady. If your cadence is consistent, you'll stay more efficient as your speed increases.

Here's a sample 4-mile tempo run. If you're training to run a half marathon at an average pace of 9:00 per mile, you would start off running slower than the average and end up running faster than the average.

Mile 1: 9:06

Mile 2: 9:00

Mile 3: 8:55

Mile 4: 8:50

The average for these four segments is approximately a 9:00 pace.

**Race Pace Tempo Run:** When the schedule tells you to do a run at race pace, you'll need to estimate your projected race pace from your most recent Time Trial and plug in that number as the overall average you're shooting for. Then follow all the same instructions for the tempo run, above.

## HILL RUNS

This workout will build great cardiovascular conditioning as well as improve your uphill and downhill running techniques. Find a place where you can run low rolling hills. Your heart rate increases significantly on each uphill section, and the downhill sections allow your heart to return to your basic aerobic rate. Whenever you're running downhill on easy grades, where you're not required to brake, it's a good time to practice your pelvic rotation. Trails are okay if you're used to them and as long as the climbs are gradual and no more than twenty-five to fifty feet in total elevation gain.

*How to:* Warm up for five to ten minutes on level ground, if possible, before starting up your first hill.

*Uphill running focuses:* Whenever going uphill, shift to a lower gear (shorter stride length) and swing your arms forward and up (instead of to the rear). Lean into the hill from the ankles and keep your heels down at all times.

*Downhill running focuses:* Whenever you crest a hill, always sustain your lean over the top of the hill until you begin heading downhill again. If the downhill is runnable, lean into it, allowing your legs to relax and your stride to lengthen. Also, allow your pelvis to rotate more. If it is a steep downhill, meaning that you have to put on your brakes, run more upright, pick up your heels, take shorter strides, and roll heel to toe as you descend.

## FUN RUNS (RECOVERY RUNS)

This workout is a recovery run to be done the day after your LSD run. Just let your mind rest and your body relax! Take yourself on a tour of some new area you'd like to explore. Keep your pace mellow and the terrain flat. This run is just to clean out your legs, loosen your muscles, and free up your spirit. You can substitute a bike ride for this workout, as long as it's at an easy speed. I've used Fun Runs for everything from studying architecture to window-shopping. Think of it as uncontrived running.

### CROSS-TRAINING WORKOUTS

In these workouts we encourage you to take a low-intensity break from running. Our favorites are cycling (road or mountain), walking, swimming, or hiking. If you have a favorite yoga or Pilates class, that's great too. Cross-training workouts shouldn't be intense. You should see them instead as a break from the focus of running and a time to freshen your body in other ways. Have fun with these workouts. And if you don't feel the need to cross-train, then don't. You'll still show up in great shape for your event.

As you can see, the conditioning phase has a lot to it. It's where the beef is, so to speak. All the work you did during the technique phase was preparation for this phase, where you actually learn how to run a half or full marathon and how to get your body in great shape to succeed at long-distance running. As the distances get longer it's time to dig deeper, but not into your physical energy; instead, draw on your vision, body-intelligence, and intuition.

This phase is preparation for the mastery phase, where you'll fine-tune your running skills even further by taking the depth of your technique and conditioning base and applying it specifically to your event. The mastery phase will help ensure that your event is pain-free and a thrilling and joyful experience because *you* have created the conditions for it to become a reality.

# CHAPTER FIVE

# Phase IV

## The Mastery Phase

Your body knows its heritage and its rightful need and will not be
    deceived.
And your body is the harp of your soul,
And it is yours to bring forth sweet music from it or confused sounds.
—KAHLIL GIBRAN

*M*astery is a big word in our lexicon. People see the word and immediately conjure up images of a person who is so far beyond
the skill levels of normal people as to be godlike. George Xu
is a grandmaster of T'ai Chi, but he would be the first to tell you that
it's all relative to where you're at in your learning process. If you want
to have good posture, you must first master standing in good alignment
until it becomes easy, natural, and intuitive. Once that happens you
might want to master the act of running slowly with good posture, or
master the ability to effortlessly hold a 90-degree bend in your arms as
they swing. Heck, I've known people who have mastered making a good
cup of coffee . . . at least in their own minds. Mastery is mostly about
being so practiced at something that it becomes an increasingly effortless

and intuitive act because of your own physical, mental, and emotional familiarity with the subject.

Why would you want to master a marathon? I'll answer that with another question: why not? In your process of mindfully training for a marathon, you're constantly working to make your running technique more efficient, to minimize the effect running long distances has on your body, to always have the appropriate response to every challenge along the way, and to finish with a smile on your face because you feel so good (and not just because you're finished). Mastery isn't only about what you do in challenging situations; it's also about what you do when you're feeling good. It's about gaining the advantage in *every* situation.

I recently attended a piano recital. This was after I'd come up with the piano metaphor that I use earlier in this book for explaining training for a marathon, but it was a fortuitous coincidence. Rachel, our eight-year-old friend, walked in dressed in a beautiful long dress and sat down at the piano like a concert pianist (except for the box at her feet, since her feet didn't reach the ground).

She played ten beautiful pieces; none of them was easy, and the final piece was quite difficult and complicated indeed. Her hands were positioned flawlessly on the keys. She made a few mistakes, but she was very practiced at finding a place she could remember and moving forward with grace. She played for at least half an hour, without consulting any sheet music.

Rachel had spent three years training, and over that time I had spoken often with her parents, who were unsure about whether they wanted to have her continue with the piano. She has a teacher who is a stickler for details, to say the least, and is quite demanding of good technique before anything else. Well, from my vantage point on the day of the recital, the composure, grace, and joy of that eight-year-old when she was done made all doubts disappear. And it immediately made me think of the marathon experience, particularly the mastery phase.

## Race-Specific Training

In the mastery phase you'll design your own training program, in which all the workouts will mimic the specific terrain and conditions in the event you'll be running and you'll apply the Form Focuses that best suit those conditions. We call this technique-based, race-specific training, and you'll experience how powerful it can be for running any distance. When race day comes around, you'll feel what it means to be at the peak of confidence and conditioning, just as Rachel did.

Most marathon training programs will tell you how many miles to run each week and how much strength training to do, and then leave it at that. But if your marathon is hilly, it seems logical that you should be training to run lots of hills. Or if it's flat, it makes sense to train yourself to run for hours on flat roads.

I remember running my first ultra marathon, the JFK 50 Mile. I was living in Boulder at the time and doing lots of trail running to get in shape for the race. What I didn't realize was that in the middle of the race course there was a 26-mile stretch of completely flat running, which I had done none of during my training. Needless to say, it was the most difficult part of my race. That was in 1995, and I have done race-specific training for every race since then.

You have already begun your process of mastery by taking the incremental steps through the first three phases of this training program, and now you're ready to add the final nuances. With all that preliminary work under your waistband, you can truly master your event.

## Assess Yourself: Physically, Mentally, and Emotionally

You're at the beginning of another phase, so now's the time to do another personal assessment of your present condition, just as you did at the beginning of the previous phases. Review your vision and goals. Make any needed adjustments or corrections to your original plan. As you know, a complete assessment involves a thorough check-in with all the thoughts, feelings, and physical sensations around your training up to this point. You might think of it as an end-of-phase review, where you look back on what went well since the beginning of the conditioning phase and what still needs improvement. So take some time to review all that has happened up to this point in your training.

You have just finished many weeks of aerobic training. Your lungs are highly efficient and your heart is strong. Your body is now more capable of maintaining a consistent pace with less effort. Write some notes in your log on your current level of conditioning.

This involves a two-part inquiry. First you must look at the results of your most recent Time Trial. Then ask yourself, in general terms, if you have any physical problems or concerns. Note all significant entries in your training log. The personal data you collect, along with the answers to the questions about the specifics of your race, will be helpful in accurately designing your upcoming workouts.

Calculate or measure the following and note the results in your log.

- Your current resting heart rate (RHR) (see instructions page 32)
- Your maximum heart rate (MHR) (see instructions page 107)
- Your maximum aerobic heart rate (MAHR) and associated training pace (see instructions page 107)
- The average pace or heart rate you'd like to hold during your race (see instructions page 125)
- Your most recent Time Trial results

The conditioning phase and the mastery phase can have some overlap, especially if you want to run multiple marathons or if you're focused on performance. For example, in the intermediate twenty-week full marathon program (not included in this book but available through our website), even though we have you begin the mastery phase in week fourteen, feel free to design your training program ahead of time and incorporate any race-specific focuses into your conditioning workouts as early as week twelve. This would give you nine weeks to fine-tune your skills for the race. I would recommend this approach only if you're a repeat marathoner or interested in performance.

If you're a novice half marathoner, we begin the mastery phase at week eleven in your sixteen-week training program. But if you're a repeat half marathoner, feel free to begin the mastery phase of your training as early as week eight.

## The Mastery Phase Time Trial

It's time to do another Time Trial, but it is slightly different this time. For those of you shooting for a specific finishing time, this will give you an idea of the pace your body is currently capable of running for a marathon or half marathon.

I'll start off by saying that a Time Trial isn't about seeing how fast you can run. So empty your brain of that idea. It's about finding out what speed you can run and still remain comfortably within your aerobic heart rate zone. Remember, anytime you go beyond your aerobic threshold and enter your anaerobic zone, you deplete your available fuel supply at a rapid rate. It's fine to run anaerobically at the very end of your marathon *if* your body is trained to do so *and* if you're feeling good. But the rest of your half or full marathon should be run at an aerobic pace, and no faster than your aerobic threshold.

Here's how the mastery phase Time Trial is done. First, pick the day you're going to run your Time Trial and make that a special day. Block out the time (preferably the same time of day as the start of your marathon) and don't schedule anything else before or after. This is a test and you don't want to be rushed with it.

This Time Trial will be 5 miles for half marathoners and 8 miles for marathoners. Do your Time Trial on a track if possible. If you don't live near a track, measure a course on a stretch of flat road or bike path and mark every mile (or kilometer) point as accurately as possible.

Do your Body Looseners followed by a ten-minute warm-up. While you're doing these, imagine you're warming up at your event, being focused and relaxed. This is the mind-set you want for this Time Trial: even though you're running only 5 or 8 miles, you should nonetheless imagine you're about to run your full event distance. When you're ready to begin your Time Trial, start your watch and take off running at the pace at which you feel you could run your event on race day. During the first mile, Body Sense what your pace feels like by running slightly faster and then slightly slower. Then allow yourself to settle into whatever pace feels just right. Your PRE should hover around 5 or 6 on a scale of 1 to 10—somewhere in third gear. However, if this is your first half marathon or marathon or if you intend to run your event in second gear, it is more valuable to be focused on having an enjoyable time than a fast time, so you might want to keep your PRE between 4 and 5 (midrange aerobic HR) to ensure you stay relaxed for the whole distance.

If you're on a track, take a split on your watch every lap so you can see if your pace is steady and not varying a whole lot. If you're not on a track, take a split every mile (or kilometer). Your goal is to feel comfortable and relaxed at all times. Body Sense your steadiness, your consistency, and your ease of running. If you're really consistent, your mile split times shouldn't vary by more than 10 seconds. If you're on a track, it's a fun challenge to see if you can run every lap within one or two seconds of each other.

At the end of your run, stop your watch and drop into a cool-down pace. Take your total time and divide by the number of miles you ran to get your average pace. From now until race day, you will be running this pace or faster on all of your daily workouts, with the exception of your LSD run, which will always be run slightly *slower* than this pace.

If you have an HR monitor, check your average HR just to make sure it wasn't too fast. It shouldn't be higher than what you figured your MAHR to be.

Whether or not you're a repeat half or full marathoner, you should always run at least the first third of your event at a lower PRE than the rest of your race so that your body slips into its highly efficient "economy" mode early on.

A note to half marathoners and marathoners alike: No matter what level of runner you are—novice, intermediate, or elite—as your distance increases your overall pace gets slower. This means it is unreasonable to expect your half marathon pace to be as fast as your 10K pace. And it is just as unreasonable to expect your marathon pace to be as fast as your half marathon pace. So whatever pace you run in shorter races pretty much has to go out the window when you increase your distance. Resist letting your mind think otherwise.

## Race Planning: Know the Territory Ahead and Train Accordingly

To create the design of your race-specific training plan, gather information about your specific race. If you'd like to improve your odds of having a successful marathon, it's a good idea to know everything you're in for and leave as little as possible to chance.

### BUILDING YOUR RACE DOSSIER

This is really the most useful tool in designing your race-specific training plan. Without knowing ahead of time what you'll be facing on race day, you'll be shooting in the dark. Imagine driving through unknown territory in your car without a map. There are times for that, but why would you want to do that in a marathon, especially if it's your first? Running a marathon should be a challenge, not a risk.

**The Marathon Course Map:** I use a Google Maps satellite map printout and use colored pens to mark the following:

- The race course
- Start/finish areas
- Mile markers
- Aid station locations and frequency

Do some research and ask the race organizers about water, sports drinks, food, and glycogen replacement. (Never use any food or fuel during a race that you haven't previously tested on your body—have we reminded you of that enough times yet?)

**Terrain Challenges:** Take the time to visualize the course in your head. At the Walt Disney World Marathon there's a blinding 2-mile stretch that heads directly into the rising sun. The first year I ran this race I didn't have a hat with a sunshade. The second year I made sure I did. The littlest details can sometimes make the biggest difference.

- **Check the elevation gain.** How much elevation gain and loss does your race have?
- **Is the start uphill, flat, or downhill?** Know what it will be for the first 6 miles and train accordingly. The first 6 miles of a marathon (or the first 3 miles of a half marathon) are the most crucial stage of the race. If you go out too fast, you'll risk overextending yourself and paying for it later, big time. Use your midweek runs to practice mock-ups of your start and practice your starting pace
- **Where are the hilly sections?** Know the length, height, and frequency of the hills and add the same type of hills into your training runs. Use these workouts to practice all of your uphill and downhill ChiRunning focuses.
- **What type of road surfaces will you be running on?** Do the majority of your training on whatever kind of surface you'll be on in your race—concrete, asphalt, dirt, sidewalks, and so on. If there's going to be lots of concrete, train on concrete so you can practice running with minimal impact. If you'll be running on canted roads, practice on canted roads, switching sides frequently. During your event try to run in the middle of the road, where it's relatively flat.
- **Are there many open spaces?** Be aware that wind can have a big effect on your effort level. Open spaces are more subject to being windy than city environments. Racecourses near large bodies of water or bridges can be predictably windy (as in the Chicago, San Diego, and Big Sur marathons).

- **Will you be on city streets?** Running on city streets can present all kinds of challenges. Curbs, crowded or narrow running conditions, spectators, heat, uneven surfaces, and even potholes can present lots of opportunities for you to keep your wits about you. If you don't live in a city, you might be challenged to get some city running practice as a part of your training. If you think it might be a problem, schedule one or two city runs during this phase. Do your city workouts early in the morning, so you can run on city surfaces without the crowds.
- **Will you encounter any bridges?** If there is a big bridge on your racecourse, be aware that it is, in no uncertain terms, a hill . . . and sometimes a big one. If you've ever run across the Golden Gate Bridge, you know what I mean. Bridges are usually windy as well, so be prepared for a windy hill and train accordingly.

### DESIGN A RACE-SPECIFIC TRAINING PLAN

**Create Course Mock-ups:** If you happen to live near your marathon or half marathon course, your design work is pretty much done for you. All you have to do is divide your course into the sections mentioned below and run on the course as often as you can. This gives you a huge advantage over all the non-local runners because you can familiarize yourself with the course, leaving very little unknown for race day.

If you're not lucky enough to live near your marathon course, you can still prepare yourself for the terrain challenges in your race. I've used this method to train for every distance from a half marathon to 100 miles, and it always works. Here are three steps to designing a great race-specific training program in which nothing is left out.

Begin by dividing your marathon map into the following four quadrants:

**Half Marathon**
1. Start to mile 3 (or 5K)
2. Mile 3 to mile 6 (5K to 10K)
3. Mile 6 to mile 10 (10K to 16K)
4. Mile 10 to mile 13.1 (16K to 21K)

**Full Marathon**
1. Start line to mile 6 (or 10K)
2. Mile 6 to the half marathon mark (10K to 20K)
3. Half marathon to mile 20 (32K)
4. Mile 20 to the finish (32K to 42K)

Look at the characteristics of each segment of your race and trace each section in a different color onto your course map. Then, using the data compiled in your race dossier, design a mock-up of each race section using the terrain where you live. Make sure each section has characteristics similar to the actual racecourse. For the sake of convenience, try to make it a loop course that has most of the basic aspects yet brings you back to where you started your workout. It doesn't have to be a perfect match as long as you feel it is somewhat similar and equally challenging.

**Make a Route Description of Each Section:** Write up route descriptions for each section. Include street names, landmarks, and mile markers. If you have access to a computer, you can print out a Google Map of the area of your run and trace each of your four routes on a separate map. You can then either memorize your route map or take it with you on your training runs.

During this mastery phase, run each of the four sections in consecutive weekly tempo runs. In other words, if your tempo run is Thursday, then every Thursday you'll practice one quadrant. Repeat the sections that are the most challenging for you. If you're a half marathoner, the mastery phase will be four weeks, so you'll be able to do one section each week. If you need more practice on any given section, you'll have the time to do consecutive quadrants of your course during your weekly LSD runs. Run each section at a second-gear training pace, then finish the last 2–3 miles in third gear (race pace) if you're feeling good.

**Pacing of Your Mock-up Course:** Based on your projected finish time, calculate the pace you'd like to run in each of the four sections of your race and the corresponding time it will take. Be aware that the four sections might have very different paces and times depending on how many hills and flats each has.

When you train on a specific section, do your normal warm-up and then run that section at your projected race *only* during your weekly tempo run. The sole exception to this rule: if you're feeling strong in the last 3–4 miles of your LSD run, you can slowly bring your speed up to race pace to finish your workout.

Of all the sections of the marathon, I'd say without a doubt that the first 6 miles is the most important to pace correctly—and that means not too fast. There's a term I've heard many times describing what happens to those who start too fast: they "fly and die." Trust me, you don't want to end up in that crowd. The first thirty to forty minutes of a marathon have a huge effect on the rest of the race. It boils down to two options: start faster and finish slower, or start slower and finish faster. It's your choice.

Use your LSD runs in this phase to perfect the fueling, hydration, and electrolyte replacement schedule you began to explore and test in the conditioning phase. By the time you get to the event, you should have a very clear "sustenance" plan to follow.

## Weekly Workouts in the Mastery Phase

During the mastery phase there are four weekly training workouts. (For a day-to-day weekly workout schedule, please refer to Appendixes A and B.)

- Speed intervals
- Hill Runs
- Tempo runs
- LSD runs

Two of the workouts (speed intervals and Hill Runs) will be a continuation of the conditioning phase, and the other two (tempo runs and LSD runs) will be race-specific workouts.

### CONDITIONING WORKOUTS

In the mastery phase you'll continue improving your strength and speed with your interval workouts and Hill Runs.

**Speed Intervals:** These workouts will continue to build your cardio conditioning by running 800-meter repeats at your aerobic threshold pace, finishing the last 50–100 meters of each interval at an anaerobic pace. Generally, the maximum number of repeats you'll do is six; if you're a performance runner, you can build up to ten intervals as long as your body says it's okay. Just Body Sense how many you can handle; if your split times start to get slower, you're done for the day. Make note of how many you did and start with that many the following week. (See Appendixes A and B for a training schedule and a more complete description of this run.)

**Hill Runs:** If you live in a hilly area, you'll use the uphill sections of these training runs to further build your cardio conditioning and develop your uphill running form. On the downhills you'll practice pelvic rotation, lengthening your stride, and running at higher speeds while relaxing your legs and keeping your cadence steady.

## RACE-SPECIFIC WORKOUTS

The other two weekly workouts (tempo run and LSD run) are dedicated to race-specific training where you'll practice pacing, fueling, hydration, and technique at race pace (on your tempo run) and for longer distances (on your LSD run). If you're a performance-minded runner training for a personal record, you'll use these two workouts to attain your goal. Your tempo run can be used to practice running at race pace and your LSD run can be used to practice holding a faster pace without increasing your HR.

**Tempo Runs:** This workout is your opportunity to practice running at race pace. The first mile should be the same as your projected starting pace for the marathon or half marathon. The middle miles will be at race pace and the last mile will be faster than race pace. This run is also a good opportunity to practice running one of the mock-up sections of your marathon. (For a complete description of this workout, see Appendixes A and B.)

**LSD Runs:** You'll run *consecutive* mock-up sections; practice hydrating, fueling, consistent pacing, and race-specific technique; and last but not least, you'll practice dealing with adversity in the many forms it takes (fatigue, pain, weather, or whatever). You'll be doing dress rehearsals of your event in every way except speed, which should always be slightly slower than race pace.

---

### INSTRUCTOR STORY

ChiRunning makes me feel like a 14-year-old. My shadow doesn't look forty-seven. I am always smiling, and the crowd really responds to my smiling and running strong at the end of a marathon. While many other people are suffering and slowing, thanks to ChiRunning I am usually picking it up near the end and enjoying the moment. Keep the focus on the form and you can get to the finish smiling.

—Dave Saltmarsh

The fifth training day is a Fun Run or cross-training day, which is intended more as a mental and physical break from your routine.

## Tips and Suggestions

Here are a few suggestions for those who live in an area that doesn't match your race course.

### HOW TO CREATE HILLS
### IF YOU LIVE IN A FLAT AREA

If you live in a flat area and need to mimic hills, it helps to have a creative mind and a penchant for the unusual. I've tried all of the following with varying success: multilevel parking garages, freeway on-ramps, a treadmill set at a low angle (only if you're desperate), and taking numerous trips to visit hilly towns near you.

### HOW TO CREATE FLAT WORKOUTS
### IF YOU LIVE IN A HILLY AREA

If you live in a hilly area and you're running a predominantly flat marathon or half marathon, you'll need to get your body used to running on flat ground. I've used a local track, parking lots, and shopping mall perimeters to practice the repetitive motion of flat running.

### HAVE A SUPPORT CREW

I know this might sound a bit over the top for some of you, but having a support crew is one of the biggest luxuries you can give yourself and a really good idea for a first-timer. It takes a lot of energy to do everything right and manage all the details. It also takes a lot of energy to keep up with your training schedule. So don't be afraid to ask for help, whether it's during your pre-race week, on race day, or post-race.

There's nothing better than to have a friend drive you to the start, hand you your favorite energy drink along the course, or hold a sign with your name on it and yell your name somewhere along the course. Friends can meet you at the finish and cheer you on or bring you a change of clean, dry clothes to slip into at the finish. On race day your crew can handle the logistical details so you can relax and focus on your race. Having others support you is not a sign of weakness but an expression of caring and trust, and the bonds that you build will most likely outlast the memory of the race itself.

Go through your list of race week and race day logistics and fill in every necessary detail that is specific to you and your race. Go over the list and assign jobs to your crew members. Some jobs on the list will involve being at a certain place at a certain time, while some jobs will require predetermined items. Be very specific in your instructions to your crew. Good communication should be a top priority. Ask yourself questions around every item on your list. For instance, if someone is meeting you along the course, how will you find him or her? If it's a race with huge crowds, your friend might need to tie a helium balloon to his or her wrist in order to be visible.

One last but important note about your crew: the devil is in the details, but the angels are on your crew. Treat them that way.

## LAST-MINUTE DETAILS

Chapter 6 has the list of things to think about the week before the race, and Chapter 7 covers race weekend logistics thoroughly. Make sure everything is planned ahead of time so you can relax as much as possible the days before your event. Relaxation is the key component to a pain-free marathon and needs to be practiced while you run—and during the rest of your life as well.

The vision of this book is to help you run a *pain-free* marathon. We've used this term because the marathon event is so often associated with pain, and now you know it doesn't have to be that way. In the future, when the concept of a pain-free marathon becomes obvious and blasé because everyone is running marathons that way, we'll be able to use terms such as *outstanding*, *ecstatic*, and *exceptional*.

The end of the mastery phase is the peak point in your training, when the pieces of the puzzle all come together. By the time you complete your mastery phase and go into taper time, you'll begin to feel a sense of relaxed spaciousness underlying your upcoming race because you'll have the confidence to know what to do, when to do it, and, best of all, how to remain centered in the midst of any challenges you weren't able to foresee. The mastery phase is your own private testing ground, where you set the tone of your coming event. Your vision and goals are now supported with concrete training and information, and you will learn what the unifying harmony of body, mind, and spirit is truly capable of. As you use the *Chi Marathon* program for more events, your training during the mastery phase will become more and more subtle and drive your Chi skills deeper and deeper into the core of how you move, how you run, and how you live.

# Phase V

## Taper Time

Strength is defined not by what you can resist, but by how much you can expand.

—ANONYMOUS

Taper time for most people starts out as a welcome relief. Most of the hard work is behind you, and you've come to the phase in your training when you scale back on your training to build energy for your event. The main Chi focus during the taper phase is Containment—containing your energy, your enthusiasm, your nerves, and your desire for a successful outcome. Or perhaps, like a woman who is nine months pregnant, with the nursery prepared and the baby clothes and blankets sorted and ready, you just can't wait for the day to finally come!

Although taper time can be a welcome relief from the longer runs, it has within it the potential for you to feel pent up and with fewer outlets for your energy to move and flow. If you are an overachiever, you may find that running *less* is hard to do. Your mind might try to convince you that you need a few more long runs. If you are an underachiever, you might tend to slip into too much relaxation and not keep focused and crisp in your runs.

In this phase, finding the balance point within, Body Sensing, and utilizing Needle in Cotton (the Chi principle of holding to your center and letting everything else relax and be responsive) are needed just as much as they are during a long run. Now is *not* the time to slip into unconsciousness about your training. On the contrary, it is more important than ever to manage your energy, watch yourself from the eyes of your Observer, and use each run to practice for your event and to continue your own personal development.

Our T'ai Chi master, George Xu, often speaks of energy like money in the bank. You only have so much, and the wise person spends that money carefully. Use what is needed at the time, but also save enough for the future. During taper time, you are amassing your money in the bank. You spend enough to keep yourself in good shape, but you are also preparing for the big expenditure of race day. If you are tempted to train more than suggested in the training programs, stop, Body Sense, and think how disappointing it would be to be broke on race day rather than having plenty to spend.

## Your Training During Taper Time

Our training programs (Appendixes A and B, or on our website) will give you specific distances and workouts for this phase. You'll be scaling back your mileage on every workout, but you won't reduce the intensity or pace of your runs. This allows you to stay mentally and physically sharp without depleting your energy stores. In the workout schedule you'll be carrying over the race-specific focuses you were practicing in the mastery phase. You'll also be spending lots of time in every run practicing your starting pace and your race pace. Keep focused, sharp, and aware of anything in your technique that you feel you need to continue working on. You'll no longer do any workouts to build strength or conditioning. At this point, whatever level of conditioning you've achieved won't change. It would actually be counterproductive to think otherwise. It's time to just hold on to what you've got and pour it all into your race.

As you'll see in the workout schedule, you will be mostly limited to focus intervals at either your starting pace or your race pace. The only thing to build in this phase is *trust*. Trust that you have all the necessary conditioning, mental skills, and experience to do all the right things on race day. You've been practicing and rehearsing for weeks. Now is the time to simply trust that you have everything you need to run a successful race.

Set yourself up well for every run, and practice your y'chi. Do your Body Looseners to relax and liberate tight muscles. Warm up well, feeling your center and feeling the light pull of gravity as you fall into a comfortable lean, just as you will on race day. Practice your one-legged posture stance with every stride and do regular Body Scans.

We've mentioned it before, and we'll say it again in this and the next chapter: don't make the mistake of starting too fast. You can easily get caught up in the excitement of the day and take off too fast from the starting line. You'll feel the buzz of adrenaline pumping through your veins, which will make it even less likely that you will feel how fast you're actually running at the start. For this reason, be very aware that on race day any pace you run for the first mile or two will feel easy. Your start is the most important time to practice containing your enthusiasm and energy. Allow all that good energy to be stored in your *dantien*, your center—your central bank account. Manage it carefully, like the pot of gold it is. This is why we emphasize practicing your start pace during taper time. If you're like me and don't trust yourself to hold a conservative pace in the early miles, try this trick: use a heart monitor during both taper time and your race and never let your heart rate go higher than your MAHR—no matter how easy it feels, no matter how many people are passing you, no matter what. Make an agreement with yourself and just stick to your agreement. Done.

If you're running a marathon, two days before the event is a rest day and a great time to do Body Looseners and gently stretch, maybe take a walk. The day before your event you'll do a short run, 2–4 miles, to practice your start pace and to loosen up and relax.

If the half marathon is your event, you'll be practicing your start pace two days before your race day and resting the day before your event.

Taper time is not the time to be worried about your performance, no matter how lofty your goals. Like Muhammad Ali and all the best athletes, you can visualize your success. See yourself crossing the finish line, feeling healthy and elated. Feel those feelings and make it as real as you can. Use those images to put *more* energy in your bank account. Even more important, Body Sense what you need in the now. If you make the best choices for your moment-to-moment needs leading up to your race, you will run your very best.

## Rest, Relax, Flow—but No Funny Stuff

Taper time is about resting your body. Make sure you get plenty of sleep and use the extra time in your life (ha!) to stretch and keep limber and loose. If you sit at a desk, make sure you stand up and walk around as often as possible. This phase can bring up some "niggles," as Catherina McKiernan (an Olympian, winner of the London, Berlin, and Amsterdam marathons, and a ChiRunning Master Instructor in Ireland) calls the small aches and pains that seem to pop up out of nowhere during taper time. Niggles are small pockets of undirected energy. You might feel achy or have the feeling of a live electrical wire in your body. Don't get concerned. Niggles are to be expected during taper time. Just trust that they'll all be out of your system by the time race day rolls around. They always are. Do your runs, walk a bit, move gently, loosen and relax, take warm baths, and they'll pass.

The goal is to remain alert while also keeping composed and building a reserve of energy. Think of being a solar battery: soak up energy to create a positive charge.

It is crucial that you don't try anything new during this phase or participate in a lot of additional physical exertion. No funny stuff! This is not the time to start a new yoga or Pilates class. If you haven't played tennis for a while, wait until after the event to pick up your racket again. Strenuous or unusual physical labor is not a great idea. Don't try any new foods you aren't used to eating—no new gels, energy bars, or sports drinks. And no new shoes, for that matter. That should all have taken place during your conditioning and mastery phases. This is the time for stability and doing what is tried, true, and reliable. You'll get a lot of last-minute advice, some of which may be great ideas, but Body Sense if this is the time to try out the newest hydration system when your belt and water bottle have served you well until now.

It is also important to avoid doing needless activities and harboring worries that can cause energy leaks. Containment is your mantra . . . gathering is your focus.

Just follow your training schedule as closely as you can. Trust that you don't need to, and shouldn't, make any significant departures from your routine.

## Race Week Pre-Race Diet

Your diet the week before your race should not have any surprises. We hope that by this time you have eliminated most foods that are detrimental to your training and your health (you'll read more about nutritional guidelines in Chapter 10). If you haven't, don't start changing anything now. Just let your digestive system process what it's used to. If you have always eaten white rice and white bread, don't change to brown rice and whole-wheat bread at this point. (But consider doing so *after* your event!) In the week before your event you should follow your previous patterns of eating.

The food plan for this week is to eat good protein meals early in the week. For the last three days before your event, load up on nutrient-rich carbohydrates and avoid protein and fat. You can find great recipes for meals on our website. Just make sure you choose meals that your body responds well to. Whole grains, whole-wheat pastas, and lots of fruits and vegetables are the best food choices for carb loading.

## Preparing for Race Day

Taper time is also when you'll be doing last-minute preparations for your event. Refer back to your race dossier and make sure everything on your pre-race list is checked off by the end of this week. Pay your bills, call your mother, and take care of business early in the week so you don't have to do *anything* non-race-related right before the race. Check the weather and make sure you have all the necessary clothes. Finalize all travel plans early in the week. Try to travel at least two days before the event to give yourself one full day at your destination. Traveling the day before is not the best for your body, your mind, or your energy. In the next chapter we'll talk about things to be aware of during race weekend.

# Race Week Logistics: The Big List

The week leading up to your race is a special time to rest your body, relax your mind, and trust the process that got you to this point. By then you will have done your homework and you'll be better prepared than the vast majority of the other participants. For precisely this reason it is of the utmost importance that the logistics of race week are taken care of well ahead of time. Finalizing all the details of your event week will put your mind at ease and help you avoid any last-minute emergencies that could inhibit your ability to fully relax during this week.

In your race dossier start a checklist, take notes, and write reminders to yourself of all the things you need to do during this pre-race week. (We'll refer to these notes in Chapter 7.) To spark your thinking, look at all the items on the following list and start your own to-do list; add any relevant data that I've left out. After each item list the date when you plan to have the necessary arrangements completed. Get help if you need it. Don't think for a moment that running a marathon is a solo event. We all need the help of others to get to that finish line, no matter how far from that finish line our journey begins. You want your mind to be focused but spacious on race day.

- How far away is your event? How much travel is involved?
- What is the location of your lodging relative to the race start? Arrange pre- and post-race lodging if necessary.
- What transportation will you need to and from the race? Cars, planes, trains, taxis, etc.? Include schedules and timetables if needed.
- Do you have any child-care or job-related factors or other life matters to consider during your race weekend?
- What is the bib packet pickup date and location? What are the pickup hours? If you can, arrange to have someone do it for you.
- What is your meal schedule for the pre-race week?
- What is the expected weather on race day, including the expected temperature at starting time? Check closer to race day to see if there have been any changes.
- What clothing will you wear while waiting for the start and during the race? Include throwaways.
- What items will you have at the start line that you don't want to carry during the race?

- What items will you need during the race that you won't have at the start line? At what specific location along the course will you need to connect with your crew and for what? (As with all race day details, estimate as accurately as you can the time of day when your crew can expect to see you. Give them a window to shoot for, using the best possible pace you can imagine to estimate the earliest time they can expect to see you.
- What are your post-race logistics? Consider clothing needs, meeting people, heading home, and so on.

Taper time is a great time to practice internal and external states of balance, resting without losing your edge, and taking care of logistics without it being an energy drain. This is a time to really enjoy the results of all your work, including your great conditioning. Experience what it feels like to be in great shape, maybe the best of your life, and appreciate this. Realize how much you have cultivated the intelligent athlete, knowing that you can rely on the wisdom of your mind and body to fully enjoy your event.

# CHAPTER SEVEN

# Phase VI

## Race Weekend

Confidence is preparation. Everything else is beyond your
control.

—RICHARD KLINE

The weekend toward which you have worked so hard is here. This
is the time when staying focused and centered is most important.
There will be many distractions to pull you off your center: traveling, the pre-race expo and events, last-minute goodwill suggestions and
recommendations, your own anticipation and nervous excitement. There
is also a lot of positive energy that is supportive of you doing well. You
want to stay open and receptive to all there is that can inspire you for
the event. As you walk through the airport or the expo hall, think of the
Window Exercise and keep your chest open to allow all the good energy
in. Let it drop to your center, into the container of your dantien. At the
expo hall, you will be surrounded by perhaps thousands of people who
have also worked hard and are also feeling excited and ready to go. Enjoy
it all, without being pulled off your own plan, purpose, and vision.

As we noted early on in this book, being in a theatrical performance is a fitting analogy for all that goes into running a marathon event. Many variables contribute to the experience and the performance: the delivery of the dialogue, blocking, stage chemistry, costumes, makeup, scenery, lighting, and so forth. For months and months, actors build toward the premiere of their show. They begin by memorizing lines and getting deeply in touch with their characters. They learn when and where to move onstage and how to interact with fellow cast members. Once they master the fundamentals, they add more and more theatrical elements to create a unique world onstage. Finally, the dress rehearsal puts it all together to prepare for the live show. The cast works hard to address the smallest details, and then the curtain goes up and . . . it's show time!

## Pre-race Preparation

We've broken down race weekend into three stages: day before, race day, and day after. In this first stage we offer pre-race guidelines to consider during your marathon weekend. Some suggestions may seem small, and some may only apply to those traveling to their race, but keep the play analogy in the back of your mind as you prepare. After putting in months of great training, you don't want to do anything in the last days before your race that could throw you off your stride, so to speak.

### PACKING

If your event isn't local, check the race day weather beforehand and pack accordingly. Bring running clothes that span the spectrum of what you might need, given the climate of the race location. Don't wear anything on race day that you haven't run in before. If it looks like you'll be standing around in the rain at the start, bring a hat and a large plastic leaf bag to use as a disposable raincoat and windbreak.

If you get new shoes before your marathon, give yourself at least three weeks to break them in. Don't wear brand-new shoes on race day—your feet will thank you.

If your race provides a drop bag service, pack a pair of shoes or flip-flops and a set of clothes to change into after your finish. It's also a good idea to pack your cell phone and an energy bar in your drop bag as well.

Plan out how many fuel supplements and electrolyte replacements you'll need for your marathon and pack accordingly. Don't forget your hydration belt, fanny pack, and water bottles if you've trained with them. If you use electrolyte caps, pack some masking tape so you can tape them to your race bib for convenient access during your race.

Bring any other items you think may keep you comfortable, such as sunscreen, a hat, gloves, sunglasses, Vaseline, Band-Aids, et cetera. These, of course, will vary according to the season.

## TRAVEL

If your race is more than an hour's drive away, we suggest traveling a day or two beforehand so you won't have to make a long trip the morning of your race. If you do have to drive on the day of the event, be sure you know what you'll be doing with your car when you arrive. Pre-race parking can sometimes be a nightmare, so find out ahead of time what to expect and plan your arrival time accordingly.

If you are driving several hours to get to your race, stop frequently and do some Body Looseners and stretches, especially for your legs. Be mindful of when you start feeling uncomfortable from sitting too long. That's your body telling you to stop and take a rest/stretching break.

Many larger races put on expos beforehand where you'll pick up your race packet. You'll be tempted to check out everything when you go to pick up your race packet, but just be mindful and don't spend too much time on your feet looking at everything.

If you travel to a new destination that is of particular interest to you, again, give yourself some time to explore without overdoing. Don't do anything too strenuous before your event. Enjoy yourself, eat well, and relax before the big day.

## FOOD AND HYDRATION

Carb loading is the key to getting ready for a marathon; however, it is even more important to eat what you practiced during your training. Many of the best ChiRunners break the rules, including myself. It's considered a real no-no to eat protein, fats, or dairy before your event, but my favorite pre-race dinner is a big bowl of brown rice and pinto beans with cheese, so I break all the rules (but it works for *me*). I might even indulge in some ice cream!

We asked some Certified Instructors about their favorite pre- and post-race meals:

*Alan Miller:* Pasta and veggies for pre-race and pizza and beer afterward.

*Ryan Miller:* I normally do not eat anything solid before a long run. I normally just drink a large glass of fresh juice, celery or apple. If I wake up hungry, I eat a banana. On the run I bring raisins and nuts soaked in honey. Sometimes I'll throw in a few raw cacao nibs as well. The night before a long race I will fuel up with a huge salad and protein shake.

*Bryan Huberty:* The week before, I focus on eating as much fruit as possible, especially calorie-rich fruits such as bananas and dates blended in a water-based smoothie with celery for natural sodium and blueberries for color, flavor, and vitamins. You can use coconut water instead of water also. I eat watermelon every morning for a week leading up to the marathon to stay hydrated, and the lycopene in the red flesh helps your cardiovascular system. At night, I focus on big salads with spinach, lettuce, and other greens; fruit; and brown rice with veggies. During the race I use coconut water blended with bananas, and sometimes I just use fresh-squeezed orange juice. For the post-event meal, first I eat a lot of fruit to get my carbs replenished, then an hour later I have a fish or chicken meal for protein—along with a beer!

*Aracely Areas:* Oatmeal, walnuts, almonds, and berries for breakfast the day before.

*Dave Saltmarsh:* Pre-race dinner is pasta and lots of it. After every long race I have Campbell's chicken noodle soup in a thermos, a peanut butter and jelly sandwich, a banana, and applesauce. I eat it as soon as possible after finishing. After that I'm ready to enjoy anything I can get my hands on, and usually this includes a good donut.

*Doug Dapo:* One of my favorite post event meals is what I call my "St. Patrick's Day" smoothie. When I get home after running a marathon, I am not ready for a big meal right away but I feel that my body needs some refueling. So I have a cool, refreshing, and very nutritious smoothie. I use almond milk with a whole orange, frozen pineapple, frozen mango, frozen organic spinach, flaxseed, nutritional yeast, and protein powder. I put this in my Vitamix blender and the smoothie turns a lovely shade of green from the spinach (hence the name St. Patrick's Day smoothie). This really hits the spot. Later in the day, I get together with my running group and we go to our favorite Mexican restaurant to celebrate.

*Joel Matalon:* On the day of the race, I have a bowl of oatmeal two hours before race start, and I make sure I go to the bathroom to move my bowels. I eat fruit as much as possible during the race, at least every hour. After the race I have a fruit drink. Then one hour after race completion I have a full meal: steak, veggies, sweet potato, and a full glass of red wine.

*Laura Houston:* Post-race, I try to drink chocolate soy milk within thirty minutes of finishing. Coconut water is good too—it helps flush out the kidneys. After that, don't stand between me and food!

*Vince Vaccaro:* During the race I use sodium-potassium pills (S! Caps) and chia seeds mixed with water and maple syrup. I drink only water. I've had some great races on a pre-race dinner of sushi.

Know what kinds of food you need to eat for your pre-race dinner. The traditional pre-race pasta feed may work for some, but it might not work for you. Learn what works best for *your* body by experimenting with different meals before your LSD runs throughout your training. Each body functions differently—you may find that brown rice and veggies work best for you, or peanut butter and jelly sandwiches. Whatever you decide to eat on the day before your race, stick with what you know. Don't eat any new foods you haven't previously tested out.

If you're traveling, research restaurants in the area that serve good pre-race meals. Read reviews online to get a sense of the food quality, and give yourself two or three options in case your first choice doesn't pan out.

Bring snacks to refuel when necessary before the race. We recommend foods that are easily digested and absorbed, such as bananas, peanut butter, honey, and so on. The pre-race meal is important, but having these snacks available will come in handy if you need something in the evening. Try to keep yourself consistently fueled the day before your marathon, but resist eating protein because it requires more time and energy to digest than carbs.

Hydrate as much as possible on the day before your race. Keep a water bottle with you all day and drink often.

### MENTAL PREPARATION

First, schedule plenty of spaciousness into the day and evening before your race.

Go back to your race dossier and revisit your vision for yourself and for your race. Review that vision to remind yourself of your goals, and assess your current strengths and weaknesses. Go over the Form Focuses, paying special attention to those focuses that you feel will help you the most during your race.

Stay relaxed and positive, and visualize yourself achieving everything you hope to accomplish during your marathon.

Refresh yourself on your race strategy: pacing, significant mile splits, staying within your aerobic capacity, when to hydrate, and so on. Set the countdown timer on your watch to remind you when to drink, refuel, and do your focus check-ins.

Engage in relaxing and centering activities: meditation or sitting quietly, yoga, slow walks, reading.

If you're running a local race, you may have already been practicing on the course, which is to your advantage. If not, review where the hills and flat areas are, where the start and finish lines are, where to park, and other details. Drive the course in the days before the race if you can.

Try not to let your excitement or nerves get the best of you. Do something relaxing the evening before and get to bed early. Don't do any emailing and texting as you approach your bedtime. Whether or not it's your first marathon, you might be so excited that you have some trouble getting to sleep, so do whatever it takes to set up the conditions for sleep to happen: make yourself a hot cup of herbal tea, or listen to some relaxing music.

Of course, you can't prepare for every surprise, but you can create optimal marathon conditions by planning for what you *can* control.

## What *Not* to Do the Day Before Your Race

Here are a few reminders of what not to do on the day before the event. Some of these may compromise your body in some way, and some are mental leaks that could shatter your mental focus.

- **No massages.** You need to show up at the start line with your mind relaxed and your body toned. Massages can leave you *too* relaxed and undo some of your muscle tonus. Massages also release toxins stored in your muscles and move them into your circulatory system, which is good, but not the day before your marathon. Reward yourself with a massage afterward.
- **Don't eat any weird foods.** All foods should be easy to digest. Avoid gluten, meat, deep-fried foods, and spicy foods. Remember, don't eat anything unfamiliar.
- **Don't drink alcohol the night before your race.** Alcoholic beverages can have a dehydrating effect.
- **No yard work, gardening, or other strenuous physical labor.** Don't do any work that involves lifting, bending, stooping, or kneeling.
- **Avoid doing things that you don't want to do.** This will keep your mental and emotional stress to a minimum.
- **No video games, email, Web surfing, computer, or iPod the evening before.** Quiet your mind. If you have to think, think about what you've been through in your training and what you'd like to do in your race.
- **No energy leaks.** "Containment" is your mantra. The day before your race should be absent of any unnecessary activity. I've heard from many runners, and I agree with them, that the day before a marathon or half marathon should be spent around the *least* number of people possible. A few friends or training partners, or family, is plenty. Save your social time for celebrating your success the evening after your marathon.

## Race Day

This is the day you finally get to apply everything you've been practicing for months. The hardest work has been done. Instead of going into your event with performance anxiety (that's an energy leak), approach this day with a sense of curiosity and open-mindedness, and with the intention to take in all the great energy of the runners around you, the spectators, and the course itself.

## MORNING ROUTINE
On the day of the race:

- Set one or two alarms to wake you up.
- Give yourself plenty of time to do your pre-race routine and get to the start without being rushed.
- Do a ritual of preparation that includes focused but relaxing things, such as yoga or light stretching, meditation, and alone time to gather your focuses and your intentions. Feel your own integrity, your own inner strength built from months of focused work. Trust that everything you need to do what you need to do is within you.
- Ask yourself what *you* want out of the day. It's a special event. Treat it that way.
- Follow your typical long run routine for eating. Remember, any food before a long run should be highly digestible.
- Write on your arm any focuses that you need to remember during your race.
- If you're shooting for specific mile split times, write them on your arm or upside down on your bib (so you can see them when you look down).
- Put everything you'll need for your race in a pack or drop bag.
- Finalize any last-minute race and post-race arrangements with your crew.
- Drink 8–16 fluid ounces of water at least an hour before the start.
- Eat in accordance with how you've trained yourself. Don't eat anything that will still be in your stomach at the finish line.
- Set your countdown timer to beep every ten minutes.

## THE RACE
You've practiced it all many times, but here are some general reminders.

- Do all of your Body Looseners before you enter the starting corral.
- Keep moving while you're waiting for the gun to go off. Don't just stand there.

- Shake out any nervousness.
- Zero out your watch and make sure your chronometer is set to start.
- Check to make sure your watch starts when you press the button at the start line.
- Settle into your starting pace and pay no attention to what other people around you are doing.
- Check in with your pace at the first mile marker. If it's too fast, *slow down immediately*. There'll be a temptation to hold the pace because it feels so easy. Don't be fooled into thinking you can hold it for the whole race.
- If your first mile is a little slow, don't worry. You have 25 more miles to make up any lost seconds. It's not a big deal.
- Start your countdown timer and start your focuses. Check in with your posture, take a sip of water, and refresh your focus every time you hear the beep.
- Thank as many race volunteers as you can.
- Run conservatively for the first 6 miles (or 5K for half marathoners) and then check to see how you're doing relative to your projected starting pace.
- During the last quarter of your race pay extra attention to reinstating your posture focuses. This will take the workload off your legs and keep them fresher longer.
- Smile often, give thanks, and take in the energy of your surroundings, the runners around you, the spectators cheering you on, and especially the aid station workers. They were out there before you came by and they'll be out there when you cross the finish line.

## Crossing the Finish Line

You've done it! Congratulations. So much focus and energy has gone into this particular moment, that wonderful feeling of completing a marathon. The medal you receive is a tangible symbol of your accomplishment. Wear it with pride.

What you do in the first hour after your event is important to your recovery, so here are some reminders.

- **After you cross the finish line, walk for a while.** This will help flush the lactic acid from your muscles. Drink lots of water and avoid eating until you are completely cooled down from running. Wait at least fifteen minutes before consuming solid food. Juice is best right after your finish, to help replenish your blood glucose levels.

- **If you feel dizziness or any unnatural discomfort, go directly to the first-aid tent.** Get yourself checked out; don't take any chances.
- **Do some post-run stretches** once your body has cooled down.
- **Find your friends and your drop bag.** Change clothes as soon as you get a chance.
- **Eat something.** A majority of the nutritionists with whom we've consulted have emphasized the importance of ingesting a hearty snack or small meal consisting of approximately 45 percent liquid protein and 55 percent carbohydrates within forty-five minutes after finishing your event. The protein will aid in rebuilding any muscle tissue broken down over the course of your run, and the carbohydrates will help replenish your blood glucose levels to normal. If you don't plan to eat right away, consider drinking a sports drink that has a mix of proteins and carbs immediately after your event.

## TIME TO CELEBRATE

### INSTRUCTOR STORY

Before ChiRunning I would complete a marathon and limp around for three weeks. At the New York City Marathon expo, in preparation of my three weeks in pain, I began collecting reading material. The ChiRunning information intrigued me enough to purchase the book and DVD. Then I signed up for a workshop. ChiRunning has turned marathoning into fun. With ChiRunning I have completed thirty-three marathons and two ultras, including three Goofy Challenges, the Lake Tahoe Triple, the JFK 50 Mile, and six marathons in six weeks. I no longer look for the ice bath. I am now looking for a post-race party!

—Vince Vaccaro

Katherine has taught me what it means to celebrate. She makes sure we punctuate our lives by taking time to stop, pause, and enjoy our accomplishments. And I've gotten to like celebrating with good food, good friends, and an inner realization that celebrating is an important part of life. Katherine likes to make toasts, a great way to acknowledge your own or other people's achievements.

Whether it's your first or fiftieth marathon, relax, enjoy yourself, show off, and dance a jig—because you can!

## The Day After

When you wake up the day after your event give yourself some time to lie peacefully in bed and soak up your accomplishment. Do a Body Scan before you get out of bed, stretch, and take in what you have accomplished. Do a mental review of the previous day: watch it as a movie in your mind, and allow yourself to feel the full magnitude of running 13.1 or 26.2 miles. Relive crossing the finish line, getting your medal, and the evening's celebration. At some point within the next day or so, write a journal entry about your experience. It will be something you will appreciate reading in the future, a great reminder of what you learned and helpful for training for future events.

When you stand up, do so with self-awareness. The first steps might be a little stiff or sore, or they may not be. Walk around a bit and Body Sense. The second day after your event can be when the full brunt of muscle soreness sets in, if there is any. You can minimize it by doing your Body Looseners on the day after the event. Do leg drains. My favorite post-race day activity is to go for a relaxing bike ride on a level stretch of road or bike path. It allows my legs to get flushed out and it's easy on my body. A warm bath with Epsom salts is always a good idea no matter what.

Most of the letters we get are from people who are blown away that they are not sore. We often get comments like the following from people who are new to ChiRunning:

At the end of the marathon I still had so much more in me. The next day I felt fine and I realized I could have gone even faster.

—Eliza

We usually reply with a word of caution and encouragement. Running a marathon does not have to be about burning through all your energy. It should not be about depleting all your resources, unless you are going for a personal best and have chosen this one event to pull out all the stops. Having energy after a marathon is a sign that you did it right.

Keep energy moving through your body all day. Rest, but take breaks from resting by walking and gently stretching. Continue to fuel and hydrate well. You are entering the rest and renewal phase (see Chapter 8), and no matter how good you feel, you need downtime. It's good for body, mind, and spirit. If you're one of those people who don't like to stop, consider that it might be a skill worth learning. If all you want to do is lay down all day, know that gentle movement is the key to recovery.

If you have to travel home, take lots of stretch breaks. If you're flying, walk up and down the aisle when it's safe to do so. If you're driving, pull over to walk and loosen every hour. When you walk, ChiWalk: pick up your feet, relax your lower legs, engage your core, and let your pelvis rotate.

## ENJOY THE HIGH

After completing a half or full marathon, you may well feel like you can accomplish anything, and you're right, you can. When you combine intelligence with mindful awareness (no, they are not the same thing) and biomechanically correct movement, you are moving from the strength of your whole person, and from that place ease and grace will follow. Soak up how good it feels. Look at the world from this new vantage point.

> Someone came up behind me and said, "You are making this look too easy! You look like you could go on forever." I felt like I could. I am so grateful for this gift of ChiRunning. I have no idea what my times were, nor do I care. What matters most to me is that I am a fifty-year-old woman tearing up the course, having the time of my life! Thank you!
>
> —Annie Valerioti

I can always tell when my daughter is feeling really good about an accomplishment. She has a very quiet pride and she holds herself tall and strong. She practically glows with the knowledge that she's done well, and when she's particularly satisfied with an accomplishment, she's all the more quiet about it and the energy pours out of her whole being. Express your good feelings in your particular way: calling your parents, telling your significant other every detail, posting it to Facebook, smiling and sharing positive energy with everyone you come in contact with. Sharing that good feeling is a great way to enjoy it even more.

# CHAPTER EIGHT

# Phase VII

## Rest and Renewal

What we achieve inwardly will change outer reality.

—PLUTARCH

Whether you've been keeping a journal of your end-of-run reviews or not, writing will help you gain insight into your training, into the experience of the event, and into yourself. Journaling has the same effect as eating a delicious meal *very* slowly: taking your time to savor each bite, letting the flavors and aromas fill your body and nourish you beyond the level of mere sustenance. When you write about your event, take the time to savor everything that went on. Feel and write about the entire spectrum of your experience, and it will become a part of you that you'll carry with you always. Look back at what you did so you can bring it into your future.

Here's a sample of some notes and end-of-run reviews from Danny's running journal. Two of these entries are end-of-event reviews.

*April 9, 2011:* I ran the Dupont Half Marathon today. I ran it as a training run for the Boston Marathon, next weekend. Only a few more miles than a normal taper time run, but it was a damn hilly course. I love hills, but because I traveled last weekend I didn't get in the training runs I needed. Taking a red-eye home Monday night didn't help. All I got in over the weekend was two short runs around Vancouver. This past week my body was low energy, and by mile 9 in the race today, I was feeling the lack of energy even more.

I decided to choose one Form Focus, one thing that would help me the most. So I pulled out my metronome and focused on my cadence and nothing else. It did the trick. My mind latched on to the rhythmic sound and my body followed suit. Once mind and body synched with the metronome my energy was moving again. I ran the last 4 miles totally focused on my cadence and crossed the finish line feeling great and won my age group (sixty to sixty-five)—which was pretty easy to do, since there was only one other guy in my age group!

When I found the right focus, in this case the metronome, all my conditioning and all my training were right there. My energy was moving and I was flowing up those hills, and enjoying it immensely. I had a great time.

*April 10, 2011:* Day after the Dupont Half Marathon: My whole body feels great today. I just confirmed my splits. I ran negative splits, running the first half in 61:00 and the second half in 58:00. I'm glad I found the key to turning on the energy in my body. Ate plenty of protein and good carbs after the run. I was hungry. Eight days until Boston and even though I know I'm going to be standing at our booth at the expo and talking to people for three days before the event, I think it will go well. I'm just looking forward to being part of the crowd and enjoying myself.

*April 18, 2011:* On the plane home from Boston: What a great day. After all the energy expenditure of talking to hundreds of people, standing and walking around a lot, and giving a couple of talks, I was a bit concerned about running the marathon, but I had a great time. I did not push the pace and ran a 3:36. It was crowded and I kept my pace steady and just enjoyed watching the crowds and all the runners. Ryan Miller (Certified Instructor and one of our

Chi-tahs—fast ChiRunners) picked me up at mile 8 and ran with me for a few miles.

My body is definitely tired, but pleasantly so. I'm going to sit back, take in the day, nap a little, and relax as much as possible. Ahhh . . . heading home.

*April 19, 2011:* Day one after Boston. I thought I would be sore from standing at the expo booth for three days and then running a marathon, but I feel surprisingly good. Only the slightest tinge of soreness on the lateral side of my quads (probably from the miles of downhill); feet are in good shape. Just rode my bike through the local neighborhoods with my dog, to loosen up and get some fresh air. My legs feel a little fatigue, but no soreness at all.

*April 20, 2011:* Day two after Boston. I did a 4-mile loosening run . . . really relaxed. My feet and legs felt fine. Any quad soreness I felt yesterday is gone, but I do still feel some fatigue in my body. Felt good to take a soak in the hot tub and do a little T'ai Chi to get limber and grounded. I've felt emotionally raw for the past two days, like my skin is a bit thinner than normal, and I'm more sensitive to my surroundings and my feelings. I just tell Katherine I'm premenstrual.

The few days after an event may leave you feeling as I felt after running Boston—as if your nerve endings are just a bit closer to the surface than usual. This emotional transparency and fragility may be a bit uncomfortable, but if you can make the time to allow yourself to feel all that you are going through, physically and emotionally, it is the best time to gain access to your inner experience. The phase after completing your event is rich and full of opportunity. You can let down, relax even more deeply, and relish your accomplishment. It can be an amazing high. While you might feel vulnerable in some ways, you also might feel invincible, like you can accomplish anything. And now you really do have the skills under your belt to create anything you want in your life.

## Your End-of-Event Review

Review your vision and your goals. How did you do? How do you feel about the process and the outcome? What unexpected benefits have there been that you did not anticipate? The letter that follows, to Christopher Griffin, Certified Instructor, is an example of what other people have experienced:

> Wow! Can I send you guys another check? Write a chapter for the next book? I just finished the Steamtown Marathon on Sunday with a chip time of 3:36:11, a personal record by 35 minutes over last year's New York City Marathon. Just 12 seconds shy of qualifying for Boston. The difference? You. ChiRunning. Body Sensing. Form. (A bit of solid training time on my part too.) And I don't think I've ever sprinted so fast across a finish line! I can't thank you enough. I actually *ran* a marathon this time! And had fun. Now for those 12 seconds . . .
>
> —Dan Burrier

Make sure your end-of-event review includes a thorough assessment of your physical health. Continue to hydrate and eat nutrient-rich foods to help your body replenish its energy.

## The Fringe Benefits of Failure

It is up to you to decide what is a failure in your pursuit of running a half or full marathon. You may consider yourself a failure if you get injured, if you don't complete the event, or if you stopped partway through your training. You may feel as if you failed if you didn't run the time you were shooting for, qualify for Boston, or finish with your running group. *Failure* is a loaded word. Most of us are terrified of failing, and yet it is when we fail, when we are not as successful as we hoped, that we often find a better path to real success. If you don't ever fail, it means you've never really stretched yourself, never really taken a risk. For many people, running the half marathon or marathon distance is taking a big risk. Taking that risk is a courageous act.

J. K. Rowling gave the 2008 commencement address at Harvard. This is what she said about how she felt about herself before her books were written:

I was the biggest failure I knew. Now, I am not going to stand here and tell you that failure is fun. That period of my life was a dark one, and I had no idea that there was going to be what the press has since represented as a kind of fairy-tale resolution. I had no idea then how far the tunnel extended, and for a long time, any light at the end of it was a hope rather than a reality.

So why do I talk about the benefits of failure? Because failure simply meant a stripping away of the inessential. I stopped pretending to myself that I was anything other than what I was, and began to direct all my energy into finishing the only work that mattered to me. Had I really succeeded at anything else, I might never have found the determination to succeed in the one arena I believed I truly belonged. I was set free, because my greatest fear had been realized, and I was still alive, and I still had a daughter whom I adored, and I had an old typewriter and a big idea. And so rock bottom became the solid foundation on which I rebuilt my life.

Pain, injury, quitting—these experiences may not feel good, but within every experience is an opportunity to do something else, to try again, to find a path that suits who you are. If life is our classroom, so is training for and running a distance event. In this process you will find many of life's lessons, including failure, and from that place you may just find your greatest strengths.

## Keep Moving

You may be tempted to just stop doing anything physical after all your focus and training, but keeping your body moving is better for you than sitting still. It is crucial that you allow yourself all the time you need to restore your reserves. Rest is essential. But so is gentle movement. In the first weeks after running a marathon, you may not want to run. So walk. Ride a bike. Swim. Go to a yoga class. Keep moving enough to keep the energy flowing, but know that this is definitely not a time to push yourself.

You might feel ready to get back into your running routine sooner than you'd expect. In many marathon books it suggests you not run for a week or more, but if your body has *not* been misused and if you feel like running, you most certainly can. Body Sensing is essential. Just listen to your body. It will tell you in no uncertain terms when you're going too far or too fast. Fun Runs and form runs are the best kinds of runs for the first week or two after your event. Relaxed movement will help your body recover and will help you to move forward into whatever is next in your life.

## Moving Forward

As you write your end-of-run review, notice what little sparks may be coming up about your future. Notice what really excited you about your event and training, and pay attention to the ideas and imaginings that pop into your mind. Create some spaciousness in your life in the next several weeks as you move into a maintenance program for your fitness and see what feels truly important to you.

We just made the assumption that no matter what, you will stay committed to a consistent fitness program and enter, at the very least, a maintenance phase. We know it's a bold assumption, but more than anything we hope that mindful fitness becomes a mainstay in your life, no matter what else you do. You can accomplish anything if you have your health, and the best way to keep your health is to create and follow a consistent exercise routine. Eating well is right up there, and we want that for you as well, but keeping active is our number one hope for you as we write this book. And if running is your main way to keep active, then we want to keep you injury- and pain-free so that you can run for the rest of your life.

As we neared the completion of this book, Katherine and I were discussing the little urges in our lives that are moving us forward. Katherine has been talking about her interest in doing more with nutrition and lifestyle. I've been feeling the desire to deepen my T'ai Chi practice again. We have several video projects we're excited about (*Hills and Trails* and the *Chi Walk-Run* video program, both of which should be done by the time this book is released). We're also looking forward to a few weeks off with our daughter this summer. She has been so patient as we focus intently on this marathon-like project.

You don't have to make any bold decisions right away, but then again, you just might find that you have the energy, focus, and drive to take on something truly significant. If you ran a half marathon, you might feel you have a faster half or even a full marathon in you, or a triathlon.

You might feel the desire to write your own book, go for that new job, renew your commitment to your family, or run for office (we could use some centered, grounded people in politics). When you tap into your innate ability to run, it can trigger other areas in your life where you have innate skills and natural potential. Focusing for several months on strengthening your core and moving from your center can stir up your creative juices. Who knows what might come forth.

> I ran my first half marathon in January 2008 and another the next year. I continually reminded myself to make sure I had good posture, that I was relaxed, that I was taking in the energy around me . . . it was *fun*! I have now begun to train for my first marathon. ChiRunning has really allowed me to believe that anything is possible.
> —Kelly G.

## Multiple Marathons

For those who run multiple marathons in a season or a year, the issue is not to keep moving but to recognize the need for regeneration. For good maintenance between events you need downtime, quiet time—stillness. Practice slow, loosening, gentle runs, but be hyperaware of the potential for doing too much too soon. Some ChiRunners use this phase as the visioning and planning phase for their next event. Use this period to go more deeply into your body to uncover the vision and goals that will keep you training in a mindful balance, with the best interests of your whole life in mind. As you move forward into your next training cycle, give yourself the gift of another technique phase and don't jump right into a conditioning phase. Spend some time refining your technique. I'm constantly working on my technique—learning, adjusting, and discovering new ways to add ease to my stride. Pace yourself and enjoy the process.

## Upward Spiral of Chi

You've probably noticed that we have come full circle, back to Phase I, visioning and planning, but from a different vantage point, a different launching pad. That is what growth is all about. It's like watching a child's growth from one birthday celebration to the next. Every time

**Figure 43—The Upward Spiral of Chi**

around the child has more experience of life, stands a few inches taller, and has a year's worth of learning and understanding in her mind and heart. We call it the Upward Spiral of Chi. (See figure 43.) You don't just start over every time around. Rather, you grow up and into your potential. Going back to our piano analogy, it's like playing octave scales where the end of one octave is the beginning of a higher octave. It's the same note, but the vibration is higher.

Who knows—you may want to join the ranks of our Certified Chi-Running Instructors and help other people recognize their innate ability to run. Or you may want to take what you've learned and apply it to other endeavors that will enrich your life. No matter what, you have accomplished something significant.

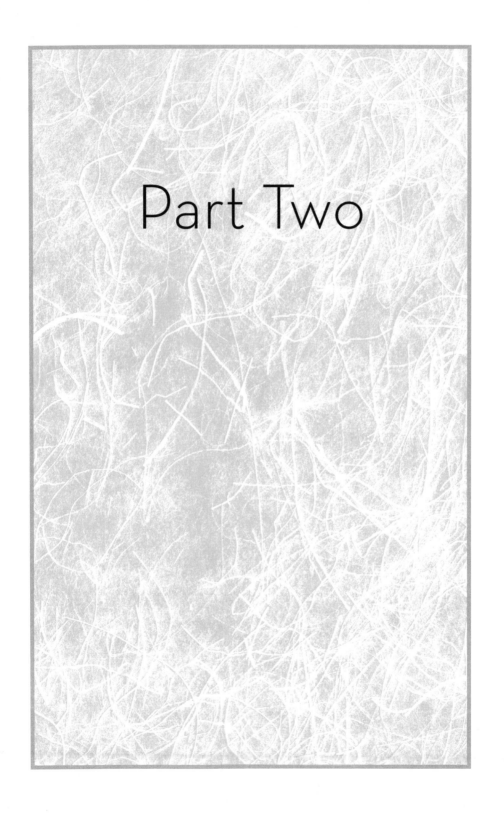

# Part Two

# CHAPTER NINE

# Advanced ChiRunning Techniques

It isn't in accomplishing something of greatness that you gain your worth; it's in appreciating your true worth that imbues everything you do with great value.

—MICHAEL TAMURA

This chapter is dedicated to the advanced runner in you. At some point, no matter who you are, you'll probably want to see your marathon times get faster, while still adding the adjective *pain-free* to that additional speed. So how exactly *do* you run faster without your PRE going through the roof? I'll give you a hint: it's not about having stronger legs. To increase your speed you need to cooperate with the pull of gravity by increasing your lean. To hold more of a lean requires stronger core muscles (lower abs) to hold your Column intact. In order to avoid any braking with the force of the oncoming road, your feet have to land directly beneath your center of mass and move rearward as they strike the ground. You'll need to relax your legs more so they can swing more easily at higher speeds. But there's much more, as you'll soon find out.

Any amount of advanced training requires a strong foundation in all aspects of your ChiRunning technique and the conditioning of your body and mind. It is almost a guarantee that once you've integrated the basics of the technique into your body, you'll be a more efficient distance runner. You've worked to reduce your effort by eliminating wasted motion; your "machine" is finely tuned to run beautifully; and your PRE is generally lower than before because you're using less muscle than you used to. You can now tweak that machine to set up the conditions for speed to happen by adding back in a small amount of muscle usage directed by some powerful mental backup.

All of the focuses and workouts in this chapter are recommended for taking your ChiRunning practice to the performance level. You can use as many or as few of these instructions as you feel necessary, given your goals. But whether you use a lot or a little of what follows, the overarching rule is that your basic ChiRunning form first needs to be well integrated into your body.

## The Five-Element Theory of ChiRunning

The best way I've found to describe the progression of novice to master of ChiRunning is to talk about it in terms of the five elements found throughout Chinese philosophy: earth, water, fire, air, and ether. These are the five elements I was taught, though I know there are many variations on these. In order to take your running to the next level it helps to have an overview of what you are working toward.

These elements have a hierarchy according to their density; earth being the most dense element and ether being the least dense. Each has a very distinctive characteristic and is represented by a specific area of the body. If you're working toward mastery of your running, you'll need to develop the grossest level first, earth, which means establishing a solid structural foundation upon which your technique will be built. Your further work will involve refining the subtleties of your movement so that eventually you can run with speed and fluidity, and with your mind and body truly unified during your movement.

### EARTH

Earth is the densest element, the one that represents physical support and stability. It is represented by the bones, ligaments, and tendons. This means the brunt of the support falls to the pelvis, legs, and feet (the feet are the only part of your body that touches the earth when you run). In

ChiRunning terms, this foundational support needs to be in place during the *support phase* of your stride. That's why, in the beginning lessons, you spend lots of time working on the alignment of your pelvis, legs, and feet.

## WATER

Water is the element that provides fluidity to your motion. It is less dense than earth because it has no innate structure. Your water band is located directly above your pelvis where all of your "water" organs reside: kidneys, bladder, and small intestine. It is often considered the "moving center" of the body. It's this area of your spine that your pelvis swings from, like the cable that supports a chandelier. When this area is relaxed and movable (as in pelvic rotation) your stride takes on a much more *fluid* feel with less bounce and impact. It's true: the easiest way to move earth is to simply add water.

## FIRE

Fire is universally recognized as the symbol for work and transformation. This element is less dense than water because you can see it but you can't grab it and hold it. The fire band of your body houses your hardest-working organs and muscles: your heart and liver, your obliques and transverse abdominals. When you want to run faster, this is the area of your body to turn to. But in order for this work to be efficient and effective you must first have the two lower levels (earth and water) in full cooperation or you'll end up working harder than is necessary. As Maryanne Roller, one of our longtime friends, has said, "Fire can cook your dinner or it can burn your house down."

## AIR

Air is invisible and represents the power of the mind and of thoughts. You can't grab air and you can't see it, but you can feel it, as the wind in your face or as it passes into your lungs. When you have the qualities of earth, water, and fire integrated into your body's movement, you can then run from inspiration, which is also the word for the in-breath. When you get proficient at this level of running you'll truly be a master and use your mind to create speed. I have moments of feeling this way, but I do not consider myself a master at this level. Air is related to the thought process and ideas. When your body is truly aligned and in tune with your mind, then just a thought can create truly magical and effortless motion.

## ETHER

Ether is the fifth element and in many ways is like chi itself. I am still working to grasp its full sense. At this level your whole body is physically and energetically integrated, not just internally but with your external environment and energies as well. The energy of ether is faster than thought; oneness with one's surroundings creates stillness in the midst of action. When Master George Xu enters this state he becomes so unified with his opponent that there is no separation between the two and no perceived struggle.

## PROGRESSION OF ELEMENTS

As you can see, the progression of elements relative to their density moves from the bottom of the body to the top of the body.

My main point here is to illustrate why it is so important to build a strong base in your technique before moving on to the next level of ChiRunning. Each level is dependent on the quality of work you put into the preceding level. All of the elements mentioned above are at work, in varying degrees, at all times. But being aware and mindful of how they work together allows you to apply their qualities in any given circumstance. The degree to which you can blend the use of all these elements defines your level of expertise. The more balance you have between all the elements within you, the more effortless your running will become—at any speed.

# Are You an Advanced ChiRunner?

The practices in this chapter are best utilized for advanced ChiRunners. If this is your first time using the ChiRunning method for a marathon or half marathon, we do not suggest using the advanced techniques yet. Your training time is best spent learning and familiarizing your body with the Form Focuses. If you take on some of the advanced focuses before you have learned the basic ChiRunning focuses, you might inadvertently slip into using *more* effort instead of less to run. If you take the time up front to learn the basic ChiRunning focuses, these advanced focuses will come to you more quickly and easily when the time is right.

If you are an advanced runner but new to ChiRunning, you will need to shift and learn how to run using progressively less leg strength. Over-reliance on your legs will in the long term impede your speed and at the very least burn through your available fuel at a faster rate.

Here's a testimonial we recently received from a ChiRunning marathoner:

> Thanks to ChiRunning, I've been injury-free the past three years and just finished the 2011 Boston Marathon in 2:59, my fastest marathon since I was twenty-one years old back in 1989. I'm now forty-two and have been running since I was eleven, but only in the last few years, after reading *ChiRunning* and putting in practice its techniques, has running really been as pain-free and enjoyable as when I first started three decades ago. I suffered severe quad pain for years after any hard or long run due to overstriding and heavy heel striking. My time progression at the Boston Marathon the past three years has been 3:14, 3:05, and 2:59, and I know I can knock some more time off in the coming years!
>
> Thanks to ChiRunning, I shifted my running form and my entire approach to training. It's not about the miles; it's about efficiency and no pain. I also ditched the bulky running shoes. It definitely works!
>
> —Neil Cucuzzella

The principle of Gradual Progress tells us that as you progress through anything it is not wise to skip ahead to a new level without first being adept at your current level of expertise. If you feel any pain or soreness that lasts longer than twenty-four hours after any training run, it means you don't yet have the foundational techniques in your body to begin using the advanced techniques.

In order for you to be ready for advanced ChiRunning, you'll need to have everything on the list below in place with your running:

- **Injury-free running.** In order to begin adding speed to your workouts and eventually to your marathon, it is crucial to enter into this phase with no injuries that will be aggravated in any way by running faster. If you have any injuries you're working with, do yourself a huge favor and give them time to heal before asking more of your body. You'll never make a wiser running choice.

- **Cardio/aerobic conditioning and core strength.** You have good cardio/aerobic conditioning and have strengthened the muscles that are used in ChiRunning. These include:
  - **Core muscle strength.** In order for weight-bearing to be evenly distributed throughout your skeletal structure during your support stance, your core muscles (especially your transverse abdominis and rectus abdominis muscles) need to be strong enough to hold your posture line straight while you're balancing yourself in an increased angle of forward lean. If these core muscles are not engaged, these advanced techniques will not work as well as they could.
  - **Hip flexors.** The elastic recoil of your hip flexors is what returns your leg to the support stance after swinging to the rear, so these muscles and tendons need to be healthy and resilient.
  - **Intrinsic muscles of the feet and ankles.** These are the deep muscles that dorsiflex the toes and plantarflex the foot. These add stability to your stance as well as elastic recoil during your foot strike and liftoff.
- **Postural alignment.** Your postural alignment and one-legged posture stance are totally self-supporting—a completely solid base with minimal muscle engagement (your postural support should be predominantly coming from skeletal structure, core muscles, and connective tissue).
- **Arm swing.** You can comfortably hold a 90-degree arm bend and run without holding any tension in your shoulders. Your arms swing freely and your shoulders have no rotation.
- **Body Sensing skills.** You are able to Body Sense everything previously mentioned in this book. You don't just understand the focuses but feel them working in your body. You are now at Level II Body Sensing, where your body quickly and intuitively responds to terrain challenges.
- **Pelvic rotation.** You allow pelvic rotation to happen. You can feel it working, but you're not forcing it. You are aware of when you lose it (due to fatigue or lack of focus) and can easily get it back again. You can clearly feel your entire lower body rotating below T12/L1.
- **Midfoot strike.** You have a solid midfoot strike and you can feel the strength and support of your ankles. (Note: If you have just moved to a minimal shoe and have a solid feel for the midfoot strike, you will

still need three to six months of running this way before your foot is fully strengthened and adapted to long distance running.)

# Advanced Topics

In this chapter we take the principle of Gathering and Issuing (mentioned in Chapter 4) to a whole new level by applying it to create speed. Here are the topics we'll cover in this chapter; some of which we'll be applying to this valuable principle.

1. Elastic recoil: gain speed without increasing your effort
2. Use of the obliques for speed and hills
3. Using breathwork and cadence to maximize issuing of energy
4. Advanced performance training: speed workouts
5. Advanced strategies: using speed wisely
6. Advanced gathering and issuing: "Balloon Power"
7. Fueling for speed: keeping ahead of your glycogen expenditure

## 1. ELASTIC RECOIL: GAIN SPEED WITHOUT INCREASING YOUR EFFORT

I know you're probably thinking that speed without effort is an oxymoron. It's not. You simply need to learn to set up the conditions for speed to happen instead of thinking it all has to come from pushing harder with your legs.

Conventional wisdom says your legs are responsible for your propulsion, and your cadence increases along with your speed. Sound familiar? It works, but it's an inefficient way to run; you can't keep a high cadence going for long because of the additional strength needed to turn your legs over faster. So whatever you might gain in speed you lose in efficiency. And, as your efficiency level goes down, your effort level goes up. It's basic physics.

ChiRunning, on the other hand, allows you to run more efficiently because you're no longer using your leg muscles for propulsion. Your propulsion instead comes from the fact that you're falling forward in a balanced lean. The result is that your legs are needed only for momentary support between strides.

But aren't your leg muscles needed to swing your legs forward? Nope. Your legs are swung forward by the elastic recoil of your ligaments and tendons. Pelvic rotation is a crucial part of this equation because it creates a twisting motion along your spine. This, in turn, stretches the elastic "spring" of your ligaments, tendons, and the myofascial tissue extending from your shoulders to your toes. The stretching of all of this connective tissue creates something like a series of rubber bands wanting to return your spinal twist (and the rest of your skeleton) to its neutral position, the support phase of your stride. Now your arms and legs are returned from their extended position by the elastic recoil of your tendons, *not* the contraction of your muscles. Because your ligaments and tendons do not burn fuel, this non-muscular action results in an extremely energy-efficient running technique. And since your muscles are not being broken down, there is less recovery time needed between workouts. As you run, your muscles learn to relax and let go of tension while your tendons become more elastic and resilient. Gravity pulls your body forward while your legs are driven rearward by the force of the oncoming road. The only real "work" you're doing is balancing yourself in a nice forward lean. Everything else is being taken care of for you.

Using this technique I have been able to run marathons on relatively low-mileage training weeks (30 miles per week). Nowadays I spend most of my time working on my technique and no time consciously strengthening my leg muscles. What I have just described creates enough efficiency for you to run at your current PRE with what I would safely guess could be 30 percent of your current energy output! If you're looking for faster race times, this translates into greater speed with relatively less effort than you're currently used to.

At the base of your elastic recoil system are your feet, where the stretch of your elastic chain begins. Barefoot running is currently enjoying an upsurge in interest across a wide spectrum of runners, and for good reason. Running barefoot, or in minimal shoes, allows the tendons in your foot and ankle to reawaken and become more resilient and elastic while at the same time strengthening all the muscles in your foot, improving your stability. Additionally, the loading and recoil of the plantar fascia and the Achilles tendon create a small amount of free propulsion at toe-off. Big, bulky running shoes have been "dumbing down" the innate elasticity in the feet of runners for the past forty years, resulting in a lessening of the elastic properties in the foot. What many people in this new movement haven't yet realized is that the recoil is not only in your feet and legs but spread the full length of your body, essentially creating a huge rubber band to power the return motion of your legs. A very creative and thorough explanation of how the body moves as an interconnected unit can be found in Tom Myers' book *Anatomy Trains*, which I highly recommend.

## 2. USE OF THE OBLIQUES FOR SPEED AND HILLS

What I described in the previous section was how to run faster with less effort by increasing your lean angle and your elastic recoil. But what if you want to run faster uphill or pick up your speed in the last 10K of a marathon? Wouldn't that require some increase in muscle usage?

The short answer is yes, but it's not what you're thinking. It doesn't mean you'll be increasing the work of your *legs*. The muscle group you'll use to make quick work of hills or other challenges is your *obliques*, which are associated with the fire element. Your obliques are two powerful sets of core muscles on either side of your belly that most people never think about when they're running. (See figure 44.) Specifically, they're called your *internal obliques* and *external obliques*, and they're normally used to rotate your torso in either direction. But when you sta-

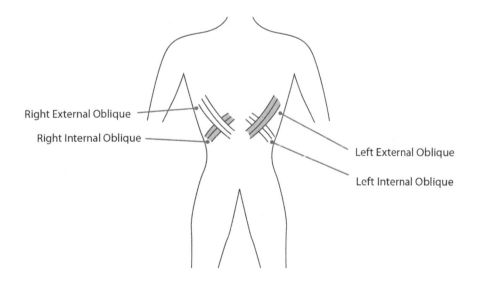

Right External Oblique

Right Internal Oblique

Left External Oblique

Left Internal Oblique

**Figure 44—The internal and external obliques**

The Right Internal Oblique works with the Left External Oblique.
The Right External Oblique works with the Left Internal Oblique.

bilize your torso they can be used quite effectively to rotate your pelvis in either direction, which drives your hips, which drives your legs.

These two sets of muscles are the only place in the human body where two different muscles are engaged to do the *same* job. The right internal oblique works in tandem with the left external oblique to rotate your left shoulder toward your right hip. Or, in ChiRunning, with your shoulders stabilized, your right internal oblique and your left external oblique both contract to drive your left hip rearward, sending propulsion to your legs. Then, as long as your legs are aligned but relaxed, the power from your obliques is transferred directly to the earth, and voilà! You run up the hill without using your leg muscles for propulsion because your obliques are doing the job. Since your obliques work in tandem, it's nearly impossible to wear them out. I ran the Shut-in Trail Race (an 18-mile uphill race, with 5,000 feet of vertical gain, in Asheville, North Carolina) using this technique and finished strong. The next day, my obliques were slightly sore, but my legs were fine!

The trick to using your obliques for propulsion is to first be able to run with your legs aligned and providing momentary support between strides while remaining very relaxed from hip to toe, especially your ankles, hamstrings, and glutes. You must also be able to clearly feel your pelvis rotate freely below T12/L1. Once you have thoroughly integrated these two focuses into your body, you can slowly begin to add in a small amount of driving your pelvis with your obliques. As you feel increasingly comfortable with driving your pelvis, you can increase the amount of drive by practicing on an uphill slope. Lean into the hill and feel your obliques pushing your legs. A slight amount of soreness in your obliques is to be expected in advanced training. It means you're doing something right.

In terms of applying the Chi principle of Gathering and Issuing, driving your pelvis with your obliques falls under the heading of issuing. The accompanying gathering is the recoil of your connective tissue returning your legs to the support stance.

### 3. USING BREATHWORK AND CADENCE TO MAXIMIZE ISSUING OF ENERGY

T'ai Chi and many other martial arts use the breath to add power during the issuing phase. We are taught to breathe out from our belly every time we issue a punch or kick. It's actually not just breathing out, but quickly exhaling through the lips while visualizing a balloon expanding in all directions from the *dantien*, the energy center of the body (located just below the navel). This slight adjustment in mental focus and breathing can turn what would be a hit into a damaging blow.

The same concept works incredibly well when you're running at faster speeds or up hills. And when you synchronize your breath with your cadence, it adds a rhythmical, machine-like, and powerful sense in your body. Your running will take on a combination of power and ease, and you'll be watching your competitors in your rearview mirror. Here's how to do it.

When I'm running at faster speeds, my breath rate naturally increases to a three-stride breath rate. That means I'm forcefully exhaling for one stride and inhaling for two. On the exhale I'm focusing on my arm swinging forward (in a short, upward punching motion) while the same-side leg swings rearward. Both are moving in opposite directions, creating the "balloon-expanding" effect. When I add in the use of my obliques driving my leg to the rear, the whole combination feels like an explosion of power from my center, through my legs, and directly into the earth passing rearward beneath me. In this case my gathering is my in-breath and my issuing is my forceful out-breath.

Carefully go through what I've just said and visualize it in your body. Then, in your next workout, try it out once you've warmed up.

- Begin with synching your breath to your stride in a three-count pattern: breathe out for one stride and in for two strides.
- Once you settle into the rhythm of breathing and cadence, start emphasizing the out-breath by blowing out through pursed lips.
- Every time you breathe out, drive your rear leg rearward with your obliques while doing a short forward punch with your same-side arm. You'll have to bring your elbow back farther than usual so that when you swing your arm forward your elbow doesn't ever swing past your ribs.

## 4. ADVANCED PERFORMANCE TRAINING: SPEED WORKOUTS

As an advanced ChiRunner, you can raise the ante in your speed workouts. Because I follow the training formula of form, distance, and *then* speed, I am conservative and don't give people more than their body is prepared for. It takes time to get the basics. As you master the mix of relaxation and recoil with powering with your obliques, speed can become play. In order to increase your half marathon or marathon pace, you'll practice holding more of a lean and relaxing ever more deeply for longer periods of time.

The following are suggested workouts for increasing your speed for a half or full marathon event. (For complete advanced programs, visit our website.) LSD runs should be run at aerobic threshold pace (PRE 5–6) and all other runs are *faster* than race pace (PRE 6–7).

### Workout #1: Cardio/aerobic workout (PRE 6-7)

**800s:** This workout is best done at a track or on a measured level road or bike path. Begin with six repeats and build up to ten repeats with a gradual negative progression of splits. When you get up to ten repeats use your speed focuses to gradually bring your split times down evenly in all ten repeats.

or

**Hill repeats:** Cardio workout (PRE 6–8). Same progression as 800s.
Find a gradual hill that is 200 meters long. Each repeat is to the top and back. At the bottom of the hill, before starting up again, do a one-minute jog break between repeats. On the uphill sections focus on forward/upward arm swing, driving with the obliques, and relaxing your legs. On the downhill sections focus on pelvic rotation, extension of the hip flexors (open up your rearward stride), bending your knees more, and holding a forward lean with your abs. Cadence should be 180 spm up *and* down. (Note: if you want to have a six-day workout schedule, this can become your sixth workout.)

### Workout #2: Cardio/aerobic workout (PRE 6-7)

**1,600-meter repeats:** Five 1,600-meter repeats with three-minute breaks, run with negative splits. This workout is best done at a track or on a measured level road or bike path. Start the set of intervals with the first couple of repeats run slightly slower than your average projected race pace. Gradually work toward finishing the set with your pace faster than your projected race pace. This is a great workout to practice setting up the conditions for speed to happen. Use all the same focuses as Workout #1.

**Workout #3:** Cardio workout (PRE 6-8)
**Ladders:** Sets of 200 meters, 400 meters, 400 meters, 800 meters, 800 meters, 1,600 meters, 800 meters, 800 meters, 400 meters, 400 meters with a one-lap jog break between each interval. This workout is best done at a track or on a measured level road or bike path. Just gauge your effort level in this workout. Your PRE should never be lower or higher than the suggested PRE range.

**Workout #4:** High-end aerobic workout (PRE 5)
**LSD run:** Train at or just below aerobic threshold for 16 to 20 miles, followed the next day by 10 miles at projected average race pace. Do as many of these back-to-back runs as possible during the mastery phase. If you'd like, you can alternate every other week with 16 miles at race pace on a mock-up of the most challenging section of your race.

**Workout #5:** Aerobic threshold workout (PRE 6-7)
**Tempo run:** This workout should be run the day after your LSD run. A Saturday/Sunday combination works best. Start with 8 miles and work up to a half marathon at your projected average race pace (based on your most recent Time Trial results).

## 5. ADVANCED STRATEGIES: USING SPEED WISELY

If you haven't yet seen the movie *Apollo 13*, I strongly suggest you rent it some evening, make yourself a big bowl of popcorn, and watch it . . . for two reasons. The first reason is that it is a really well-done nail-biter of a film with a happy ending. The second reason is because it's the perfect example of how to make a little fuel go a long way, and that's the way you should be thinking about running a marathon with speed: how to get the most speed from the least amount of fuel.

In this true story, the astronauts are in a tiny, damaged space capsule that normally needs 60 amps for it to function. In order to get these men home from their position close to the moon, they have to get the power usage down to 12 amps—barely enough to run a vacuum cleaner, as they say in the movie. And in order to set their space capsule in the right trajectory for reentry they'll need to fire the thrusters, which will cost them valuable fuel. They get the go-ahead from Houston, but they can only "step on the gas" for a few seconds, after which they have to drop back into cruise mode. This is very similar to the image you should have during your marathon. You have to be incredibly discerning about when to throw in speed and how much to use, because your fuel supply is limited and the distance is long. The first half of your marathon is not the time to be macho. It's the time to use your wisdom.

In order to use speed wisely, you have to intimately know the course you'll be running and know exactly when and how to safely and effectively throw in speed. Here are some strategic moves I've observed in elite runners over the years.

- Even if you keep your speed constant throughout the marathon, your heart rate will drift up. In the last 5 miles, if you have that intuitive sense that you have something left in your tank, it's a great time to rise to the occasion and spend whatever you've got left in your energy bank. It's a palatable distance to finish hard, if you're a racer. And at some point you've just got to take a risk and give it your best shot. If you fail, you still come away having learned something about yourself. In the 2011 Boston Marathon, what went on in Ryan Hall's brain that made him trust his own sense of what he could do to try to catch the Kenyans late in the race? He didn't win the race, but he caught the Kenyans, bested the previous course record, and ran a personal record. He dug deep for that one, and I'm sure he came away from the race much more satisfied than he would have been had he not committed himself to putting the hammer down when he did.
- Downhill stretches are strategic spots to throw in some speed because you've got the pull of gravity working in your favor. Lean into the downhill and let your legs swing big out the back. If you want to catch the Kenyans, you need to run like the Kenyans.
- Here's a basic rule of speed that I follow in races: you can run as fast as you want to as long as you can maintain abdominal breathing (as opposed to shallower breathing) *and* as long as you're replacing your glycogen stores at a rate that keeps up with your expenditure. As long as you're doing abdominal breathing you're probably safely within your aerobic zone. Monitoring your breathing will give you something relaxing and positive to focus on. Don't let yourself get into the fight-or-flight mode or you could quickly go into oxygen debt.
- If you're trying to catch someone ahead of you, accelerate slowly to catch that person, and then once you're there, settle back into cruise mode again. Just say to yourself, *When I get there I'm going to relax.*

- At the start of a race, when you're trying to gain or hold a good position, any Surges should be very relaxed. Avoid any sudden or sustained accelerations. If you're smart at the start and don't waste any energy, that up-front patience will work in your favor in the last miles, when most of your competitors will be running out of gas.
- Run the tangents by following the straightest line between curves in your course. This can cut minutes off your time.
- Don't use your speed on uphills or you will burn through more fuel per stride than almost anything else you'll ever do while running. Stay steady on the uphills by engaging your obliques and save your speed for the downhills, where it's a free ride.
- I've seen elite marathoners throw in light Surges followed by relatively slower "rest" periods to make their competitors think they're tiring. When they throw in the Surge they gain some distance on their competitors; when they slow down, their competitors seize the opportunity and speed up to catch them. But just as a competitor gets close they throw in another Surge and demoralize the chaser. It's a bit of a cat-and-mouse ploy.
- Your y'chi is one of your best allies for running faster speeds As an advanced runner, you should be using y'chi for all kinds of race challenges, such as fatigue, hills, passing, and reinstating focuses after you pass through aid stations. By focusing your intent through your eyes to a point ahead of you, you can override the multitude of distractions that could throw off your focus. When I'm working with my y'chi I feel my entire body relax and I can taste a pervasive sense of stillness underlying my entire experience. You can also use an internal y'chi to see your vision of success. An advanced athlete should be using the element of air, the thought process, even more than regular athletes. Your internal vision will help pull you forward toward your goal.

## 6. ADVANCED GATHERING AND ISSUING: "BALLOON POWER"

The following advanced technique is a powerful way to combine everything you've learned so far. In order to master this exercise you'll be required to simultaneously use your skills of focus, relaxation, visualization, symmetry, and alignment. Have fun with it.

This mental version of the gathering and issuing of my chi was taught to me by George Xu. Imagine your energy field being like a balloon. As your energy issues outward from your center, the balloon expands. As your energy gathers back inward, your balloon contracts.

The images of yin and yang can be found woven through everything in existence. For simplicity's sake, we can say that yin represents the principle of gathering energy inward, toward a center. The complement to this is yang, which represents energy expanding out from a center. In order to be balanced and efficient in your movement, you need to have these two elements always in balance. I'm speaking of a balance between gathering (rest) and issuing (effort). We see the principle of gathering and issuing energy in everything from the change of seasons (outward in summer and inward in winter) to the simple act of breathing (in-breath and out-breath). If, in your running, you do only half of the equation—let's say only gathering—you won't go anywhere. On the other hand, if all you do is issue, it'll be all work and no rest, and you'll fizzle faster than cheap champagne.

In ChiRunning, every time your leg swings to the rear imagine you're issuing energy, and as your leg returns to the support phase of your stride, imagine you're gathering energy. There's a way to use this balloon image to your advantage during long training runs and marathons. When you're feeling the need for some rest and recovery, focus on gathering energy each time your arms and legs are swinging toward your center (the return phase of your stride). With your Observer, simply follow the inward movement of your arms and legs as they return to your center. Envision gathering energy with each stride, like a sponge sucking up water in a rhythmical way. By running with this image in your mind, you'll eventually feel your limbs beginning to recharge with energy. When you sense that your body is sufficiently recharged, gradually return to your normal gait.

Remember that gathering does not mean contracting (as in contracting your muscles to bring your arms and legs to your center). It means relaxing and allowing your arms and legs to return to your center by the recoil action of your ligaments and tendons. It's an important distinction.

If, on the other hand, you need some power to get up a hill or to catch a runner ahead of you, focus on the expanding mode of this balloon image and visualize energy issuing out of your body in all directions. For example, during each rearward swing of your leg, your energy is expanding out, away from your center. This rearward swing of your leg is then balanced by a simultaneous forward swing of your same-side arm.

In figure 43, note that even though my arms are swinging forward, my elbows never swing ahead of my ribs.

The outward expansion of your energy is what drives your arms and legs away from your center and moves you down the road or up the hill, as the case might be. To make this easier to do, I set my metronome to beep on every third stride so I'm issuing on a different leg each time I hear a beep. I issue for one stride and gather for two. So I feel my energy expand on my right side, arm forward and leg rearward. Then I take two strides where I focus on gathering energy in toward my center, relaxing my body, allowing the recoil of my ligaments and tendons to bring my arms and legs back to my Column. Then I issue on my left side, arm forward and leg rearward . . . followed by two strides of gathering, resting, recoiling. With each issuing I breath out through pursed lips and with each gathering I inhale through my nose. It's a very powerful way to direct your mind, your breath, and your chi to produce power when you really need it. This is a way to gain power without increasing the work of your muscles because it is based on mental focus, not on physical strength. You are truly running at the speed of thought.

The reason why I call this an advanced technique is because of what your legs are doing in this situation: *nothing*. Your legs must be aligned and relaxed, and in order to do this exercise well it is crucial to first develop the skill of using your legs *only* for support. When you're issuing your "balloon power," you're not pushing with your quads, calves, or feet. They are simply acting as an extension of the power coming from your center.

### 7. FUELING FOR SPEED: KEEPING AHEAD OF YOUR GLYCOGEN EXPENDITURE

When you are running at peak performance levels, two areas to really stay on top of are the rate at which you burn glycogen and the rate at which you replace your glycogen. If you're pushing the pace, you'll need to be taking in calories, because when you're running at your aerobic threshold, your blood glucose supply is good for only about ninety minutes.

This brings up an important point. I just mentioned running at your aerobic threshold, *not* your anaerobic threshold. If you want maximum performance in a marathon or half marathon, it is crucial that you hold off doing any anaerobic running until you are within 5K of the finish of a half marathon or at 20 miles in the marathon (and feeling good, I might add).

This is precisely why, if you are a performance runner, it is so important for you to be doing most of your LSD runs at your aerobic threshold pace. If you do, you're effort level will remain constant and your speed will increase as your level of conditioning improves.

To keep up with your glycogen burn rate, take a glycogen replacement gel at the 10K mark and another every half hour after that for the duration of your marathon. Some gels work better than others, so I recommend trying out different ones during your LSD runs to find what works best for you.

With these advanced focuses and workouts in your arsenal of training tools, you'll take your performance to a new level and begin to feel your body's potential to truly *run like the wind*. By practicing these strategies in your training you'll feel ease in your effort and joy in your speed.

# CHAPTER TEN

# Training the Whole Person

## Lifestyle Components for Success

Live in each season as it passes: breathe the air, drink the
drink, taste the fruit.

—HENRY DAVID THOREAU

Running a marathon is a common metaphor for anything that takes
a long time and a lot of hard work. Life itself is often compared to
the marathon experience: think of writing a book, marriage, child
rearing, finishing college, or putting together a business plan. Choos
ing how and where we spend our time creates the framework of our
life. Choosing to run and train is a fabulous way to gain a tremendous
amount for the time spent: good health, a strong core, a focused mind, a
relaxed and accepting attitude, a responsive body, discipline, patience . . .
the list goes on. The real beauty is that because of the time commitment
of any marathon-type project, the internal growth and transformation
that take place can be deep and long-lasting, and in some cases perma-
nent.

I am now "practicing" ChiRunning principles in all aspects of my life, and the more I learn and do, the more I love what it has done for me!

—Connie D.

In this chapter we'll look at the phrase "life is a marathon" and how training for a marathon *mindfully* can both challenge and support you in the process of creating the best life possible for you and those you care about. The real marathon challenge, although realized in the running of your half or full marathon, is truly lived in your everyday life. That is where you do the training, such as practicing your posture, learning to relax, and eating a healthful diet, while still doing your regular work and nurturing the relationships that sustain you. The key to making it all happen in a good way is to throw yourself fully into each moment and make *quality* the keyword of everything you do.

## Creating a Life with Flow

In ChiRunning all the Form Focuses help to create a smooth and flowing running form that makes it easy to move down the road with grace and ease. Those same principles will help you create a flow in your everyday life. Just as ChiRunning takes some time to practice and learn, it takes some effort to create a more effortless flow to your life. On the following page you'll find a wheel, the sections of which represent various aspects of your life. Create a similar wheel for yourself and modify the sections to represent areas of your life that are important to you. Rate your level of fulfillment or personal satisfaction between 1 and 10. Then, using the center of the wheel as zero and the outer circumference as 10, draw a line in each section to represent your rating. Remember, you are rating your current personal satisfaction.

In order to create a smooth ride, strive to have a wheel that is balanced. Everything might not be at an 8, 9, or 10, but if some important aspects of your life are at a 2 or 3, you may feel that your life isn't flowing the way you'd like it to, creating a bumpy, imbalanced ride. It's a helpful way to see which areas of your life need focus and attention so that your "wheel" can roll smoothly.

Another wheel you will want to create and fill in is the support system you need to complete a pain-free marathon. We'll review each of these areas in more depth in this chapter. For now, rate your current level

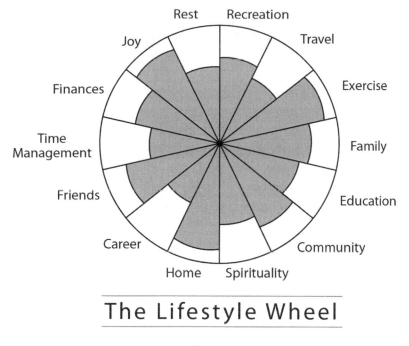

## The Lifestyle Wheel

**Figure 45**

of personal satisfaction in each of these areas, and then we'll help you find ways to create balance within these key components to a successful marathon:

- A consistent, sustainable schedule
- Support from friends and family
- Support in your training
- Rest and recuperation
- Energy management
- A mindful mind-set (approach)

## Nutrition

Whole books are devoted to nutritional information, and you can find a lot of information and recipes on our website, but here are some general guidelines.

Sound nutrition that supports body, mind, and spirit plays as important a role in running a marathon as your training. Actually, there is no area of your life that will not benefit from healthy, nourishing foods. Eating a clean, high-octane diet, allows you to gain access to greater amounts of chi, leaving you more energized, mentally focused, and enjoying an increased level of health. Good nutrition stabilizes mood swings, aids in weight loss, and will even help you to get a more restful night's sleep, all of which can help you in your training. Building the deep nutritional base to run a marathon pain-free is long-term practice, not a quick fix. And the sooner you get started, the better.

Unfortunately for many, food has become a loaded subject. In an attempt to lose weight, run faster, or become healthier you may have already tried a variety of diets that confuse you and your body about which foods are *good* for you. It can often feel like a bumpy ride up and down the hills of a low-carb, high-carb, low-fat, high-fat, high-protein roller coaster.

Our passion for a healthy lifestyle has led Katherine and me into the study and practice of getting the most from the foods we eat. We've discovered that just as you need to set up the right conditions in your running and training, you need to do the same with your diet. Here we'll share what we've learned over the years to provide you with guidelines for creating the best diet for you. We've also consulted with Dick Felton, a Certified ChiRunning Instructor who is also a Certified Nutritionist.

### PRACTICAL STEPS FOR A HEALTHFUL DIET

If you want to have a high-quality life, then eat high-quality foods. Eating poor-quality foods is like putting low-octane gasoline into a fine sports car. The car will move, but it won't function at anywhere near its capacity. You will get a much higher performance out of your body if it's running on premium fuel. Ask yourself, "How much life does this food have in it?" There can be no question that the most beautiful section of the grocery store is the produce section. It is always alive with vibrant colors and fresh smells because fresh foods are filled with chi. Compare this image with the aisle lined with cans and heavily processed foods wrapped in foil and plastic. The processed foods might seem quick and convenient, but they have lost much of their nutritional value in the processing.

Fresh, wholesome foods don't need anything added to them to be perfectly aligned with your body's nutritional needs. Processed foods with their added flavors, colors, preservatives, and low-fat or sugar-free formulations aren't really an improvement on nature. It's like taking a gorgeous landscape in Yellowstone Park and bringing in artificial flowers, fake trees, and stuffed birds.

The best fruits and vegetables to eat are organic and fresh, grown without chemical fertilizers, pesticides, and fungicides. Organic meats, eggs from free-range chickens, and organic dairy products are also your first choices because they are cleaner, come from animals that have been fed high-quality feed, and do not contain growth hormones, artificial colors, or other additives.

In summary, high-chi foods are:

- Organic foods
- Fresh, whole foods
- Freshly prepared foods

Low-chi or no-chi foods include:

- Most canned foods
- Overcooked foods
- Processed and refined foods (white sugar, white flour, white rice)
- Deep-fried foods (light sautéing is fine)
- Hydrogenated oil
- Microwaved foods
- Foods with additives, preservatives, or artificial coloring
- Pickled foods
- Commercially produced condiments
- Smoked foods
- Foods sweetened with high-fructose corn syrup or artificial sweeteners (aspartame, sorbitol, etc.)
- Soft drinks, including low-calorie versions

## TRAINING AND WEIGHT LOSS

Training for a marathon or half marathon is a great way to get in shape, but we never suggest using any exercise program as a means to lose weight. Regular exercise can help you manage and lose weight; however, your diet is the most important place to focus for weight loss. Many people have gained weight while training for an event because of the false assumption that since they are exercising they can eat whatever they want. When you're running long miles your body needs nutrient-rich foods more than ever, but not necessarily more food. At the same time, you do not want to hold back on needed nutrients and calories while training long distances. Be sensible and treat yourself to really good, healthful food after a long run, rather than high-sugar, high-fat treats.

### DIET FOR OPTIMAL AND SUSTAINABLE PERFORMANCE

Training for a marathon is also no time for a low-carb or a low-fat diet. A healthful balance of slow-burning carbs is an important fuel. You also need protein to repair and rebuild muscle tissue. Healthful fats are essential for your body to function well. A ratio of 55–60 percent carbs, 20–25 percent protein, and 20–25 percent fats is a good ratio to aim for.

Although many of today's diets suggest eating lots of small meals, we believe in the three-square-meals-a-day routine. Even at the peak of my training, I stick with this. The stomach is a periodic organ, meaning there are times when it should work and times when it needs to take a break. If you are eating all day, the acids in your stomach are at work all day long. I like to get hungry, eat until pleasantly satisfied, and then stop eating until the next meal.

I treat breakfast as the most important meal of the day. After my morning workout I eat a hearty and substantial meal. Three times a week I have a big bowl of hot whole-grain cereal loaded with nuts, seeds, and dried fruit. Once or twice a week I have eggs, and twice a week I have a cooked grain and vegetable with nuts and sometimes cheese (yes, for breakfast). Once a week I have a big bowl of yogurt with lots of nuts, seeds, raisins, and fruit.

At midday I eat a light lunch, which might include dried fruit with nuts, fresh fruit with cheese, or peanut butter with vegetable slices.

My weekly dinner menu looks something like this: lean meat or chicken once a week, fish once a week, a huge salad once or twice a week, and legumes (beans or lentils) with brown rice once or twice a week. On the other nights I have grain-and-vegetable meals, sometimes with nuts, seeds, and/or cheese.

Since I do my long runs on Saturdays, I eat higher-protein meals early in the week and nutrient-rich carbs in the two to three days before my long run or before the marathon.

After a long run, it is important to eat a good meal consisting of about 45 percent protein and 55 percent healthy carbs within forty-five minutes of the workout to support and speed up recovery. This is vitally important when your long runs are longer than two hours. A turkey sandwich on whole-wheat bread is a simple and effective meal to satisfy that post-run nutritional need.

Fueling during your long runs and during your event is covered in Chapter 4. Pre-race meals are in Chapter 7.

### THE DIETARY VERSION OF GRADUAL PROGRESS

If you want to eat a cleaner, more wholesome diet, allow yourself and your body some time to develop new dietary habits. Don't expect to have the perfect nutrition program right away. Instead, be gentle with yourself and make small, progressive changes, allowing your body time to adjust. If you try to follow a training diet that is too different from the one you are used to, it will be difficult to stick to and could cause some digestive stress. Instead, create good habits by making small changes at first and allowing these changes to become cumulative. Learning to eat nutritiously is like learning the ChiRunning focuses—they are easier if you practice them one at a time. Once each change becomes habit, you can add another brick to the foundation. Take your time and do it right. You will get the most chi from your food by being solid with each step along the way and moving forward with gradual progress. Don't decide to stop eating sugar and drinking coffee the week you have to prepare an important presentation at work. Just work on eliminating sugar, and when you're solid with that, begin to reduce your caffeine intake. The amount of chi gained by improving one aspect of your diet will give you the confidence to take on additional improvements.

The best tool I know of to make changes to your diet is keeping a diet journal. You don't have to do it forever, but if you've never done it before, try it for two weeks. Write down everything you put into your mouth, including how much water your drink (okay, that may be going a bit far, but if you do that for one day, you might notice that you drink too little water). Even though you don't have to show anyone your journal, you'll think about it whenever you eat something, and it will start supporting positive change right away.

A place to start to upgrade your diet is by eliminating foods that are not good for you. By the time of your event, you want to have eliminated some of the worst dietary culprits. You choose, but at the top of our list is high-fructose corn syrup and hydrogenated oils. When you eliminate these from your diet, you'll be amazed at how much your whole diet is cleaned up. And add in some of the high-energy foods that we should all be eating more of; vegetables (especially greens) and fruits are at the top of the list here.

Don't forget to listen to your body while you are modifying your food program. You may find that you do better with a little less animal protein, or that you just can't tolerate dairy at all. Allow your general health, sense of well-being, energy levels, and sleep patterns to be your guide. Pay extra-close attention to your cravings. However, it's one thing to crave a candy bar and another thing altogether to crave a piece of fish or a pile of broccoli. Just remember: whenever you're aware of a food choice to be made, follow the path of more chi and that's exactly what you'll end up with.

## Have a Consistent Schedule: An Exercise in Rate and Rhythm

Your mind, body, and emotions love rhythm, routine, and consistency. Creating a consistent schedule may sound like an oxymoron in this day and age, where the word *consistent* would more likely describe your level of distraction. Katherine and I have crazy lives as well. We both travel, we have a daughter whose life keeps getting busier, we run a business, we write books, and we have a dog, a cat, and a house in which something always needs to be fixed. What keeps our lives sane is a foundational schedule that we come back to and rely on heavily to keep our lives grounded and moving in the direction we want. Some things are sacred. We exercise regularly. Keeping our chi flowing with physical activity is a mainstay. We focus on eating meals together, as much as possible, and at the same time each day. Katherine and I both meditate and take personal quiet time. Katherine gets Journey off to school on Mondays, Wednesdays, and Fridays while I run with the dog. She takes the dog Tuesdays and Thursdays while I get Journey off to school. This way we each get to run with and without the dog, which is a real blessing. If I cook, she does dishes, and vice versa. It's taken years of working at it, and we still have to check in all the time about who can cover what, but the basics of exercise, meditation, good food, time with our daughter, and regular time together is the foundation of our lives. If those things are not fitting into the schedule, the schedule has to change.

Your exercise program is a framework and physical foundation for a healthy lifestyle. Training for a marathon is a good incentive to create a consistent schedule for your long-term well-being. Whether you're training four or six days a week, consistency is the key. As much as possible, it is best to follow a similar schedule each week, something to this effect:

Monday: Rest, walk, or other cross-training

Tuesday: Form Focus intervals

Wednesday: Speed intervals

Thursday: Hill Run

Friday: Rest, walk, or other cross-training

Saturday: Long run

Sunday: Fun run or rest

Use the schedule from the novice training programs in Appendixes A and B, or from one of our online programs for intermediate or advanced training, and modify it to fit your needs. Do your best to keep the consistency from week to week. The weekly routine will allow your body to get into a regular rhythm and you'll be able to more easily discern what is affecting your body if you eliminate as many variables as possible, a change in schedule being a big variable. As your mileage increases and your nutritional needs become more important, you'll also eat specific meals before and after various runs. We recommend eating a nutrient-dense carbohydrate meal the evening before a long run and a protein-rich, mineral-replenishing meal afterward. The human body loves regularity, in what and how much we eat, in when and how we exercise, in when we work and focus, or when we play and relax. We call it your rate (how much: whether it's exercise, food, or sleep) and rhythm (when: the times at which you eat, sleep, or exercise). Even positive changes should be made gradually. So pay attention to the rate and rhythm cycles that work best for you. Then stick with it, making changes gradually so your body can adjust.

## SCHEDULING TIME FOR YOUR LONG RUNS

For all of us, training for a half or full marathon is a commitment on many levels. But in this fast-paced day and age, finding the time to train can be one of the biggest challenges we come up against. The fact that you're planning on training for a long-distance event tells me that you already have at least some semblance of a weekly running schedule. You're used to doing your weekly runs of thirty to forty-five minutes, which are usually not a problem to fit into even the busiest of schedules. The long run, however, presents a logistical challenge of its own. Not only does the run itself take up a significant part of one day each week, but when you add on your pre-run prep time and post-run recovery time, including sitting down to a nourishing meal afterward, you're looking at the better part of a day.

Because of all these factors, it is important to schedule your long runs on a day of the week where you can pretty much do your own thing and not have lots of extraneous commitments to anyone except maybe your training partners. For most runners who have a day job, this means they're running long either Saturday or Sunday. If you choose to do your LSD run on Saturdays, you have all of Sunday to recover before heading back to work on Monday. If you train on Sundays, you have all day Saturday to run errands or do house projects, but it tends to inhibit your Saturday night social scene, if you have one. Running long on Sundays has never affected my ability to put in a good day's work on Monday. I'm as ready to get to work as most people who *didn't* run the day before. Whichever day you choose to do your long run, make it a day when you can schedule lots of space on either side *and* when you are most likely to have the least number of obstructions before, during, and after.

For most runners the long run is the most challenging. So your job is to set up the conditions for this run to have the least number of external challenges, whatever that means for you.

## Support from Friends and Family

In the chapter on the mastery phase we discuss putting together a crew for support at your event. In order to accomplish your goals, you might need a "crew" throughout your training, especially for your first marathon: friends and family and co-workers who support and encourage you to keep at your training, who ask questions, listen to you, and cover for you when needed.

Establishing your crew is an important step in your process. For the most part, you will probably find that people respect and are excited about your decision to run a marathon and want to help you as much as possible; however, you have to be willing to give back as well and to listen and understand their point of view if they don't seem as enthusiastic as you hoped they would be. Katherine has been very supportive of my training and racing over the years, but when our daughter was very little and my race schedule very full, she got fed up with holding down the fort more than her share. Your colleagues at work might be willing to cover for you if you need them to once in a while, but at the same time, you don't want your running to interfere with your work.

If there is any real resistance from your family or friends, follow Stephen Covey's suggestion to "seek first to understand." Getting back on track with your health and getting strong and centered might create some fear in those who aren't in the same place as you. They might feel threatened that you're changing and growing. If your family begins to feel the stress of your Saturday long runs, it's time to stop, listen, and problem-solve, just as you would if you were out on a run and your hip begins to hurt. The goal is for your running to add to your life, rather than becoming a burdensome sacrifice that you and your loved ones are making. If you come home too tired to do anything else with them all day, they may feel resentful. So as you run, you'll work to conserve energy and relax for more than just yourself; you'll be doing so to have energy for the people and other meaningful endeavors in your life.

Here are some ways to make your family and friends part of your team.

- **Share your vision and goals.** Let them know how important running is to you. Fill them in on your plan and schedule.
- **Ask for clear and specific support.** Make sure you do this in advance.
- **Invite them to join you on this grand adventure.** They don't have to run a marathon to share a run or two with you.
- **Share aspects of the ChiRunning technique while ChiWalking.** It isn't threatening to non-runners, and ChiWalking is the best way to practice ChiRunning when you're not out on a run.
- **Support them in something they want to do.** Give to them the same support you'd like to get from them.
- **Share your discoveries.** Also, listen to what is important for them.

Joe found that being aware of his wife's needs deepened his own ChiRunning skills:

Your recent newsletter article on performance is very important to me. Your last paragraph suggests the greatest truth: Running is not about competition with others or ourselves; rather, running is to serve the purpose of helping us each to fulfill our calling in life.

Years ago my wife, Dana, gave me your book, and over that time I have slowly come to understand more of what you both are getting at with ChiRunning. Dana read from the book often, but only in the last year, of six years of your book with us, has she started to run. Now she is running close to 3 miles, and I have the pleasure of running with her.

But only by shortening my stride as I maintain my cadence have I been able to stay a tiny bit behind her so as not to pressure her into running faster than her form and endurance allows. At this non-competitive pace I have deepened the feeling of controlling my speed with the lean. I sense more fully the needle and the cotton; not spilling the chi while keeping the shoulders, hands, and legs relaxed; the breath, deep and easy.

After all these years I am experiencing relaxation in the run, and hours later I am energized by the run, rather than made tired. This energy is carrying over into my work and relationships.

—Joe

## Rest and Recuperation

Overtraining is a big issue in running and training for a marathon. Rest is equally as important as training. Rest days need to be part of your schedule. With ChiRunning many people find that their recovery time after a run is much shorter than it used to be; it's one of the great benefits of being so energy-efficient in your movement. It doesn't mean that you don't need to recover, however. If running long distances is new to you, you need to be especially aware of the need for downtime. Sometimes a higher level of activity will make your sleep deeper, and sometimes the extra energy moving through your body can create a lighter, less restful sleep. Sleep is not the only way to rest, however. There are other quiet activities, and even doing nothing (sacrilege!). Even when you're doing nothing, you can be Body Sensing, and on those days when you do take a break from physical activity or spend five minutes just looking at the sky and doing nothing but enjoying the view and feeling yourself, you'll learn more about the rest you need than you can ever learn in a book. Take a minute (or five or ten or twenty) to feel yourself right now; feel if you are well rested, if your body is at a good place with the amount of physical activity it needs. Do this often, and remember that if your mind is working at full speed all the time, you're probably not Body Sensing enough. Body Sensing rests the mind, which is equally important.

## The Multiple Marathon Lifestyle

If you run marathons regularly, or are feeling that that is a possibility for you, all the issues around lifestyle are even more important. We live the multiple marathon lifestyle, maintaining a fairly high level of conditioning (while still making sure we have enough physical rest), eating well as a part of how we live, and moving through the various phases of training as a matter of course. I suggest running a maximum of four marathons a year. There may be a time or a reason to do more, but to do four a year, you should be at a fairly high level with your technique, with Body Sensing, with sound nutritional intake, and with your conditioning in order to remain pain- and injury-free. It can be a great way to move through life—if you remain centered and non-identified, and if you keep your Observer on the alert for overtraining.

## Energy Management and the Mindful Lifestyle

In many ways, this entire book is about managing energy. Focusing your mind, building a strong core, learning to relax, and being as responsive and flexible as possible are all tools to help direct and manage the chi that flows through your body. These tools work whether you're running, at the computer, or being present for your child when she is going through an emotional meltdown. One of the best ways to maintain good flow of chi is to stop the leaks in your life. If you are at work and thinking about how to handle a difficult neighbor, you're not giving your work the focus and attention it needs, so the focus on your neighbor is an energy leak. Equally, when you're talking with that difficult neighbor, you need to keep your center, be aware of your tone, and keep focused on dealing with that issue, rather than wishing you could escape to the safety of your office at work.

Every time your focus is divided or going down into a negative spiral, you're leaking precious energy. You can also leak energy by getting too excited or overly dramatic. But don't take that to mean you shouldn't celebrate successes. Celebration and enjoying your success are very positive ways to build energy. What matters most is how you feel during and after any experience. We all have a lot more available energy than we realize. And there are many sources of great energy in our lives: the air we breathe, good food, good friends, a beautiful day. You may feel tired doing the laundry, but then your best friend says, "Let's meet downtown for tea and catch up," and suddenly the energy is flowing in your veins again. On the other hand, you may be going out the door for a run with your training group when your wife says your son has a fever and she has a meeting she has to go to. Double whammy: your son is sick and you can't run. The energy that doesn't leak out can help you find creative solutions and appropriate responses no matter what the world throws at you. You address your son's fever by giving him your full, loving attention. Nothing will help him heal faster, and it will give your energy a healthy place to move and flow instead of leaking away in frustration or fear.

Managing your energy requires mindfully approaching the world around you and noticing how you respond. When you watch the rise and fall of what creates energy and learn to anticipate and manage that flow, you become a master of your own self. It is always good to ask yourself, "How can my energy best be used in this situation?" Use your y'chi and find the focus that gives your energy a channel to move through rather than letting all your good energy drain away.

## KATHERINE'S STORY

When I was twenty-seven years old, a friend gave me a book on meditation. The only notion of mediation I had was what I had learned in a high school world religions course in a brief lesson from a visiting Buddhist monk. Even back then I was intrigued, so when I read the meditation book, more than ten years after that class, I devoted an afternoon to following some of the suggestions, paying close attention to everything I was doing; watching my breathing and thoughts. I went for a run, trying to be sensitive to my surroundings and how my body felt. Afterward I listened very intently to some beautiful music, then sat in front of a candle for thirty minutes, watching my thoughts. *Well,* I thought that evening, *I don't feel any different,* and I went to bed.

But the next morning on the subway, headed to work in New York City, I did feel something. It felt significant yet hard to describe. I was aware of myself in a way I never had been before; of how I was feeling and thinking, and it felt good and solid, like I had something to hold on to in myself that I had never had before. I knew it was from the focuses of the day before. I also had the realization that being aware of myself in this way was a lifetime's work, and that it was worth doing. I felt I would know myself in a way I had never imagined possible. It was a profound experience that literally changed my life.

Living a mindful life can have many meanings, but on the most basic level it means being consciously aware of yourself in any given moment, seeing yourself through the eyes of your Observer: *Oh, that made me angry. Wow, anger makes my body tense,* or *I want to eat, but I'm not really hungry. What is that sense of hunger telling me and what else would satisfy that need right now?* When you are not aware, the tension from anger might show up the next day when you get an ache in your neck, or you may just eat what's in the fridge because you didn't really notice that you weren't actually hungry for food but for something nourishing.

A helpful tool for living a mindful life is Body Sensing. Your mind can be a useful tool as well, but it is not the only source of self-knowledge. It can just as easily distort a healthy view of any situation. The mind has ideas about how things *should* be or how you *should* be, and those judgments become part of your worldview. Body Sensing and your mind make a good team for living a mindful life; this is the same team that makes it possible to run pain- and injury-free.

## Infuse Yourself with the Positive

Another important key to managing your energy is to absorb all the good things in your life. We often take our lives for granted by not savoring the food we eat, the beautiful day, the group we run with every Saturday. If you want more energy in your life, appreciate what you already have, especially a healthy body that is able to train for a marathon. Just as we suggest an end-of-run review, it's also worthwhile to have an end-of-day review (or combine the two reviews) where you contemplate the goodness of life and infuse it into your cells. Don't ignore the difficult aspects of the day, but rather treat those issues as lessons so they don't become leaks. Make a choice to appreciate yourself, your health, and all that life offers you every day. Take time to infuse into your whole self the great energy that moves through your body when you move well. Experience what it feels like and savor the sensations. Then take that feeling with you into your next activity.

For Katherine and me, and for many people who call themselves runners, running is a touchstone, something that helps us live a more centered, balanced life. It doesn't matter if you run to live well or live well to run better; either way you benefit. That is the potential of running a marathon, and the underlying drive for most people: true empowerment, true discovery, a new vision of success.

This book is meant to help you succeed at any long-term, important goal in your life. As the principles of *Chi Marathon* seep into your mind and body through your running, you may find that you don't have to change your life to run a pain-free marathon; rather, you may find that the pain-free marathon experience is changing you.

# Acknowledgments

No one person, or two people write a book. It takes a village to raise a child and it takes a team to write a book.

We want to thank our team:

First and foremost the ChiLiving Staff who work so hard with such dedication and always with the goal of pervasive integrity that is the hallmark of our vision for all the Chi services. We treasure having you in our lives, especially Ashley, Liz, Nicole, Shelly, Jeff, and Casey.

Bonnie Solow, our agent of nine years and an early believer. Thank you, many times over. Matthew Benjamin, Kiele Raymond, Cherlynne Li, Stacy Creamer, and all the folks at Simon & Schuster who have made this and all our books possible. We can't thank you enough for your support, creativity, and insights. Frank Veronsky, we love working with you as our photographer . . . you make us look so good.

To all the Certified Instructors; you are so multi-talented and the ones who make ChiRunning come to life for people all over the world. Your dedication and your desire to help others is an inspiration to both of us.

Mark Cucuzzella, when ChiRunning helped you run well again, we had no idea how much we'd get in return. Thank you for all you do to help runners run safely and spread the ChiRunning teachings.

To our friends and family, you put up with our crazy schedules, help us when we need a hand, love us when we're not all that lovable. In memory of Connie Bergin, Katherine's mother, who had picture-perfect posture and who inspires us to enjoy life as she did. With love and gratitude to Jean Longway, Danny's mother. And always last, but never ever least, thank you Journey Marie, for your unfathomable wisdom, your laughter, your music, your poetry, and for reminding us regularly how important it is to play and land lightly.

# Appendix A

## WEEKLY LONG-RUN SCHEDULE

| WEEK # | LSD DISTANCE |
| --- | --- |
| 1 (Phase II) | 3 miles |
| 2 | 4 miles |
| 3 | 5 miles |
| 4 | 6 miles |
| 5 | 6 miles/10K race |
| 6 | 7 miles |
| 7 | 8 miles |
| 8 | 9 miles |
| 9 (Phase III) | 10 miles |
| 10 | 10 miles |
| 11 | 11 miles |
| 12 | 12 miles |
| 13 | 13 miles |
| 14 (Phase IV) | 11 miles |
| 15 | 8 miles |
| 16 (Phase V)   RACE DAY | 13.1 miles |

## PHASE II: THE TECHNIQUE PHASE

### Workout Schedule: Weeks 1–8

| | Monday | Tuesday | Wednesday | Thursday | Friday | Saturday | Sunday |
|---|---|---|---|---|---|---|---|
| 1 | REST | 30 min. Form intervals + Time Trial | REST | 30–40 min. Form intervals | REST | LSD 3 miles | 30 min. Fun Run |
| 2 | REST | 30–40 min. Form intervals | REST | 30–40 min. Form intervals | REST | LSD 4 miles | 30 min. Fun Run |
| 3 | REST | 30–40 min. Form intervals | REST | 30–40 min. Form intervals | REST | LSD 5 miles | 30 min. Fun Run |
| 4 | REST | 30–40 min. Form intervals | REST | 30–40 min. Form intervals | REST | LSD 6 miles | 35 min. Fun Run |
| 5 | REST | 45 min. Form intervals | REST | 45 min. Form intervals | REST | LSD 6 miles/ 10K race | 35 min. Fun Run |
| 6 | REST | 45 min. Form intervals | REST | 45 min. Form intervals | REST | LSD 7 miles | 35 min. Fun Run |
| 7 | REST | 45 min. Form intervals | REST | 45 min. Form intervals | REST | LSD 8 miles | 35 min. Fun Run |
| 8 | REST | 45 min. Form intervals | REST | 45 min. Form intervals | REST | LSD 9 miles | 45 min. Fun Run |

# Week 1

**Goal:** Posture: Get aligned, feel aligned
**Lesson:** Posture
**DVD:** Lesson 1

**Monday: Rest**

Get a good night's sleep.

**Tuesday: 30 min. form intervals + Time Trial**

**1 min. on/off form intervals:** Practice Focus 1 for 1 min. on/1 min. off for 10 min.; then practice Focus 2 for 1 min. on/1 min. off for 10 min. Practice both focuses together for the last 10 min., 1 min. on/1 min. off.

**Focus 1:** Align your feet and legs

**Focus 2:** Create your Column (shoulders, hips, ankles aligned)

**Time Trial:** At the end of your workout, run 1 mile at a very comfortable, conversational pace. Record your overall time. This will be the pace for your Saturday LSD run. This Time Trial should be run on a track or on a measured 1-mile section of road.

**Wednesday: Rest**

**Thursday: 30–40 min. form intervals**

**1 min. on/off form intervals** (same as Tuesday, different focuses)

**Focus 1:** Level your pelvis

**Focus 2:** Lengthen the back of your neck

**Friday: Rest**

Practice The "C" Shape wherever you are.

**Saturday: 3-mile LSD run**

**Alternating form intervals:** Set watch with a 5 min. countdown timer. Every time it goes off, choose a focus from the list and stick with it for 5 min., then switch to the next focus. Practice each focus at least once.

**Suggested focuses:** Align your feet and legs • Create your Column • Level your pelvis • Lengthen the back of your neck • Feel your feet at the bottom of your Column • The "C" Shape

**Use Tuesday's Time Trial pace × 3 to determine total run time** (i.e., 9:45 [9.75 min.] × 3 = ~30 min.). This is approximately the total time for today's 3-mile LSD run.

**Make a cheat sheet** of the focuses or write them on your hand. You can do this every week if you need help remembering them.

**Sunday: Optional 30 min. Fun Run or cross-training workout**

# Week 2

**Goal:** Moving from your Center
**Lesson:** Engage your core
**DVD:** Lesson 1, Step 3

## Monday: Rest

Learn the Body Looseners and do them before each run this week.

## Tuesday: 30-40 min. form intervals

**1 min. on/off form intervals:** Practice Focus 1 for 1 min. on/1 min. off for the first third of the run; then, practice Focus 2 for 1 min. on/1 min. off for second third of run. Practice both focuses together for the last third, 1 min. on/1 min. off.

**Focus 1:** Level your pelvis
**Focus 2:** Feel your feet at the bottom of your Column

## Wednesday: Rest

## Thursday: 30-40 min. form intervals

**1 min. on/off form intervals** (same as Tuesday, different focuses)
**Focus 1:** Level your pelvis
**Focus 2:** Lengthen the back of your neck

## Friday: Rest

Practice leveling your pelvis whenever you think about it.

## Saturday: 4-mile LSD run

**10 min. alternating form intervals:** Using the four focuses from today's focus list, practice every focus for 10 min. each, using your watch timer. With remaining time, repeat any that you found most challenging.

**Suggested focuses:** Level your pelvis • Feel your feet at the bottom of your Column • Lengthen the back of your neck • The "C" Shape

**Total run time** = (Time Trial pace or average aerobic pace) × 4

## Sunday: Optional 30 min. Fun Run or cross-training workout

# Week 3

**Goal:** Engage gravity
**Lesson:** Lean
**DVD:** Lesson 2
**Fueling:** For information on fueling, please refer to Chapter 4, page 109
**Three steps to engage your lean**
    Step 1: Check in with your posture line
    Step 2: Feel your feet supporting your one-legged posture stance
    Step 3: Let your Column fall in front of where your feet are hitting
**Practice the three steps to engage your lean** every time you start running and every time you go up a gear

### Monday: Rest

### Tuesday: 30–40 min. form intervals
**1 min. on/off form intervals:** Practice Focus 1 for 1 min. on/1 min. off for the first third of the run; then, practice Focus 2 for 1 min. on/1 min. off for middle of run. Practice both focuses together for the last third, 1 min. on/1 min. off. **At the beginning of your run,** practice the three steps to engage your lean from a standing position as many times as possible in 5 min., jogging only 10 yards between each time. Then begin your workout.
    **Focus 1:** One-legged posture stance
    **Focus 2:** The "C" Shape

### Wednesday: Rest

### Thursday: 30–40 min. form intervals
    **1 min. on/off form intervals** (same as Tuesday, different focuses)
    **Focus 1:** The "C" Shape
    **Focus 2:** Land midfoot

### Friday: Rest

### Saturday: 5-mile LSD run
    **10 min. alternating form intervals**
    **Suggested focuses:** One-legged posture stance • Three steps to engage

your lean • Balance in the "window of lean" • The "C" Shape • Land midfoot

**Total run time** = (Time Trial pace or average aerobic pace) × 5

**Mindful maintenance:** Hydrate every 10 min. after the first hour. If you think your LSD run will take longer than an hour, plan to take electrolytes.

### Sunday: 30 min. Fun Run or cross-training workout

# Week 4

**Goal:** The passive lower leg
**Lesson:** Lower body, cadence, and metronome
**DVD:** Lesson 1, Step 3
**Drill:** Knee-Bending Exercise (DVD: Lesson 3)
**Drill:** Determine your cadence (see Chapter 3, page 87)

### Monday: Rest

### Tuesday: 30–40 min. form intervals

**1 min. on/off form intervals:** Do the Knee-Bending Exercise at the beginning of your workout, repeating the entire sequence three times. Then begin your run.

**Focus 1:** Limp lower legs: calves, shins, ankles, feet, toes
**Focus 2:** Heels up, knees down

### Wednesday: Rest

### Thursday: 30–40 min. form intervals + determine your cadence

**1 min. on/off form intervals** (same as Tuesday, different focuses)
**Focus 1:** The "C" Shape
**Focus 2:** Heels up, knees down

**At the end of your run,** take 5 min. to determine your cadence. Match your metronome to your cadence. This will tell you your cadence. If it is below 170 spm, set your metronome to 170 spm and shorten your stride until your steps match the beat. If your cadence falls between 170–180 spm you're fine.

**Friday: Rest**

**Saturday: 6-mile LSD run**

**10 min. alternating form intervals:** Remember to do pre-run Body Looseners and post-run stretches today. Use your metronome throughout the run to make sure your cadence is steady.

**Suggested focuses:** Limp lower legs • Circular feet • Let your hip swing back with your leg • The "C" Shape • Heels up, knees down • Balance in the "window of lean"

**Total run time** = (Time Trial pace or average aerobic pace) × 6

**Mindful maintenance:** Hydrate every 10 min. after the first hour. Replace electrolytes if needed.

**Sunday: 35 min. Fun Run or cross-training workout**

# Week 5

**Goal:** Adding fluidity to your form
**Lesson:** Pelvic rotation
**DVD:** Lesson 4
**Drill:** Pool Running Exercise (same as Pelvic Rotation Drill, DVD: Lesson 4)
**Set your metronome** to the same cadence as last week and use it on every run.

**Monday: Rest**

**Tuesday: 45 min. form intervals**

**Start the workout** with the Pool Running Exercise. Then walk briskly for 200m, feeling your pelvis rotate. Next, break into a slow jog while keeping your pelvis rotating. Jog for 3 min., then slow to a walk for 1 min. Repeat this cycle for the duration of the workout. Best done on a track.

**Focus 1:** Level your pelvis
**Focus 2:** Feel your Pivot Point at T12/L1

**Wednesday: Rest**

**Thursday: 45 min. form intervals**

**1 min. on/off form intervals:** Remember your pelvic rotation from Tuesday and try to re-create that today as you run.

**Focus 1:** The "C" Shape

**Focus 2:** Let your hip swing back with your leg

**Friday: Rest**

Teach someone else the Pool Running Exercise and watch those hips swing.

**Saturday: 6-mile LSD run** (or run in a 10K race, but don't race)

**10 min. alternating form intervals** (If you're running a race, change focuses at every mile marker.)

**Suggested focuses:** Level your pelvis • Feel your Pivot Point at T12/ L1 • The "C" Shape • Rotate entire lower body below Pivot Point • Let your hip swing back with your leg • Let your Column fall in front of where your feet are hitting.

**Total run time** = (Time Trial pace or average aerobic pace) × 6

**Mindful maintenance:** Hydrate every 10 min. after the first hour. Replace electrolytes if needed.

**Sunday: 35 min. Fun Run or cross-training workout**

# Week 6

**Goal:** Have your upper body join the fun

**Lesson:** Upper body

**DVD:** Lesson 5

**Review:** Using your y'chi (see Chapter 4, page 113)

**Set your metronome** same as last week.

**Monday: Rest**

**Tuesday: 45 min. form intervals**

**1 min. on/off form intervals**

**Focus 1:** Bend your elbows 90 degrees (swing your arms, don't pump them)

**Focus 2:** Shoulders fall forward

**Wednesday: Rest**

**Thursday: 45 min. form intervals**

**1 min. on/off form intervals:** Focus 2 introduces focus pairs: try to focus on elbows and legs swinging to the rear gracefully

**Focus 1:** Keep your upper body ahead of your feet

**Focus 2:** Swing elbows to the rear/Let legs swing to the rear

**Friday: Rest**

**Saturday: 7-mile LSD run**

**5 min. alternating form intervals:** On this run, lower body focuses are combined with upper body focuses to form pairs; during each section, focus on each pair for the entire 20 min. Set your countdown timer for 5 min. increments to remind you to stay focused.

**Set 1 focuses (20 min.):** Let your hip swing back with your leg/ Shoulders fall forward

**Set 2 focuses (20 min.):** Rotate entire lower body below Pivot Point/ Y'chi directs energy forward through your eyes

**Set 3 focuses (20 min.):** The "C" Shape/Swing elbows to the rear

If you have remaining time, practice focuses that are particularly challenging for you.

**Total run time** = (Time Trial pace or average aerobic pace) × 7

**Mindful maintenance:** Hydrate every 10 min. after the first hour. Refuel and replace electrolytes as needed.

This is an important week to practice writing an end-of-week review.

**Sunday: 35 min. Fun Run or cross-training workout**

# Week 7

**Goal:** Feel the rhythm
**Lesson:** Gears
**DVD:** Lesson 6
**Set your metronome** same as last week and use it on *every run*.

**Monday: Rest**

**Tuesday: 45 min. form intervals**

**Warm-up for 5 min. in first gear.** Set a 1 min. countdown timer. Every time it goes off, shift one gear. Follow this gear pattern throughout the entire run: 1-2-3-2-1-2-3-2-1-2-3, etc. Change gears by leaning 1" more or 1" less. Keep your lower legs as relaxed as possible as you shift gears.

**Focus:** Change gears

**Wednesday: Rest**

**Thursday: 45 min. form intervals**

**1 min. on/off form intervals:** During Focus 1 intervals, match your heel as it comes up with the metronome beep. Practice with both heels.

**Focus 1:** Heels up, knees down

**Focus 2:** Swing elbows to the rear

**Friday: Rest**

**Saturday: 8-mile LSD run**

**10 min. alternating form intervals** (you'll alternate focus pairs today instead of individual focuses)

**Focus pairs 1 and 2:** Choose four lower body focuses to be used in pairs (see Appendix C)

**Total run time** = (Time Trial pace or average aerobic pace) × 8

**Mindful maintenance:** Hydrate every 10 min. after the first hour. Refuel and replace electrolytes as needed.

**Sunday: 35 min. Fun Run or cross-training workout**

# Week 8

**Goal:** Adjust your stride length to your speed
**Lesson:** Stride length
**DVD:** Lesson 6
**Set your metronome** same as last week and use it on every run.

**Monday: Rest**

Practice your pelvic rotation whenever you walk today.

Tuesday: 45 min. form intervals

**2 min. on/off form intervals:** Practice Focus 1 for 2 min. on/2 min. off for the first third of run; then, practice Focus 2 for 2 min. on/2 min. off for middle third of run. Practice both focuses together for the last third, 2 min. on/2 min. off.

**Focus 1:** Balance in the "window of lean"

**Focus 2:** Allow pelvic rotation to happen

Wednesday: Rest

Thursday: 45 min. form intervals

**10 min. alternating form intervals**

**Focuses 1 and 2:** You choose (see Appendix C for suggestions)

Friday: Rest

Saturday: 9-mile LSD run

**10 min. alternating form intervals**

**Suggested focuses:** Rotate your pelvis • Balance in the "window of lean" • Three steps to engage your lean

**Total run time** = (Time Trial pace or average aerobic pace) × 9

**Mindful maintenance:** Hydrate every 10 min. after the first hour. Refuel and replace electrolytes as needed.

Sunday: 45 min. Fun Run or cross-training workout

## PHASE III: THE CONDITIONING PHASE

### Workout Schedule: Weeks 9–13

|   | Monday | Tuesday | Wednesday | Thursday | Friday | Saturday | Sunday |
|---|--------|---------|-----------|----------|--------|----------|--------|
| 9 | REST | 40 min. Form intervals + Time Trial | REST | 45 min. Easy Hill Run | REST | LSD 10 miles | 40 min. Fun Run |

|    | Monday | Tuesday | Wednesday | Thursday | Friday | Saturday | Sunday |
|----|--------|---------|-----------|----------|--------|----------|--------|
| 10 | REST | 40 min. Surges | REST | 45 min. Easy Hill Run | REST | LSD 10 miles | 45 min. Fun Run |
| 11 | REST | 45 min. Surges | REST | 40 min. Easy Hill Run | REST | LSD | 45 min. Fun Run |
| 12 | REST | 5 × 800m intervals | REST | 40 min. Easy Hill Run | REST | LSD 12 miles | 40 min. Fun Run |
| 13 | REST | 5 × 800m intervals + Time Trial | REST | 40 min. Easy Hill Run | REST | LSD 13 miles | 30 min. Fun Run |

# Week 9

**Goal:** Hold your form over longer distances
**Lesson:** Hill Runs
**Description of Hill Run:** see Chapter 4, page 126
**Review:** Body Looseners and stretches
**Set your metronome** same as last week and use it on every run.

## Monday: Rest

## Tuesday: 40 min. form intervals + Time Trial

**4 min. alternating form intervals:** Alternate focus pairs at beginning of each interval.

**Focus pairs 1 and 2:** Choose any four focuses that best address your needs; put them in pairs. Each pair should have one easy focus and one challenging focus.

**At the end of your run,** do a 1-mile Time Trial and write the pace down in your journal.

## Wednesday: Rest

**Thursday: 45 min. easy Hill Run**

**5 min. warm-up on level ground.** Run 10 min. in second gear on flat before beginning hills, change focus pair relative to terrain. These hills should be short and low.

**Focus pair 1:** Choose two uphill focuses.

**Focus pair 2:** Choose two downhill focuses.

**If you don't have hills, do the following workout:**

**4 min. alternating form intervals:** Alternate between second and third gears; pick one upper body focus and one lower body focus for each focus pair.

**Friday: Rest**

Practice The "C" Shape wherever you are.

**Saturday: 10-mile LSD run**

**10 min. alternating form intervals**

**Suggested focuses:** Review any two focus pairs that you need to work on, and don't forget to have fun. Or, try these:

**Focus 1:** Allow your pelvic rotation to happen

**Focus 2:** Balance in the "window of lean"

**Total run time** – (Time Trial pace or average aerobic pace) × 10

**Mindful maintenance:** Hydrate every 10 min. after the first hour. Refuel and replace electrolytes as needed.

**Stop your watch** whenever you take a break during the run. Restart it when you begin running again.

**Sunday: 40 min. Fun Run or cross-training workout**

# Week 10

**Goal:** Master your gears

**Lesson:** Surges

**Description of Surges:** see Chapter 4, page 124

**Review:** Gears

**Review:** Body Looseners and stretches

**Set your metronome** same as last week and use it on every run.

**Monday: Rest**

### Tuesday: 40 min. Surges

**1 min. alternating form intervals:** Alternate between second gear and third gear. Reinstate focus pair every time you switch gears.

**Focus pair:** Balance in the "window of lean"/Lengthen the back of your neck.

### Wednesday: Rest

### Thursday: 45 min. easy Hill Run

**5 min. warm-up on level ground.** Run 10 min. in second gear on flat before beginning hills, change focus pair relative to terrain. These hills should be short and low.

**Focus pair 1:** Choose two uphill focuses
**Focus pair 2:** Choose two downhill focuses
**If you don't have hills, do the following workout:**
**4 min. alternating form intervals:** Alternate between second and third gears; pick one upper body focus and one lower body focus for each focus pair.

### Friday: Rest

### Saturday: 10-mile LSD run

**10 min. alternating form intervals:** Second gear entire run; run as much of the last 10 min. in third gear as you can.

**Focus pairs 1 and 2:** Pick two focus pairs that best address your current needs. Each focus pair should have one upper body focus and one lower body focus.

**Total run time** = (Time Trial pace or average aerobic pace) × 10

**Mindful maintenance:** Hydrate every 10 min. after the first hour. Refuel and replace electrolytes as needed.

### Sunday: 45 min. Fun Run or cross-training workout

# Week 11

**Goal:** Keep on swinging with great pelvic rotation
**Lesson:** Practice pelvic rotation
**DVD:** Lesson 4

**Drill:** Pool Running Exercise
**Set your metronome** same as last week and use it on every run.

## Monday: Rest

## Tuesday: 45 min. Surges

**1 min. alternating form intervals:** Alternate between second gear and third gear. Reinstate focus pair every time you switch gears.

**Focus pair:** Lean from your ankles/Allow pelvic rotation to increase (as you lean more)

## Wednesday: Rest

## Thursday: 40 min. easy Hill Run

**5 min. warm-up on level ground.** Run 10 min. in second gear on flat before beginning hills, change focus pair relative to terrain. These hills should be short and low.

**Focus pair 1:** Choose two uphill focuses
**Focus pair 2:** Choose two downhill focuses
**If you don't have hills, do the following workout:**
**4 min. alternating form intervals:** Alternate between second gear and third gear; pick one upper body focus and one lower body focus for each focus pair.

## Friday: Rest

## Saturday: 11-mile LSD run

**10 min. alternating form intervals:** Second gear entire run; run as much of the last 10 min. in third gear as you can.

**Focus pairs 1 and 2:** Pick two focus pairs that best address your current needs. Each focus pair should have one upper body focus and one lower body focus.

**Total run time** = (Time Trial pace or average aerobic pace) × 11

**Mindful maintenance:** Hydrate every 10 min. after the first hour. Refuel and replace electrolytes as needed.

## Sunday: 45 min. Fun Run

# Week 12

**Goal:** Upper body and Lower body: Know when to use each
**Lesson:** Lower body and Upper body
**DVD:** Lesson 3 and Lesson 5
**Set your metronome** same as last week and use it on every run.
**This week will help you** feel the importance of both upper body and lower body focuses and how to feel them working together to run most efficiently.

### Monday: Rest

### Tuesday: 5 × 800m form intervals

**Warm up for 5 min.** Start each interval in second gear and gradually increase to third gear for the last 200m. Jog for 1 min. in first gear. Repeat. Lean and relax to speed up; don't use muscle. Best done on a track. Use focus pair 1 for intervals 1 and 2, focus pair 2 for intervals 3 and 4, both pairs for interval 5.

**Focus pairs 1 and 2:** For each pair, choose 2 focuses: one that you like and one that is more challenging.

### Wednesday: Rest

### Thursday: 40 min. easy Hill Run

**Warm-up for 5 min.** Run 10 min. in second gear on flat before beginning hills; change focus pair relative to terrain. These hills should be short and low. Remember your metronome.

**Focus pair 1:** Choose two uphill focuses
**Focus pair 2:** Choose two downhill focuses
**If you don't have hills, do the following workout:**
**4 min. alternating form intervals:** Alternate between second and third gear; pick one upper body focus and one lower body focus for each focus pair. Remember your metronome.

### Friday: Rest

Use your arms to create balance between your upper and lower body. Anytime your upper and lower body move fluidly, in a balanced, flexible manner, no part of your body will offer any hindrance to your forward motion.

### Saturday: 12-mile LSD run

**10 min. alternating form intervals:** Second gear entire run; run as much of the last 10 min. in third gear as you can. First half of run, cycle through focuses individually; second half, alternate focus pairs.

**Focuses:** Pick four favorite focuses from the past two weeks (two upper body and two lower body). Each focus pair should have one upper body focus and one lower body focus.

**Total run time** = (Time Trial pace or average aerobic pace) × 12

**Mindful maintenance:** Hydrate every 10 min. after the first hour. Refuel and replace electrolytes as needed.

### Sunday: 40 min. Fun Run

# Week 13

**Goal:** Do your homework
**Lesson:** Practice race-specific focuses
**Practice the course:** Create a list of your half marathon's course characteristics by mile marker. Example: Start: downhill first 3 miles; Mile 6: major uphill, 1 mile long; Mile 9: flat, uphill finish for 1.1 miles. If your course is hilly, practice hill focuses. If your course is flat, practice focuses that work best for you. You can also practice the fatigue fixes found in Chapter 4, page 116.
**Set your metronome** and use it on every run.

### Monday: Rest

Get a good night's sleep.

### Tuesday: 5 x 800m form intervals

**Warm up for 5 min.** Start each interval in second gear and gradually increase to third gear for the last 200m. Jog for 1 min. in first gear. Repeat. Lean and relax to speed up, don't use muscle. Best done on a track. Use focus pair 1 for intervals 1 and 2, focus pair 2 for intervals 3 and 4, both pairs for interval 5.

**Focus pairs 1 and 2:** For each pair, choose 2 focuses: one that you like and one that is more challenging.

**At the end of your run,** do a 1-mile Time Trial in second gear.

## Wednesday: Rest

## Thursdays: 40 min. easy Hill Run

**No speed.** Work arms and upper body on uphills; lean and pelvic rotation on downhills. Start flat, finish flat. Change focus pairs relative to terrain. These hills should be short and low.

**Focus pair 1:** Choose two uphill focuses

**Focus pair 2:** Choose two downhill focuses

**If you don't have hills, do this workout:**

**5 min. alternating form intervals:** Exaggerate practicing the focuses in each pair. Since you won't be running hills, this will really help you feel your upper and lower body working together.

**Focus pair 1:** Upper body focuses

**Focus pair 2:** Lower body focuses

## Friday: Rest

## Saturday: 13-mile LSD run: Your first half marathon!

**10 min. alternating form intervals:** Design a 13-mile course resembling a mock-up of your event. Every major detail should be included at approximate mile markers of the real course. Second gear entire run; run as much of the last 10 min. in third gear as you can.

**Focus pairs 1 and 2:** You choose: one easy and one challenging focus per pair.

**Total run time** = (Time Trial pace or average aerobic pace) × 13

**Mindful maintenance:** Hydrate every 10 min. after the first hour. Refuel and replace electrolytes as needed.

## Sunday: 30 min. Fun Run or bike ride

## PHASE IV: MASTERY

### Workout Schedule: Weeks 14 & 15

|    | Monday | Tuesday | Wednesday | Thursday | Friday | Saturday | Sunday |
|----|--------|---------|-----------|----------|--------|----------|--------|
| 14 | REST | 6 × 800m intervals | REST | 45 min. Hill Run | REST | LSD 11 miles | 40 min. Fun Run |
| 15 | REST | 4 miles start pace | REST | 40 min. start pace | REST | LSD 8 miles | 4 mile Fun Run |

# Week 14

**Goal:** Make long-distance running relaxing and easy

**Lesson:** Three steps to engage your lean

    **Step 1:** Check in with your posture line.

    **Step 2:** Feel your feet supporting your one-legged posture stance.

    **Step 3:** Let your Column fall in front of where your feet are landing.

**Practice the three steps to engage your lean** every time you start running and every time you go up a gear.

**Review** the course mockup you designed last week.

**Set your metronome** and use it on every run.

**Make a list** of focuses you need to work on and practice them for the next two weeks.

## Monday: Rest

## Tuesday: 6 × 800m form intervals

    **Warm up for 5 min.** Start each interval in second gear and gradually increase to third gear for the last 200m. Jog for 1 min. in first gear. Repeat. Lean and relax to speed up; don't use muscle. Best done on a track. Use focus pair 1 for intervals 1 and 2, focus pair 2 for intervals 3 and 4, both pairs for intervals 5 and 6.

    **Focus pair:** Use two focuses from this week's list.

## Wednesday: Rest

### Thursday: 45 min. Hill Run

**Try to find a moderately challenging** course for this run. Work arms and upper body on uphills; lean and pelvic rotation downhill. Start flat, finish flat. Change focus pair relative to terrain. These hills should be short and low.

**Focus pair 1:** Choose two uphill focuses

**Focus pair 2:** Choose two downhill focuses

**If you don't have hills, do this workout:**

**5 min. alternating form intervals:** (Exaggerate focuses like last Thursday)

**Focus pair 1:** Upper body focuses

**Focus pair 2:** Lower body focuses

### Friday: Rest

### Saturday: 11-mile LSD run

**10 min. alternating form intervals.** Cycle through all the focuses, one at a time. Repeat cycle until time is up. Mock up an 11-mile route similar to the last 11 miles of your event. Practice your ability to recognize the changes in terrain and how to change focuses to fit the terrain. Run second gear entire run.

**Focuses:** Choose six of your most challenging focuses

**Total run time** = (Time Trial pace or average aerobic pace) × 11

**Mindful maintenance:** Hydrate every 10 min. after the first hour. Refuel and replace electrolytes as needed.

### Sunday: 40 min. Fun Run or cross-training workout

# Week 15

**Goal:** Stay the course

**Lesson:** Perfecting a mindful setup and start for your event

**Listen to your body** and thank it for all the hard work it has done.

**Start pace runs** will be a mock-up of your pre-race and the start of your event; it's just like a rehearsal.

**Set your metronome** and use it on every run.

### Monday: Rest

### Tuesday: 4-mile form intervals at start pace

**10 min. alternating form intervals.** Second gear for whole workout (third gear at the end is okay, but only if you can stay relaxed). This run should be an approximate mock-up of the first four miles of your event. Pretend this is the real event start. Visualize yourself at the start line of the race: Have you done your Body Looseners? Do you have your metronome? A clear list of focuses? As you start to run, maintain a low gear and don't get caught up in what the crowd is doing.

**Focuses:** Choose focuses relative to your specific event course.

**Total run time** = (Time Trial pace or average aerobic pace) × 4

### Wednesday: Rest

### Thursday: 40 min. form intervals at start pace

**10 min. alternating form intervals**

**Focus pairs:** Choose two focus pairs, different from Tuesday

### Friday: Rest

### Saturday: 8-mile LSD run—easy!

**Run a mock-up of the first 8 miles** of your event course. Practice 10 min. alternating form intervals: second gear for whole workout, finish in third gear. It's important to have a steady cadence, so bring your metronome. Remember to clearly Body Sense your start pace as well.

**Focuses:** Breathing focuses and favorite loosening/relaxing focuses

**Total run time** = (Time Trial pace or average aerobic pace) × 8

**Mindful maintenance:** Hydrate every 10 min. after the first hour. Refuel and replace electrolytes as needed.

### Sunday: 4-mile Fun Run or cross-training workout

## PHASE V: TAPER TIME

### Week 16 Workout

|    | Monday | Tuesday | Wednesday | Thursday | Friday | Saturday | Sunday |
|----|--------|---------|-----------|----------|--------|----------|--------|
| 16 | REST | 35 min. Form intervals | REST | 5 miles start pace | REST | (See Race Weekend phase) | |

# Week 16

**Goal:** Go the distance!
**Lesson:** You have everything you'll need
**Believe in yourself** and in the level of your mental and physical conditioning.
**Please use your metronome** for both runs this week.

**Monday: Rest**

**Tuesday: 3 min. alternating form intervals.** Run at your projected race pace or your most recent Time Trial pace.

**Suggested focuses:** Lengthen the back of your neck • One-legged posture stance • Rotate your pelvis • The "C" Shape • Swing elbows to the rear • Smile

**Wednesday: Rest**

**Thursday: 5-mile form intervals at Start Pace**

**5 min. alternating form intervals:** Run the entire workout at your projected start pace. This run should be an approximate mock-up of your start pace for your event. Pretend you're at the start line of the race: Have you done your Body Looseners? Do you have your metronome? A clear list of focuses? As you start to run, maintain a low gear and don't get caught up in what the crowd is doing.

**Focuses:** Choose focuses that will help you the most in the early stages of your race.

**Total run time** = (Projected start pace) × 5

**Friday: Rest**

# Appendix B

## WEEKLY LONG-RUN SCHEDULE

| WEEK # | LSD TIME OR DISTANCE |
| --- | --- |
| 1 (Phase II) | 70 min. |
| 2 | 70 min. |
| 3 | 80 min. |
| 4 | 90 min. |
| 5 | 1 hr 40 min. |
| 6 | 1 hr 50 min. |
| 7 | 2 hrs |
| 8 | 2 hrs |
| 9 (Phase III) | 13.1 miles |
| 10 | 14 miles |
| 11 | 15 miles |
| 12 | 16 miles |
| 13 | 17 miles |

(*continued on next page*)

| WEEK # | LSD TIME OR DISTANCE |
|---|---|
| 14 | 18 miles |
| 15 | 16 miles |
| 16 | 19 miles |
| 17 (Phase IV) | 16 miles |
| 18 | 20-mile LSD or 17-mile Hill Run |
| 19 | 22–24-mile LSD or 20–22-mile Hill Run |
| 20 | 18 miles |
| 21 | 20–22-mile LSD or 18–20-mile Hill Run |
| 22 (Phase V) | 18 miles |
| 23 | 10 miles |
| 24  **RACE DAY** | 26.2 miles |

## PHASE II: THE TECHNIQUE PHASE

### Workout Schedule: Weeks 1–8

| | Monday | Tuesday | Wednesday | Thursday | Friday | Saturday | Sunday |
|---|---|---|---|---|---|---|---|
| 1 | 35–45 min. Form intervals | REST | 35–45 min. Form intervals | 35–45 min. Form intervals | REST | LSD 70 min. | optional Fun Run or cross-train |
| 2 | 35–45 min. Form intervals | REST | 35–45 min. Form intervals | 35–45 min. Form intervals | REST | LSD 70 min. | optional Fun Run or cross-train |
| 3 | 35–45 min. Form intervals | REST | 35–45 min. Form intervals | 35–45 min. Form intervals | REST | LSD 80 min. | optional Fun Run or cross-train |

|   | Monday | Tuesday | Wednesday | Thursday | Friday | Saturday | Sunday |
|---|--------|---------|-----------|----------|--------|----------|--------|
| 4 | 35–45 min. Form intervals | REST | 35–45 min. Form intervals | 35–45 min. Form intervals | REST | LSD 90 min. | optional Fun Run or cross-train |
| 5 | 35–45 min. Form intervals | REST | 40–50 min. Form intervals | 40–50 min. Form intervals | REST | LSD 1hr 40 min. | optional Fun Run or cross-train |
| 6 | 35–45 min. Form intervals | REST | 40–50 min. Form intervals | 40–50 min. Form intervals | REST | LSD 1 hr 50 min. | optional Fun Run or cross-train |
| 7 | 35–45 min. Form intervals | REST | 40–50 min. Form intervals | 40–50 min. Form intervals | REST | LSD 2 hrs | optional Fun Run or cross-train |
| 8 | 35–45 min. Form intervals | REST | 40–50 min. Form intervals | 40–50 min. Form intervals | REST | LSD 2 hrs | optional Fun Run or cross-train |

# Week 1

**Goal:** Get aligned, feel aligned
**Lesson:** Posture
**DVD:** Lesson 1
**Set your metronome** (170–180 spm) and use it on every run.

## Monday: 35–45 min. run: form intervals

**1 min. on/off form intervals:** Practice Focus 1 for 1 min. on/1 min. off for the first third of run; then, practice Focus 2 for 1 min. on/1 min. off for second third of run. Practice both focuses together for the last third, 1 min. on/1 min. off.

**Focus 1:** Align your feet and legs

**Focus 2:** Create your Column (shoulders, hips, ankles aligned)

**Tuesday: Rest**

Get a good night's sleep.

**Wednesday: 35–45 min. run: form intervals**

**1 min. on/off form intervals:** (same as Monday, different focuses)

**Focus 1:** Level your pelvis

**Focus 2:** Lengthen the back of your neck

**Thursday: 35–45 min. run: form intervals**

**1 min. on/off form intervals:** (same as Monday and Wednesday, different focuses)

**Focus 1:** Lengthen the back of your neck

**Focus 2:** Feel your feet at the bottom of your Column

**Friday: Rest**

Practice The "C" Shape wherever you are.

**Saturday: 70 min. LSD run**

**Alternating form intervals:** Set watch with a 10 min. timer. Every time it goes off, choose a focus from the list and stick with it for 10 min., then switch to the next focus. Practice each focus at least once.

**Suggested focuses:** Align your feet and legs • Create your Column • Level your pelvis • Lengthen the back of your neck • Feel your feet at the bottom of your Column • The "C" Shape

**Make a cheat sheet** of the focuses or write them on your hand. You can do this every week if you need help remembering them.

**Sunday: Optional Fun Run or cross-training workout**

# Week 2

**Goal:** Moving from your center
**Lesson:** Engage your core
**DVD:** Lesson 1, Step 3
**Set your metronome** (170–180) and use it on every run.

**Monday: 35–45 min. run: form intervals**

**1 min. on/off form intervals:** Practice Focus 1 for 1 min. on/1 min. off for the first third of run; then, practice Focus 2 for 1 min. on/1 min.

off for the second third of run. Practice both focuses together for the last third, 1 min. on/1 min. off.

**Focus 1:** Level your pelvis

**Focus 2:** Feel your feet at the bottom of your Column

### Tuesday: Rest

Learn the Body Looseners and do them before each run.

### Wednesday: 35–45 min. run: form intervals

**1 min. on/off form intervals** (same as Monday, different focuses)

**Focus 1:** Level your pelvis

**Focus 2:** Lengthen the back of your neck

### Thursday: 35–45 min. run: form intervals

**1 min. on/off form intervals** (same as Monday and Wednesday, different focuses)

**Focus 1:** The "C" Shape

**Focus 2:** Feel your feet at the bottom of the Column

### Friday: Rest

Practice leveling your pelvis whenever you think about it.

### Saturday: 70 min. LSD run

**Alternating form intervals:** Using the four focuses from today's focus list, practice every focus for 10 min. each. With remaining time, repeat any that you found most challenging.

**Suggested focuses:** Level your pelvis • Feel your feet at the bottom of your Column • Lengthen the back of your neck • The "C" Shape

### Sunday: Optional Fun Run or cross-training workout

**Learn the post-run stretches** today and do them after every run throughout the program.

# Week 3

**Goal:** Engage gravity

**Lesson:** Lean

**DVD:** Lesson 2

**Set your metronome** (170–180 spm) and use it on every run.

**Three steps to engage your lean:**

Step 1: Check in with your posture line.

Step 2: Feel your feet supporting your one-legged posture stance.

Step 3: Let your Column fall in front of where your feet are hitting.

**Practice the three steps to engage your lean** every time you start running and every time you go up a gear.

### Monday: 35-45 min. run: form intervals

**1 min. on/off form intervals**

Practice Focus 1 for 1 min. on/1 min. off for the first third of run; then, practice Focus 2 for 1 min. on/1 min. off for the second third of run. Practice both focuses together for the last third, 1 min. on/1 min. off. **At the beginning of your run,** practice the three steps to engage your lean from a standing position as many times as possible in 5 min., jogging only 10 yards between each time. Then, begin your workout.

Focus 1: One-legged posture stance

Focus 2: The "C" Shape

### Tuesday: Rest

### Wednesday: 35-45 min. run: form intervals

**1 min. on/off form intervals** (same as Monday, different focuses)

Focus 1: Balance in the "window of lean"

Focus 2: Relax your lower legs and ankles

### Thursday: 35-45 min. run: form intervals

**1 min. on/off form intervals** (same as Monday and Wednesday, different focuses)

Focus 1: The "C" Shape

Focus 2: Land midfoot

### Friday: Rest

Keep your ankles loose any time you walk.

### Saturday: 80 min. LSD run

**10 min. alternating form intervals**

**Suggested focuses:** One-legged posture stance • Three steps to engage your lean • Balance in the "window of lean" • The "C" Shape • Land midfoot

**Hydrate** every 10 min. after the first hour; refuel as needed.

### Sunday: Optional Fun Run or cross-training workout

# Week 4

**Goal:** The passive lower leg
**Lesson:** Lower body
**DVD:** Lesson 3
**Drill:** Knee-Bending Exercise
**Set your metronome** (170–180 spm) and use it on every run.

## Monday: 35-45 min. run: form intervals

**1 min. on/off form intervals:** Practice Focus 1 for 1 min. on/1 min. off for the first third of run; then, practice Focus 2 for 1 min. on/1 min. off for the second third of run. Practice both focuses together for the last third, 1 min. on/1 min. off. Do the Knee-Bending Exercise at the beginning of your workout, repeating the entire sequence three times. Then, begin your run.

**Focus 1:** Limp lower legs: calves, shins, ankles, feet, toes
**Focus 2:** Heels up, knees down

## Tuesday: Rest

## Wednesday: 35-45 min. run: form intervals

**1 min. on/off form intervals** (same as Monday, different focuses)
**Focus 1:** Circular feet with wheels at the ends of your legs
**Focus 2:** Balance in your "window of lean"

## Thursday: 35-45 min. run: form intervals

**1 min. on/off form intervals** (same as Monday and Wednesday, different focuses)
**Focus 1:** The "C" Shape
**Focus 2:** Heels up, knees down

## Friday: Rest

## Saturday: 90 min. LSD run

**10 min. alternating form intervals:** Remember to do pre-run Body Looseners and post-run stretches today.

**Suggested focuses:** Limp lower legs • Circular feet • Let your hip swing back with your leg • The "C" Shape • Heels up, knees down • Balance in the "window of lean"

**Hydrate** every 10 min. after the first hour; refuel as needed.

**Remember** to do an end of run and end of week review today.

## Sunday: Optional Fun Run or cross-training workout

# Week 5

**Goal:** Adding fluidity to your form
**Lesson:** Pelvic rotation
**DVD:** Lesson 4
**Drill:** Pool Running Exercise
**Use your metronome** as needed.

### Monday: 35-45 min. run: form intervals

**Start the workout with the Pool Running Exercise.** Then, walk briskly for 200m, feeling your pelvis rotate. Next, break into a slow jog while keeping your pelvis rotating. Jog for a few min., then slow to a walk and repeat this for about 30 min. Best done at track.

   **Focus 1:** Level your pelvis
   **Focus 2:** Feel your Pivot Point at T12/L1

### Tuesday: Rest

### Wednesday: 40-50 min. run: form intervals

**1 min. on/off form intervals:** Practice Focus 1 for 1 min. on/1 min. off for the first third of run; then, practice Focus 2 for 1 min. on/1 min. off for the second third of run. Practice both focuses together for the last third, 1 min. on/1 min. off.

   **Focus 1:** The "C" Shape
   **Focus 2:** Rotate entire lower body below Pivot Point

### Thursday: 40-50 min. run: form intervals

**1 min. on/off form intervals** (same as Wednesday, different focuses). Remember your pelvic rotation from Monday run; try to re-create that today as you run.

   **Focus 1:** The "C" Shape
   **Focus 2:** Let your hip swing back with your leg

### Friday: Rest

Teach someone else the Pool Running Exercise and see those hips swing.

### Saturday: 1 hr 40 min. LSD run

   **10 min. alternating form intervals**
   **Suggested focuses:** Level your pelvis • Feel your Pivot Point at T12/L1 • The "C" Shape • Rotate entire lower body below Pivot Point • Let

your hip swing back with your leg • Let your Column fall in front of where your feet are hitting.

**Hydrate** every 10 min. after the first hour; refuel as needed.

**Sunday: Optional Fun Run or cross-training workout**

# Week 6

**Goal:** Have your upper body join the fun
**Lesson:** Upper body
**DVD:** Lesson 5
**Use your metronome** as needed.

**Monday: 35–40 min. run: form intervals**
   **1 min. on/off form intervals:** Practice Focus 1 for 1 min. on/1 min. off for the first third of run; then, practice Focus 2 for 1 min. on/1 min. off for the second third of run. Practice both focuses together for the last third, 1 min. on/1 min. off.
   **Focus 1:** Bend your elbows 90 degrees (swing your arms, don't pump them)
   **Focus 2:** Shoulders fall forward

**Tuesday: Rest**
   Check in with your shoulders today; are they tight and hunched or low and relaxed?

**Wednesday: 40–50 min. run: form intervals**
   **1 min. on/off form intervals** (same as Monday, different focuses)
   **Focus 1.** Y'chi directs energy forward through your eyes (see Chapter 4, page 113)
   **Focus 2:** Swing elbows to the rear

**Thursday: 40–50 min. run: form intervals**
   **1 min. on/off form intervals:** Focus 2 introduces "Focus Pairs": try to focus on elbows and legs swinging to the rear gracefully
   **Focus 1:** Keep your upper body ahead of your feet
   **Focus 2:** Swing elbows to the rear/Let legs swing to the rear

**Friday: Rest**

**Saturday: 1 hr 50 min. LSD run**

**5 min. alternating form intervals:** On this run, you'll combine lower body focuses with upper body focuses and alternate them during your workout. During each 35 min. section, alternate between upper body focus/lower body focus every 5 min.

**Set 1 focuses (35 min.):** Let your hip swing back with your leg/ Shoulders fall forward

**Set 2 focuses (35 min.):** Rotate entire lower body Pivot Point/Y'Chi directs energy forward through your eyes

**Set 3 focuses (35 min.):** The "C" Shape/Swing elbows to the rear

**Hydrate** every 10 min. after the first hour; refuel as needed. This is an important week to practice writing an end-of-week review.

**Sunday: Optional Fun Run or cross-training workout**

# Week 7

**Goal:** Feel the rhythm
**Lesson:** Gears, cadence, and metronome
**DVD:** Lesson 6
**Determine your cadence** (see Chapter 3, page 86)
**Set your metronome** and use it on *every run.*

**Monday: 35–45 min. run: form intervals**

**Warm-up** for 5 min. in first gear. **Set a 60 sec. countdown timer.** Every time it goes off, shift one gear. Follow this gear pattern throughout the entire run: 1-2-3-2-1-2-3-2-1-2-3, etc. Change gears by leaning 1" more or 1" less. Keep your lower legs as relaxed as possible as you shift gears.

**Focus:** Change gears

**Tuesday: Rest**

**Wednesday: 40–50 min. run: form intervals**

**1 min. on/off form intervals:** Practice Focus 1 for 1 min. on/1 min. off for the first third of run; then, practice Focus 2 for 1 min. on/1 min. off for the second third of run. Practice both focuses together for the last third, 1 min. on/1 min. off. **During Focus 1** intervals, match your heel as it comes up with the metronome beep. Practice with both heels.

**Focus 1:** Heels up, knees down

**Focus 2:** Swing elbows to the rear

### Thursday: 40–50 min. run: form intervals

**1 min. on/off form intervals** (same as Wednesday, different focuses)

**Focus 1 and 2:** Choose one that you like and one that is more challenging (see Appendix C for suggestions).

### Friday: Rest

### Saturday: 2 hr LSD run

**10 min. alternating form intervals** (You'll alternate focus pairs today instead of individual focuses.)

**Focus pairs 1 and 2:** Choose four lower body focuses to be used in pairs (see Appendix C for suggestions)

**Hydrate** every 10 min. after the first hour; refuel as needed. **Take electrolytes** during the last 10 min. of your run.

### Sunday: Optional Fun Run or cross-training workout

# Week 8

**Goal:** Adjust your stride length to your speed

**Lesson:** Stride length

**DVD:** Lesson 6

**Review Pelvic Rotation (DVD: Lesson 4)**

**Set your metronome** and use it on *every run.*

### Monday: 35–45 min. run: form intervals

**2 min. on/off form intervals:** Practice Focus 1 for 2 min. on/2 min. off for the first third of run; then, practice Focus 2 for 2 min. on/2 min. off for second third of run. Practice both focuses together for the last third, 2 min. on/2 min. off.

**Focus 1:** Balance in the "window of lean"

**Focus 2:** Allow pelvic rotation to happen

**Tuesday: Rest**

**Wednesday: 40–50 min. run: form intervals**

**2 min. on/off form intervals** (same as Monday, different focuses): Alternate between second gear and third gear every 2 min.

    **Focus 1:** Level your pelvis

    **Focus 2:** Feel your Pivot Point at T12/L1

**Thursday: 40–50 min. run: form intervals**

    **10 min. alternating form intervals**

    **Focuses 1 and 2:** You choose (see Appendix C for suggestions)

**Friday: Rest**

**Saturday: 2 hr LSD run**

    **10 min. alternating form intervals**

    **Suggested focuses:** Rotate your pelvis • Balance in the "window of lean" • Three steps to engage your lean

    **Hydrate** every 10 min. after the first hour; refuel as needed. **Take electrolytes** during the last 10 min. of your run.

**Sunday: Optional Fun Run or cross-training workout**

## PHASE III: THE CONDITIONING PHASE

### Workout Schedule: Weeks 9–16

|    | Monday | Tuesday | Wednesday | Thursday | Friday | Saturday | Sunday |
|----|--------|---------|-----------|----------|--------|----------|--------|
| 9  | 40 min. Form intervals + Time Trial | REST | 45 min. Form intervals | 40 min. tempo run | REST | LSD 13.1 miles | optional Fun Run or cross-train |
| 10 | 40 min. | REST | 45 min. Form intervals | 40 min. easy Hill Run | REST | LSD 14 miles | optional Fun Run or cross-train |

|    | Monday | Tuesday | Wednesday | Thursday | Friday | Saturday | Sunday |
|----|--------|---------|-----------|----------|--------|----------|--------|
| 11 | 45 min. Form intervals | REST | 50 min. Form intervals | 40 min. easy Hill Run | REST | LSD 15 miles | optional Fun Run or cross-train |
| 12 | 45 min. Form intervals | REST | 55 min. Form intervals | 40 min. easy Hill Run | REST | LSD 16 miles | optional Fun Run or cross-train |
| 13 | 45 min. Form intervals | REST | 55 min. Form intervals | 40 min. tempo or Hill Run | REST | LSD 17 miles | optional Fun Run or cross-train |
| 14 | 45 min. Form intervals | REST | 55 min. Form intervals | 50 min. tempo or Hill Run | REST | LSD 18 miles | optional Fun Run or cross-train |
| 15 | 45 min. Form intervals | REST | 45 min. Form intervals | 45 min. form intervals | REST | LSD 16 miles | optional Fun Run or cross-train |
| 16 | 4 × 800m speed intervals | REST | 50 min. Form intervals | 45 min. Surges | REST | LSD 19 miles | optional Fun Run or cross-train |

# Week 9

**Goal:** Your first half marathon!

**Lesson:** Time Trial and tempo runs

**Review:** Body Looseners and stretches and descriptions of tempo run and Time Trial (see Chapter 4, page 98)

**Set your metronome** and use it on *every run.*

**Monday: 40 min. run: form intervals + Time Trial**

**4 min. alternating form intervals:** Reinstate focus pairs at beginning of each interval.

**Focus pairs 1 and 2:** Choose any four focuses that best address your needs; put them in pairs. Each pair should have one easy focus and one challenging focus.

**At the end of your run,** do a 1-mile Time Trial in second gear. Multiply your Time Trial pace by 13.1 (i.e., 9:45 × 13.1); this is approximately the total time for this week's 13.1-mile LSD run.

**Tuesday: Rest**

Get a good night's sleep.

**Wednesday: 45 min. run: form intervals**

**10 min. alternating form intervals**

**Focus 1:** Balance in the "window of lean"

**Focus 2:** Let legs swing to the rear

**Thursday: 40 min. tempo run**

Be sure you completely understand what a tempo run is (see Chapter 4, page 125)

**Focus 1:** Allow pelvic rotation to happen

**Focus 2:** Balance in the "window of lean"

**Friday: Rest**

Practice The "C" Shape wherever you are.

**Saturday: 13.1 LSD run: Your first half marathon**

**10 min. alternating form intervals**

**Suggested focuses:** Review any two focus pairs that you need to work on, and don't forget to have fun.

**Use Monday Time Trial** pace × 13.1 to determine total run time. **Hydrate** every 10 min. after the first hour. **Refuel and replace electrolytes** as needed. Stop your watch whenever you take a break during the run. Restart it when you begin running again.

**Sunday: Optional Fun Run or cross-training workout**

# Week 10

**Goal:** Master your gears
**Lesson:** Hill Run, Surges, and Refueling
**Description of Hill Run and Surges:** see Chapter 4, page 126
**Review: Gears** (see Chapter 3, page 86)
**About refueling:** (see Chapter 4, page 109)
**Review:** Body Looseners and stretches (Refer to the ChiRunning book, pg. 210)
**Set your metronome** and use it on *every run.*

### Monday: 40 min. Surges

**1 min. alternating form intervals:** Alternate between second gear and third gear. Reinstate focus pair every time you switch gears.

**Focus pair:** Balance in the "window of lean"/Lengthen the back of your neck

### Tuesday: Rest

### Wednesday: 45 min. run: form intervals

**4 min. alternating form intervals:** Try to find similar terrain to your Saturday LSD run.

**Focus 1:** Balance in the "window of lean"
**Focus 2:** Let your legs swing to the rear

### Thursday: 40 min. easy Hill Run

**5 min. warm-up** on level ground, 10 min. second gear on flat before beginning hills, change focus pair relative to terrain. These hills should be short and low.

**Focus pair 1:** Choose two uphill focuses.
**Focus pair 2:** Choose two downhill focuses.
**If you don't have hills, do this workout:**
**4 min. alternating form intervals:** Alternate between second and third gears; pick one upper body focus and one lower body focus for each focus pair.

### Friday: Rest

**Saturday: 10 min. alternating form intervals:** Second gear entire run; run as much of the last 10 min. in third gear as you can.

**Focus pairs 1 and 2:** Pick two focus pairs that best address your current needs. Each focus pair should have one upper body focus and one lower body focus.

**Total run time** = (Time Trial pace or average aerobic pace) × 14

**Hydrate** every 10 min. after the first hour. **Refuel and replace electrolytes** as needed.

**Sunday: Optional Fun Run or cross-training workout**

# Week 11

**Goal:** Keep on swinging with great pelvic rotation
**Lesson:** Remember pelvic rotation
**DVD:** Lesson 4
**Drill:** Pool Running Exercise
**Set your metronome** and use it on *every run.*

**Monday: 45 min. run: form intervals**

**2 min. on/off form intervals:** Reinstate your focus pair at the beginning of each "on" interval. **Run second gear** first half of workout, third gear second half of workout.

**Focus pair:** Lean from your ankles/Allow pelvic rotation to increase (as you lean more)

**Tuesday: Rest**

The medical term for where the twelfth thoracic vertebra meets the first lumbar vertebra is called T12/L1. In traditional Chinese medicine, this is one of the main points where Chi enters the body. We call it your Pivot Point: feel it as you walk today.

**Wednesday: 50 min. run: form intervals**

**2 min. on/off form intervals:** Similar terrain as your LSD run. Finish last 3 min. in third gear. Today's focuses will reduce impact and relax your legs.

**Focus 1:** Rotate entire lower body below Pivot Point
**Focus 2:** Limp lower legs

### Thursday: 40 min. easy Hill Run

5 min. **warm-up** on level ground, 10 min. second gear on flat before beginning hills, change focus pair relative to terrain. These hills should be short and low.

**Focus pair 1:** Choose two uphill focuses

**Focus pair 2:** Choose two downhill focuses

**If you don't have hills, do this workout:**

**4 min. alternating form intervals:** Alternate between second gear and third gear; pick one upper body focus and one lower body focus for each focus pair.

### Friday: Rest

### Saturday: 15-mile LSD run

**10 min. alternating form intervals:** Second gear entire run; run as much of the last 10 min. in third gear as you can.

**Focus pairs 1 and 2:** Pick two focus pairs that best address your current needs. Each focus pair should have one upper body focus and one lower body focus.

**Total run time** = (average aerobic pace) × 15

**Hydrate** every 10 min. after the first hour. Refuel and replace electrolytes as needed.

### Sunday: Optional Fun Run or cross-training workout

# Week 12

**Goal:** Upper body and Lower body: Know when to use each

**Lessons:** Lower body and Upper body

DVD: Lesson 3 and Lesson 5

**Set your metronome** and use it on *every run.*

**This week** will help you feel the importance of both upper body and lower body focuses and how to feel them working together to run most efficiently

### Monday: 45 min. run: form intervals

**2 min. on off form intervals:** Run second gear first half of workout, third gear second half of workout. Reinstate your focus pair at the beginning of each "on" interval.

**Focus pair:** Lean from your ankles/Rotate entire lower body below Pivot Point

### Tuesday: Rest

### Wednesday: 55 min. run: form intervals

**5 min. alternating form intervals**

**Focus pairs 1 and 2:** Choose any four focuses that best address your needs; put them in two pairs. Each pair should have one easy focus and one challenging focus.

### Thursday: 40 min. easy Hill Run

**Warm-up** for 5 min. Run 10 min. in second gear on at before beginning hills; change focus pair relative to terrain. These hills should be short and low. **Remember** your metronome.

**Focus pair 1:** Choose two uphill focuses

**Focus pair 2:** Choose two downhill focuses

**If you don't have hills, do this workout:**

**4 min. alternating form intervals:** Alternate between second and third gears; pick one upper body focus and one lower body focus for each focus pair. Remember your metronome.

### Friday: Rest

### Saturday: 16-mile LSD run

**10 min. alternating form intervals:** Second gear entire run; run as much of the last 10 min. in third gear as you can. First half of run, cycle through focuses individually; second half, alternate focus pairs.

**Focuses:** Pick four favorite focuses from the past two weeks (two upper body and two lower body). Each focus pair should have one upper body focus and one lower body focus.

**Total run time** = (average aerobic pace) × 16

**Hydrate** every 10 min. after the first hour. **Refuel and replace electrolytes** as needed.

### Sunday: Optional Fun Run or cross-training workout

# Week 13

**Goal:** Feel your core and relax your legs more
**Lesson:** Run from your Center
**DVD:** Lesson 1, Step 3
**Set your metronome** and use it on *every run.*

### Monday: 45 min. run: form intervals

**Warm up** for 10 min. Run ½ lap in second gear, then ½ lap in third gear, then rest ½ lap in first gear. Repeat cycle for 25 min. Last 10 min., run in third gear. **Reinstate focus pair** at beginning of each gear change. Best done at track.

**Focus pair:** Pick two upper body focuses that will most help you take the work load off your legs (i.e., Shoulders fall forward/Swing elbows to the rear).

### Tuesday: Rest

Your core is the home of your Chi. Engaging your core and finding your inner balance go hand in hand. One cannot happen without the other.

### Wednesday: 55 min. run: form intervals

**2 min. alternating form intervals:** Second gear for entire run; finish last 5 min. in third gear.

**Focus 1:** Balance in the "window of lean"
**Focus 2:** The "C" Shape

### Thursday: 40 min. tempo run or Hill Run

**5 min. alternating form intervals**

First third of workout in first gear, second third in second gear, last third in third gear. Use your metronome.

**Focus 1:** Balance in "window of lean"
**Focus 2:** Allow pelvic rotation to happen

**or**

**Hill Run focuses:** Uphill focuses or downhill focuses depending on terrain; first and second gears up hills, third gear down hills. Use your metronome.

**Friday: Rest**

**Saturday: 17-mile LSD run**

**10 min. alternating form intervals:** First 9 miles, cycle through focuses one at a time. Next 8 miles, cycle through focuses in pairs. Second gear entire run; run as much of the last 10 min. in third gear as you can.

Suggested focuses: Allow pelvic rotation to happen and three favorite Focuses from the past two weeks (four total)

**Total run time** = (average aerobic pace) × 17

**Hydrate** every 10 min. after the first hour. **Refuel and replace electrolytes** as needed.

**Sunday: Optional Fun Run or cross-training workout**

# Week 14

**Goal:** Gear up
**Lesson:** Review gears, cadence, and stride length
**DVD:** Lesson 6
**Set your metronome** use it on *every run.*

**Monday: 45 min. run: form intervals**

**2 min. alternating form intervals:** Practice alternating gears in this order: 1-2-3-2-1-2-3-2-1-2-3-2 every 2 min. Reinstate focus pair each time you change gears. Gears should be practiced by changing lean angle by 1" more or 1" less.

Focus pair: Balance in the "window of lean"/Lengthen or shorten stride relative to gear

**Tuesday: Rest**

**Wednesday: 55 min. run: form intervals**

**2 min. alternating form intervals:** Make sure your heels come up with each beat of the metronome. We suggest you set your metronome to a waltz beat. Take your total strides per min. cadence and divide by 3. Then set your metronome to this cadence (i.e., 180 spm ÷ 3 = 60 bpm on the metronome).

Focus 1: Heels up with each beat
Focus 2: Lengthen the back of your neck

**Thursday: 50 min. tempo run or Hill Run**

**5 min. alternating form intervals:** First third of workout in first gear, second third in second gear, last third in third gear. Use your metronome.

**Focus 1:** Balance in "window of lean"

**Focus 2:** Allow pelvic rotation to happen

**or**

**Hill Run focuses:** Uphill focuses or downhill focuses depending on terrain; first and second gears up hills, third gear down hills. Use your metronome.

**Friday: Rest**

**Saturday: 18-mile LSD run**

**10 min. alternating form intervals:** Cycle through focuses, one at a time and repeat until workout time is completed. Second gear entire run; run as much of the last 10 min. in third gear as you can.

**Suggested focuses:** Allow pelvic rotation to happen and three favorite focuses from the past two weeks (four total)

**Total run time** = (average aerobic pace) $\times$ 18

**Hydrate** every 10 min. after the first hour. **Refuel and replace electrolytes** as needed.

**Sunday: Optional Fun Run or cross-training workout**

# Week 15

**Goal:** Find your weakest link

**Lesson:** Practice makes perfect

**Assess your focus list** and pick a handful of focuses you find most challenging.

**Set your metronome** and use it on *every run.*

**Monday: 45 min. run: form intervals**

**5 min. alternating form intervals:** Second gear+ for duration of the run. Last 10 min., practice focuses as pair in third gear.

**Focuses 1 and 2:** Pick two of your most challenging focuses.

**Tuesday: Rest**

### Wednesday: 45 min. run: form intervals

**5 min. alternating form intervals:** Second gear+ for duration of the run. Last 10 min., practice focuses as pair in third gear.

**Focuses 1 and 2:** Pick two challenging focuses, different from Monday

### Thursday: 45 min. run: form intervals

**10 min. alternating form intervals:** Alternate focus pairs every 10 min. second gear+ for duration of the run. Last 10 min., try to practice both pairs at once in third gear.

**Focus Pair 1:** Monday focuses

**Focus Pair 2:** Wednesday focuses

### Friday: Rest

### Saturday: 16-mile LSD run

**10 min. alternating form intervals:** Pay attention to your pelvic rotation while you cycle through focuses one at a time and repeat until 30 min. remain. Then, combine into focus pairs and alternate pairs for last 30 min. of the run. Second gear entire run; run as much of the last 10 min. in third gear as you can.

**Focuses:** focuses from Monday and Wednesday (four total)

**Total run time** = (average aerobic pace) × 16

**Hydrate** every 10 min. after the first hour. **Refuel and replace electrolytes** as needed.

### Sunday: Optional Fun Run or cross-training workout

# Week 16

**Goal:** Make long-distance running relaxing and easy

**Lesson:** Three steps to engage your lean

   **Step 1:** Check in with your posture line.

   **Step 2:** Feel your feet supporting your one-legged posture stance.

   **Step 3:** Let your Column fall in front of where your feet are hitting.

**Practice the three steps to engage your lean** every time you start running and every time you go up a gear.

**Set your metronome** and use it on *every run.*

**Monday: 4 × 800m: speed intervals** (see Chapter 6, page 137)

**Warm-up** for 5 min. **Run lap 1** (400m) in first gear; lap 2 (400m) in second gear; lap 3 (400m) in third gear. Rest ½ lap (200m) in first gear. Repeat 3 more times. At the beginning of each gear change, practice the three steps to engage your lean. Best done at track.

**Focus:** Three steps to engage your lean

**Tuesday: Rest**

**Wednesday: 50 min. run: form intervals**

**10 min. alternating form intervals**

**Focus pairs 1 and 2:** Choose two focus pairs to help you stay relaxed

**Thursday: 45 min. Surges**

**Second gear** with a light, gradual Surge into third gear every 5 min., holding third gear for 1 min. Drop back into second gear for 4 min. Repeat cycle for duration of workout. **Reinstate focus pair** every 5 min.

**Focus pair:** Balance in the "window of lean"/Rotate your pelvis

**Friday: Rest**

**Saturday: 19-mile LSD run**

**10 min. alternating form intervals:** Second gear entire run; run as much of the last 10 min. in third gear as you can.

**Focuses:** Pick a handful of restful and relaxing focuses

**Total run time** = (average aerobic pace) × 19

**Hydrate** every 10 min. after the first hour. **Refuel and replace electrolytes** as needed.

**Sunday: Optional Fun Run or cross-training workout**

## PHASE IV: THE MASTERY PHASE

### Workout Schedule: Weeks 17–22

|    | Monday | Tuesday | Wednesday | Thursday | Friday | Saturday | Sunday |
|----|--------|---------|-----------|----------|--------|----------|--------|
| 17 | 5 × 800m Speed intervals + Time Trial | REST | 45–55 min. easy Hill Run | 5 mile Tempo run | REST | LSD 16 miles | optional Fun Run or cross-train |
| 18 | 5 × 800m Speed intervals | REST | 45–55 min. easy Hill Run | 5–6 mile Tempo run | REST | LSD 20 miles (or 17 Hill Run) | optional Fun Run or cross-train |
| 19 | 4 × 800m Speed intervals | REST | 45 min. Fun Run | 45 min. Form intervals | REST | LSD 22–24 miles (20–22 Hill Run) | optional Fun Run or cross-train |
| 20 | 5 × 800m Speed intervals | REST | 55 min. Form intervals | 45 min. Form intervals | REST | LSD 18 miles | optional Fun Run or cross-train |
| 21 | 6 × 800m Speed intervals | REST | 45–55 min. easy Hill Run | 50 min. Tempo run | REST | LSD 20–22 miles (18–20 Hill Run) | optional Fun Run or cross-train |
| 22 | 6 × 800m Speed intervales | REST | 45–55 min. Fun Run | 45–60 min. Tempo run | REST | LSD 18 miles | optional Fun Run or cross-train |

# Week 17

**Lesson:** Practice Race-Specific focuses
**Practice the course:** Create a list of your marathon's course characteristics by mile marker. Example: start, downhill first 3 miles; mile 6, major uphill, 1 mile long; miles 10–19, flat, uphill finish for 1.5 miles.
**If your course is hilly**, practice hill focuses. If your course is flat, practice the Fatigue Fixes found in Chapter 4, page 116.
**Set your metronome** and use it on *every run.*

## Monday: 5 × 800m run: speed intervals + Time Trial

**Warm up** for 5 min. **Start each interval in second gear** and gradually increase to third gear, finishing last 10–20m in fourth gear. Jog for 1 min. in first gear. Repeat. Lean and relax to speed up, don't use muscle. Best done at track. **Use focus pair 1 for intervals 1 and 2**, focus pair 2 for intervals 3 and 4, both pairs for interval 5.

**Focus pairs 1 and 2:** For each pair, choose 2 focuses: one that you like and one that is more challenging

**Time Trial:** At the end of your run, do one mile in second gear. Compare this with the Time Trial from Monday, Week 9, to see how you are progressing.

## Tuesday: Rest

Get a good night's sleep.

## Wednesday: 45-55 min. easy Hill Run

**No speed.** Work arms and upper body on uphills; lean and pelvic rotation downhill. Start flat, finish flat. Change focus pair relative to terrain. **These hills** should be short and low.

**Focus pair 1:** Choose two uphill focuses
**Focus pair 2:** Choose two downhill focuses
**If you don't have hills, do this workout:**
**5 min. alternating form intervals:** Exaggerate practicing the focuses in each pair. Since you won't be running hills, this will really help you feel your upper and lower body working together.

**Focus pair 1:** Upper body focuses
**Focus pair 2:** Lower body focuses

**Thursday: 5-mile run: Tempo**

**5 min. alternating form intervals:** Measure 5-mile flat course, remembering each mile marker. **Warm up 5 min.**, then begin course in easy second gear. Run mile 1 in second gear. Run miles 2–5 in third gear.

**Focus 1:** Rotate your pelvis

**Focus 2:** Heels up, knees down

**Friday: Rest**

**Saturday: 16-mile LSD run**

**10 min. alternating form intervals:** Design 16-mile course resembling the most challenging portion of your event. Every major detail should be included at approximate mile marker on the real course. Second gear entire run; run as much of the last 10 min. in third gear as you can.

**Focus pairs 1 and 2:** You choose one easy and one challenging focus per pair.

**Total run time** = (average aerobic pace) × 16

**Hydrate** every 10 min. after the first hour. **Refuel and replace electrolytes** as needed.

**Sunday: Optional Fun Run or cross-training workout**

# Week 18

**Goal:** Back to basics

**Lesson:** Review your form

**DVD:** Lesson 1

**Make a list** of focuses that you need to work on; practice these for the remaining training weeks.

**Set your metronome** and use it on *every run.*

**Monday: 5 × 800m: speed intervals**

**Warm up** for 5 min. **Start each interval in second gear** and gradually increase to third gear, finish last 10–20m in fourth gear. Jog for 1 min. in first gear. Repeat. Lean and relax to speed up, don't use muscle. **Reinstate** focus pair at beginning of each gear change. **Use Focus 1** for lap 1, Focus 2 for lap 2. Best done at track.

**Focus pair:** Use two focuses from your list this week.

**Tuesday: Rest**

**Wednesday: 45–55 min. easy Hill Run**

**No speed.** Work arms and upper body on uphills; lean and pelvic rotation downhill. Start flat, finish flat. Change focus pair relative to terrain. These hills should be short and low.

    **Focus pair 1:** Choose two uphill focuses

    **Focus pair 2:** Choose two downhill focuses

    **If you don't have hills, do this workout:**

**5 min. alternating form intervals:** (Exaggerate focuses like last Wednesday)

    **Focus pair 1:** Upper body focuses

    **Focus pair 2:** Lower body focuses

**Thursday: 5-6-mile run: tempo**

**10 min. alternating form intervals:** Alternate individual focuses until last 10 min., then practice all three together. **Run mile 1** in second gear. Run miles 2–6 in third gear.

    **Focuses:** Pick three focuses from your list this week

**Friday: Rest**

**Saturday: 20-mile LSD run or 17-mile Hill Run**

**10 min. alternating form intervals:** Cycle through all the focuses, one at a time. Begin cycle over until time is up. **Mock up a 20-mile route** similar to the last 20 miles of your event. Practice your ability to recognize the changes in terrain and how to change focuses to the terrain. Run second gear entire run.

    **LSD run focuses:** Choose six of your most challenging focuses

    **Total run time** = (average aerobic pace) × 20

    **or**

**Hill Run focuses:** Choose focuses pertaining to upper/lower body, alternate pairs relative to the terrain. Stay as relaxed as possible on the uphills, stretch on the downhills.

**FOR EITHER WORKOUT:**

**Hydrate** every 10 min. after the first hour. **Refuel and replace electrolytes** as needed.

**Sunday: Optional Fun Run or cross-training workout**

# Week 19

**Goal:** Break new boundaries: How long can you stay relaxed?
**Lesson:** Get relaxed and economical with your movement
**The LSD this week** is your longest run to date; stay loose and relaxed.
**Set your metronome** and use it on *every run.*

**Monday: 4 × 800m run: form intervals**

**Warm up** for 5 min. **Run lap 1** (400m) in second gear. Run lap 2 (400m) in third gear. Rest ½ lap (200m) in first gear before beginning next interval. Use Focus 1 for second gear and Focus 2 for third gear. Best done at track.

**Focus 1:** Balance in the "window of lean"
**Focus 2:** Swing elbows to the rear

**Tuesday: Rest**

**Wednesday: 45 min. Fun Run**

**Focuses:** Body Scan and practice relaxing for the duration of the workout. **Body Scan** every 10 min.

**Thursday: 45 min. run: form intervals**

**10 min. alternating form intervals:** Try to maintain second gear+/ third gear for duration of workout.

**Focus 1:** Heels up, knees down
**Focus 2:** Lengthen back of neck

**Friday: Rest**

**Saturday: 22–24-mile LSD run or 20–22-mile Hill Run**

**10 min. alternating form intervals:** Practice focuses that apply to marathon course, second gear all the way. Practice your ability to recognize the changes in terrain and how to change focuses to fit terrain. **Body Scan** every 10 min.; stay as relaxed as possible.

**LSD run focus pairs 1 and 2:** Pick four of your favorite and most helpful/relaxing focuses; put them in pairs.

**Total run time** = (average aerobic pace) × 22 (or 24)

**or**

**Hill Run focus pairs:** Choose focus pairs pertaining to upper/lower body; alternate pairs relative to the terrain. Stay as relaxed as possible on the uphills, stretch on the downhills.

## FOR EITHER WORKOUT:

**Hydrate** every 10 min. after the first hour. **Refuel and replace electrolytes** as needed.

**Do end-of-run review:** Note any problem areas or sore spots

### Sunday: Optional Fun Run or cross-training workout (we recommend a bike ride for recovery)

If you are sore, pay attention, and try to modify next week's focuses to help you overcome stresses and soreness.

# Week 20

**Goal:** Physician, heal thyself

**Lesson:** Choose your own lesson

**Choose at least four focuses** that will help you avoid any soreness from last week's LSD run. Refer to last week's LSD run review for focus ideas.

**Review focuses** in Book and DVD.

**Set your metronome** and use it on *every run.*

### Monday: 5 × 800m run: speed intervals + Time Trial

**Warm up** for 5 min. **Run lap 1** (400m) in second gear. Run lap 2 (400m) in third gear. Rest ½ lap (200m) in first gear before beginning next interval. **Use Focus 1** for second gear, Focus 2 for third gear. Best done at track.

**Focuses 1 and 2:** Choose two focuses from this week's list

### Tuesday: Rest

### Wednesday: 55 min. run: form intervals review

**5 min. alternating form intervals:** Use this run to practice the 11 focuses. This is an opportunity to experience what it feels like to really focus your mind.

**Focuses:** Any 11 unique focuses (incorporate this week's focuses into this set)

**Make a cheat sheet** or write the focuses on your hand.

### Thursday: 45 min. run: form intervals

**10 min. alternating form intervals:** Keep a steady third gear pace throughout the entire run. **Stay focused** and relaxed.

**Focuses:** Choose two focuses from this week's list.

### Friday: Rest

### Saturday: 18-mile LSD run

**10 min. alternating form intervals:** Second gear entire run

**Focus pairs:** Choose four focuses and put them in pairs (i.e., two easy focuses, two focuses from this week's list)

**Total run time** = (average aerobic pace) × 18

**Hydrate** every 10 min. after the first hour. **Refuel and replace electrolytes** as needed.

### Sunday: Optional Fun Run or cross-training workout

# Week 21

**Goal:** Stay the course
**Lesson:** Get relaxed and focused
**Set your metronome** and use it on *every run.*

### Monday: 6 × 800m run: speed intervals

**Warm up** for 5 min. **Run lap 1** (400m) in second gear. Run lap 2 (400m) in third gear. Rest ½ lap (200m) in first gear before beginning next interval. **Reinstate focus pair** at beginning of each gear change. Best done at track.

**Focus pair:** Balance in the "window of lean"/Rotate your pelvis

### Tuesday: Rest

### Wednesday: 45–55 min. easy Hill Run

**No speed.** Work your arms and upper body on uphills; lean and pelvic rotation on downhills. Start flat, finish flat. Change focus pair relative to terrain.

**Focus pair 1:** Choose two uphill focuses
**Focus pair 2:** Choose two downhill focuses
**If you don't have hills, do 45 min. of Surges:** Every 2 min., alternate between second gear and third gear. Use lower body focuses for second gear, upper body focuses for third gear.

### Thursday: 50 min. run: tempo run

**10 min. alternating form intervals:** First 20 min. in second gear, last 30 min. in third gear. **Steady cadence:** remember your metronome.
**Focus pairs 1 and 2:** Choose two pairs of favorite focuses

### Friday: Rest

### Saturday: 20–22-mile LSD run or 18–20-mile Hill Run

**10 min. alternating form intervals:** Second gear entire run
**LSD run focus pairs 1 and 2:** Choose four focuses and put them in pairs (i.e., two relaxing focuses, two challenging focuses)
**Total run time** = (average aerobic pace) × 20 (or 22)
**or**
**Hill Run focus pairs:** Choose focus pairs pertaining to upper/lower body; alternate pairs relative to the terrain. Stay as relaxed as possible on the uphills, stretch on the downhills.

### FOR EITHER WORKOUT:

**Hydrate** every 10 min. after the first hour. **Refuel and replace electrolytes** as needed.

### Sunday: Optional Fun Run or cross-training workout

# Week 22

**Goal:** Check your accuracy
**Lesson:** Study the marathon course
**Take some time** to really study the marathon course and make a list of the focuses you will be using.
**Set your metronome** and use it on *every run.*

### Monday: 6 × 800m run: speed intervals

**Warm up** for 5 min. Run lap 1 (400m) in second gear. Run lap 2 (400m) in third gear. Rest ½ lap (200m) in first gear before beginning next interval. **Use focus pair 1** for second gear, focus pair 2 for third gear. **If you haven't been using a track**, use one for this workout. It's important for accuracy; track your split times for each 800m.

**Focus pair 1:** Balance in the "window of lean"/Rotate your pelvis

**Focus pair 2:** Lengthen back of neck/Heels up, knees down

**At the end of your workout:** Calculate your average time for all six intervals. Your average 800m interval time can help you predict your final marathon time (i.e., if 3:45 is your average 800m time, you could run a 3:45 marathon).

## Tuesday: Rest

## Wednesday: 45–55 min. Fun Run

**Focuses:** Body Scan and practice relaxing for the duration of the workout

**Body Scan every 10 min.**

## Thursday: 45–60 min. tempo run

**10 min. alternating form intervals:** Try to maintain second gear+/third gear for duration of workout.

**Focus 1:** The "C" Shape

**Focus 2:** Rotate your pelvis

## Friday: Rest

## Saturday: 18-mile LSD run

**10 min. alternating form intervals:** Run second gear entire run.

**Focus pairs:** You choose

**Total run time** = (average aerobic pace) × 18

**Hydrate** every 10 min. after the first hour. **Refuel and replace electrolytes** as needed.

## Sunday: Optional Fun Run or cross-training workout

## PHASE V: TAPER TIME

### Workout Schedule: Weeks 23-24

|    | Monday | Tuesday | Wednesday | Thursday | Friday | Saturday | Sunday |
|----|--------|---------|-----------|----------|--------|----------|--------|
| 23 | REST | 40–50 min. avg race pace | 6 miles start pace | 40 min. start pace | REST | 10 miles easy LSD | optional Fun Run or cross-train |
| 24 | REST | 30 min. form intervals | 6 miles start pace | 40 min. start pace/avg race pace | REST | (See race weekend phase) | |

# Week 23

**Goal:** Acknowledge the shape your body is in and be grateful

**Lesson:** Perfecting a mindful setup and start for your event

**Listen to your body** and thank it for all the hard work it has done.

**Start pace runs** will be a mock-up of pre-race and start of your event; it's just like a rehearsal.

**Set your metronome** and use it as needed on *every run.*

### Monday: Rest

### Tuesday: 40–50 min. run: form intervals (at race pace)

**10 min. alternating form intervals,** third gear for whole workout

**Focuses:** Choose two of your favorites

### Wednesday: 6-mile run: form intervals (at start pace)

**10 min. alternating form intervals:** Second gear for whole workout (third gear at the end is okay, but only if you can stay relaxed). This run should be an approximate mock-up of the first six miles of your event. **Pretend this is the real event start.** Visualize yourself at the start line of the race: Have you done your Body Looseners? Do you have your metronome? A clear list of focuses? As you start to run, maintain a low gear and don't get caught up in what the crowd is doing.

**Focuses:** Choose focuses relative to your specific event course

**Thursday: 40 min. run: form intervals (at start pace)**

**10 min. alternating form intervals:** Refer to yesterday's workout description for run guidelines.

**Focus pairs 1 and 2:** Choose two focus pairs, different from Wednesday

**Friday: Rest**

**Saturday: 10-mile LSD run, easy**

**10 min. alternating form intervals:** Second gear for whole workout, finish in third gear. It's important to have a steady cadence, so bring your metronome.

**Focuses:** Breathing focuses and favorite loosening/relaxing focuses

**Total run time** = (average aerobic pace) × 10

**Hydrate** every 10 min. after the first hour. **Refuel and replace electrolytes** as needed.

**Sunday: Optional Fun Run or cross-training workout**

# Week 24

**Goal:** Go the distance
**Lesson:** You have everything you'll need
Believe in yourself and in the level of your mental and physical conditioning. Please use your metronome for all your runs this week.

**Monday: Rest**

**Tuesday: 30 min. run: form intervals**

**5 min. alternating form intervals**

**Suggested focuses:** Lengthen the back of your neck • One-legged posture stance • Rotate your pelvis • The "C" Shape • Swing elbows to the rear • Smile

**Wednesday: 6-mile run: form intervals (at start pace)**

**10 min. alternating form intervals,** second gear for whole workout (third gear at the end is okay, but only if you can stay relaxed). This run should be an approximate mock-up of the first 6 miles of your event.

**Pretend this is the real event start.** Visualize yourself at the start line of the race: Have you done your Body Looseners? Do you have your metronome? A clear list of focuses? As you start to run, maintain a low gear and don't get caught up in what the crowd is doing.

    **Focuses:** Choose focuses relative to your specific event course

### Thursday: 40 min. run: form intervals

**5 min. alternating form intervals:** Run first 10 min. at start pace, followed by a 30 min. rehearsal of your race pace (whatever gear that is). Similar conditions to yesterday.

    **Focus 1:** Belly breathe

    **Focus 2:** Keep shoulders low and relaxed

### Friday: Rest

# Appendix C

## Single focuses

**Posture**
- Align your feet and legs
- Soften your knees
- Balance your feet (left/right, front/back, inside/outside)
- Lengthen the back of your neck by lifting the crown of your head
- Level your pelvis
- Relax your glutes
- Create your Column (shoulders, hips, ankles aligned)
- Feel your feet at the bottom of your Column
- Look for your shoelaces
- One-legged posture stance
- The "C" Shape
- Feel your Column with each foot strike
- Relax everything but your lower abs

**Lean**
- Three steps to engage lean:
  1. Check-in with your posture
  2. Feel your feet
  3. Fall from there
- Relax lower legs and ankles

- Lengthen the back of your neck and lead with your forehead
- Land midfoot
- Upper body ahead of your feet
- Balance in the "window of lean"
- Feel your lower abs and obliques engage more as you lean more
- Your lean is your gas pedal

## Lower body
### Legs
- Start out with short stride
- Swing your legs to the rear
- Let your hip swing back with your leg
- Rotate legs medially (toward your midline) to point feet forward

### Lower legs
- Bend your knees
- Limp lower legs: calves, shins, ankles, feet, toes
- Heels up/knees down
- Soften knees
- Passive lower legs—no push off

### Feet and ankles
- Feet point forward
- Circular feet with wheels at the ends of your legs
- Lift your ankles
- Heels up/toes down
- Peel foot off the ground
- Midfoot strike

### Pelvic rotation
- Feel your Pivot Point at T12/L1
- Level your pelvis
- Allow pelvic rotation to happen
- Rotate entire lower body below Pivot Point

**Upper body**

**Arm swing**
- Bend your elbows to 90 degrees (don't pump)
- Curl fingers with thumbs on top; relax hands
- Hands always held above your waistline
- Hands don't cross your centerline
- Swing elbows rearward
- Shoulders fall forward

**Head, neck, shoulders**
- Keep shoulders low and relaxed
- Shoulders always face forward—don't rotate
- Lengthen back of neck; lengthen spine; lift at the crown of your head
- Lead with your forehead, drop your chin
- Y'chi directs energy forward through the eyes

**Breathing**
- Belly breathe: inhale through nose, exhale through mouth as you pull your belly in
- Match breath rate to cadence: exhale for two steps, inhale for one
- Nose breathe if possible

**Gears, cadence, and stride length**

**Cadence**
- Work toward a range between 170–180 steps per min. (spm) with a metronome
- If your current cadence is below 170 spm, shorten your stride until you reach 170 spm

**Gears and stride length**
- First gear
  - 1-inch lean
  - Shortest stride length
  - Warm-up pace
  - Breath rate barely increases
- Second gear
  - 2-inch lean
  - Medium stride length

- Conversational/training pace
- Aerobic pace
- Third gear
  - 3-inch lean
  - Race pace
  - Longest stride length
  - High end of aerobic pace
- Fourth gear
  - 4-inch lean
  - Sprint pace
  - Third gear stride length
  - Anaerobic pace
  - Arms swing forward (not to the rear)
  - Drive with your hips (not your legs)
  - Slight increase in cadence but not in stride length
  - Engage The "C" Shape more, relax hips and legs more

**Focus Pairs**

**Posture**
- One-legged posture stance/Bend opposite knee
- Lengthen back of neck/Level pelvis
- Feel your Column/Feel a midfoot strike
- Connect the dots/Relax everything else

**Lean**
- Shoulders forward/Elbows back
- Upper body forward/Lower body rearward
- Hold The "C" Shape/Balance in the "window of lean"
- Level your pelvis/Lean from your ankles

**Lower body**
- Focus on the Pivot Point/Rotate lower body below T12/L1
- Midfoot strike/Let your hip swing back with leg
- Circular feet: peel heels up over opposite ankles/Knees down
- Knee bending/One-legged posture stance

## Pelvic rotation
- Rotate your pelvis/Feel yourself run level to the ground
- Small rotation at slower speeds/Large rotation at faster speeds
- Level pelvis/Rotate pelvis from T12/L1

## Upper body
- Shoulders squared forward/Elbows back
- Y'chi focused forward/Elbows back
- Lengthen back of neck/Open your chest
- Forward lean with Column/Elbows and legs swing rearward
- Lengthen back of neck/Focus your y'chi ahead

## Cadence and breathing
- Level pelvis/Belly breathing (inhale through nose, exhale through mouth)
- Match your breath rate to your cadence: 3:2 or 2:1 out/in

## Gears and stride length
- Increase lean/Lengthen stride
- Decrease lean/Shorten stride
- Sustain each gear for 1 min./Relax lower legs
- Steady cadence (metronome)/Cycle up and down through gears

## Body Sensing and relaxation
- Level your pelvis/Relax your lower back
- Rotate your pelvis/Relax your lower back
- Relax your shoulders/Lengthen your neck
- Level your pelvis/Rotate your pelvis
- Relax lower legs/The "C" Shape
- Relax your wrists/Relax your ankles
- Level your pelvis/Relax your glutes

## Uphill focuses
**These focuses can be used for runnable uphills.** The uphill focuses should involve more of your upper body, with less emphasis on lower body. For tips on non-runnable uphills, please see Chapter 4, page 126.

**Lean into the hill:** As a hill comes up in front of you, it may throw you back into an upright position. To counteract this tendency, lean into the hill and keep your upper body ahead of your hips and feet. This will feel like you've increased your lean because your Achilles tendon is stretched, but it's really because you're leaning into a hill instead of a flat road.

**Don't step ahead of your hips:** To prevent the overuse of your hamstrings, never step past your hips when running uphill. As you lean, keep your shoulders ahead of your hips and your hips ahead of your feet.

**Swing your arms forward and up:** Since you won't be using your legs much, your upper body will have to pick up the slack. As you run up hills, your arms should swing up, in the direction you are going up the hill. (We break our own rule here about swinging your arms to the rear.) Pretend you're trying to punch yourself in the chin.

**Shorten your stride length:** Running uphill is not the time to be in a hurry, so take it easy and you'll get to the top in great shape, without feeling like you're dying a slow death. The best way to reduce your lower body effort on hills is to relax everything below your waist as much as possible. This naturally shortens your stride length. If you feel fatigue in your legs, shorten your stride until you feel less fatigue.

**Relax your lower legs:** Keep your lower legs very relaxed as you run uphill. This will ensure that you don't run uphill on your toes and overwork your calf and foot muscles.

**Keep your heels down:** In order to avoid overworking your lower leg muscles, always keep your heels on the ground during the support phase of your stride. Any time spent on your forefoot is energy spent working your *small* leg muscles to do a *big* job.

**Use a mental image:** A good mental image to use when running uphill is to imagine yourself floating up the hills like you're in a hot air balloon, or let your upper body feel spacious and light, like an eagle catching an updraft. Just think, *Uphill: upper body*.

### Downhill focuses

**These focuses can be used for runnable downhills.** Most downhill focuses involve your lower body, with less emphasis on upper body. Tips on non-runnable downhills can be found in Chapter 4, page 126.

**Relax everything from the waist down:** Pay special attention to relaxing your lower back, quads, and calves.

**Keep your cadence steady:** Let your stride length increase.

**Lean downhill:** On the easy slopes, keep your upper body ahead of your foot strike. Holding The "C" Shape is the best way to accomplish this. If you keep your pelvis truly level, it will flatten your lower back and reduce the impact to your sacrum. If you feel like you're going too fast, back off of your lean until you feel comfortable. To reduce impact to your legs, increase your pelvic rotation, letting your stride open up behind you. Be sure to bend your knees as your legs swing rearward.

**Let your pelvis rotate more:** Let your entire lower body rotate and swing from T12/L1, allowing your pelvis to rotate with each stride. Every time your leg swings out the back, let your hip be pulled back with it.

**Relax your ankles:** To avoid shin splints or plantar fasciitis, it is crucial that you don't dorsiflex your ankles. I gently point my toes as my legs swing forward to avoid a hard heel strike.

**Relax your mind:** Relax, and surrender to the speed, Grasshopper.

# Appendix D

## PACE CHARTS

## HALF MARATHON PACE CHART

| Time/Mile | Distance/Time | | | | |
|---|---|---|---|---|---|
| | 1 mi | 5K | 10K | 10 mi | 13.1 mi |
| 5:44 | 5:44 | 17:46 | 35:33 | 57:00 | 1:15:00 |
| 6:07 | 6:07 | 18:57 | 37:55 | 1:01:00 | 1:20:00 |
| 6:29 | 6:29 | 20:09 | 40:17 | 1:04:00 | 1:25:00 |
| 6:52 | 6:52 | 21:20 | 42:39 | 1:08:00 | 1:30:00 |
| 7:15 | 7:15 | 22:31 | 45:01 | 1:12:00 | 1:35:00 |
| 7:38 | 7:38 | 23:42 | 47:24 | 1:16:00 | 1:40:00 |
| 8:01 | 8:01 | 24:53 | 49:46 | 1:20:00 | 1:45:00 |
| 8:24 | 8:24 | 26:04 | 52:08 | 1:24:00 | 1:50:00 |
| 8:47 | 8:47 | 27:15 | 54:30 | 1:28:00 | 1:55:00 |
| 9:10 | 9:10 | 28:26 | 56:52 | 1:31:00 | 2:00:00 |
| 9:33 | 9:33 | 29:37 | 59:15 | 1:35:00 | 2:05:00 |
| 9:56 | 9:56 | 30:48 | 1:01:00 | 1:39:00 | 2:10:00 |
| 10:18 | 10:18 | 31:59 | 1:04:00 | 1:43:00 | 2:15:00 |
| 10:41 | 10:41 | 33:11 | 1:06:00 | 1:47:00 | 2:20:00 |
| 11:04 | 11:04 | 34:22 | 1:08:00 | 1:51:00 | 2:25:00 |

*(continued)*

| Time/Mile | 1 mi | 5K | 10K | 10 mi | 13.1 mi |
|-----------|------|------|---------|---------|---------|
| 11:27 | 11:27 | 35:33 | 1:11:00 | 1:54:00 | 2:30:00 |
| 11:50 | 11:50 | 36:44 | 1:13:00 | 1:58:00 | 2:35:00 |
| 12:13 | 12:13 | 37:55 | 1:15:00 | 2:02:00 | 2:40:00 |
| 12:36 | 12:36 | 39:06 | 1:18:00 | 2:06:00 | 2:45:00 |
| 12:59 | 12:59 | 40:17 | 1:20:00 | 2:10:00 | 2:50:00 |
| 13:22 | 13:22 | 41:28 | 1:22:00 | 2:14:00 | 2:55:00 |
| 13:45 | 13:45 | 42:39 | 1:24:00 | 2:18:00 | 3:00:00 |

All times in min.:sec or hr:min.:sec format

## MARATHON PACE CHART

| Distance/Time | | | | | | |
|-----------|------|------|---------|---------|---------|---------|
| Time/Mile | 5k | 10k | 10 mi | 13.1 mi | 20 mi | 26.2 mi |
| 5:44 | 17:46 | 35:33 | 57:00 | 1:15:00 | 1:54:00 | 2:30:00 |
| 6:07 | 18:57 | 37:55 | 1:01:00 | 1:20:00 | 2:02:00 | 2:40:00 |
| 6:29 | 20:09 | 40:17 | 1:04:00 | 1:25:00 | 2:09:00 | 2:50:00 |
| 6:52 | 21:20 | 42:39 | 1:08:00 | 1:30:00 | 2:17:00 | 3:00:00 |
| 7:15 | 22:31 | 45:01 | 1:12:00 | 1:35:00 | 2:25:00 | 3:10:00 |
| 7:38 | 23:42 | 47:24 | 1:16:00 | 1:40:00 | 2:33:00 | 3:20:00 |
| 8:01 | 24:53 | 49:46 | 1:20:00 | 1:45:00 | 2:40:00 | 3:30:00 |
| 8:24 | 26:04 | 52:08 | 1:24:00 | 1:50:00 | 2:48:00 | 3:40:00 |
| 8:47 | 27:15 | 54:30 | 1:28:00 | 1:55:00 | 2:56:00 | 3:50:00 |
| 9:10 | 28:26 | 56:52 | 1:31:00 | 2:00:00 | 3:03:00 | 4:00:00 |
| 9:33 | 29:37 | 59:15 | 1:35:00 | 2:05:00 | 3:11:00 | 4:10:00 |
| 9:56 | 30:48 | 1:01:00 | 1:39:00 | 2:10:00 | 3:19:00 | 4:20:00 |
| 10:18 | 31:59 | 1:04:00 | 1:43:00 | 2:15:00 | 3:26:00 | 4:30:00 |
| 10:41 | 33:11 | 1:06:00 | 1:47:00 | 2:20:00 | 3:34:00 | 4:40:00 |
| 11:04 | 34:22 | 1:08:00 | 1:51:00 | 2:25:00 | 3:42:00 | 4:50:00 |
| 11:27 | 35:33 | 1:11:00 | 1:54:00 | 2:30:00 | 3:49:00 | 5:00:00 |
| 11:50 | 36:44 | 1:13:00 | 1:58:00 | 2:35:00 | 3:57:00 | 5:10:00 |

| Time/Mile | 5k | 10k | 10 mi | 13.1 mi | 20 mi | 26.2 mi |
|-----------|------|---------|---------|---------|---------|---------|
| 12:13 | 37:55 | 1:15:00 | 2:02:00 | 2:40:00 | 4:05:00 | 5:20:00 |
| 12:36 | 39:06 | 1:18:00 | 2:06:00 | 2:45:00 | 4:12:00 | 5:30:00 |
| 12:59 | 40:17 | 1:20:00 | 2:10:00 | 2:50:00 | 4:20:00 | 5:40:00 |
| 13:22 | 41:28 | 1:22:00 | 2:14:00 | 2:55:00 | 4:28:00 | 5:50:00 |
| 13:45 | 42:39 | 1:24:00 | 2:18:00 | 3:00:00 | 4:36:00 | 6:00:00 |

All times in min.:sec or hr:min.:sec format

# INDEX

Page numbers in *italics* refer to illustrations.